THE
STRECKFUS RIVERBOAT DYNASTY
——— Jazz and the Big Smoke Canoe ———

THE
STRECKFUS RIVERBOAT DYNASTY
—— Jazz and the Big Smoke Canoe ——

ARTHUR L. SMITH
Grandson of Captain Roy Michael Streckfus

Copyrighted Material

The Streckfus Riverboat Dynasty: Jazz and the Big Smoke Canoe

Copyright © 2023 by Arthur L. Smith. All Rights Reserved.

No part of this publication may be reproduced, stored in a retrieval system or transmitted, in any form or by any means—electronic, mechanical, photocopying, recording, or otherwise—without prior written permission from the publisher, except for the inclusion of brief quotations in a review.

For information about this title or to order other books and/or electronic media, contact the publisher:

Grand Strand Publishers
grandstrandpublishers@gmail.com

ISBNs:
979-8-218-10910-3 (hardcover)
979-8-9885466-0-3 (softcover)
979-8-9885466-1-0 (eBook)

Printed in the United States of America

Cover and Interior design: 1106 Design

This book is dedicated to my grandchildren.

Girls and boys, when reading nonfiction literature inspires you, please give this narrative your attention.

Our Streckfus patriarch, John Streckfus, a.k.a. "the Commodore" founded a fabulous excursion steamboat business in 1900. Under the creative management of his sons, Streckfus Steamers tramped the Mississippi and Ohio and played an important role in the introduction of jazz music from New Orleans to St. Paul (and farther, to Pittsburgh).

The Commodore was my great-grandfather, and Roy Michael Streckfus was my grandfather.

This book is dedicated to you, Brooke, Noah, Bennett, Emerson, McKay, and Louise (the Commodore's great-great-great grandchildren).

I believe it was my fascination with being on or near the water my entire life that inspired me to research—and endeavor to understand—my Mississippi Streckfus Steamer roots. I'm so happy I did.

"Jazz was just bursting to get out of New Orleans and swim upstream."

~ Capt. Clarke "Doc" Hawley[1]

---

1 As related by Clarke C. Hawley to the author.

TABLE OF CONTENTS

Author's Preface	xv
Preface	xvii
Introduction—Fitzgerald Jazz	xix
PART I • *Early History of the Mississippi River*	**1**
A Greatly Condensed History of the Mississippi	3
The New World & The Race for Its Control	7
Very Early History Since de Soto	11
Marquette and Jolliet—The next Disruptors	15
René-Robert Cavelier, Sieur de La Salle—Extraordinary Explorer	19
The First La Salle Expedition	19
La Salle Claims "La Louisiane"	21
The Ill-Fated Texas Expedition	22
PART II • *How the Mississippi River Was Tamed*	**25**
Corps of Engineers—Commentary	27
Levees, Locks, and Dams	29
Upper Mississippi vs. Lower Mississippi Geography	31
Abe and the Flatboats	35
Mike Fink, Keelboatman	37
The Showboat Saga	41
Construction and Destruction of the Mississippi Artery of Rivers	43
The Glory Days of Steamboat Expansion: 1820–1870	45
Lincoln and the Rock Island Railroad Bridge Lawsuit	53
Eads vs. Humphreys—Engineering Fireworks on the River	57
Humphreys	57
Eads	59
Eads and Humphreys Collide	60

PART III • *The Streckfus Family*	63
Balthazar Streckfus	65
The Freddie, 1884	71
The Verne Swain, 1889	73
Verne Swain vs. Jo Long	75
Acme Packet vs. Anchor Line	83
The City of Winona	89
The J.S.	93
Maiden Voyage—June 29, 1901	99
A Rough Patch for the *J.S.*	103
All Aboard for New Orleans, 1903	105
Houdini, the J.S., and the Muddy Mississippi, 1907	111
The *J.S.'s* Fiery Demise, June 25, 1910	115
City of Winona to *W.W.*	125
Here Comes the Jazz	129
Fate Marable	135

PART IV • *Packets to Excursion: Wood to Steel*	141
Expansion, 1911–	143
The Excursion Conversion Bonanza	156
Titanic 1912, *Eastland* 1915	161
World War I	165
The *Dubuque* Becomes the *Capitol*	167
The *Quincy* Tests the St. Louis to New Orleans Long-Haul Market	173
The 1921 Sensation—The Garden Steamer *J.S. Deluxe*	177
The *Saint Paul* Becomes the *Senator*	179
The *Senator*, 1940–1953	185
Diamond Jo Fleet Retired with Grace	189
New Blood—The *Cincinnati*: Steel & Oil	191
An Art Deco Steamship: Mazie Krebs Performs Design Magic	195

Table of Contents

Kids' Stuff and Powder Rooms: The Admiral Appeals to All	201
Calliopes, Arcades, Popcorn, and Souvenirs	204
The Brothers Collide	209
WWII & the Excess Profits Tax	214
The Jefferson Arch Challenge	216
Loose Lips Sink Ships	218
Capt. D. Walter Wisherd	220
Wisherd and the *Island Queen*	223
PART V • *The Sons Rise*	**225**
As told by Joseph Leo Streckfus	227
1926–Onward, as told by Joe Streckfus	236
In the Words of Capt. Roy Michael Streckfus Sr., 1888–1967	251
Obituary for Roy Michael Streckfus Sr.	261
Lily's Packard Travelogue, in the Words of Lily Ann Streckfus Smith	263
John Curran Streckfus (1916–1959)	266
In the Words of Capt. John Nicholas Streckfus (1891–1948)	269
In the Words of Capt. Verne Walter Streckfus (1895–1984)	273
Verne: Escape from the Commodore	274
Verne's Smoke	277
Music: More in the Words of Capt. Joseph Streckfus	281
PART VI • *Jazz & the Streckfus Steamboats*	**289**
As told by Verne Streckfus, 1960	291
The Monumental Influence of Louis Armstrong	301
"Movin' On Up"	307
Streckfus Steamer Musicians	315
Charles Wenzel "Charley" Mills	315
Fate Marable-Inspired Jazz Legends	317
Joseph Nathan "King" Oliver—Cornet	317

John Alexander "Johnny" St. Cyr—Banjo	319
Arthur James "Zutty" Singleton—Drums	320
Charles Cyril "Charlie" Creath—Trumpet, Saxophone, Accordion & Bandleader	321
John "Johnny" Dodds—Clarinet	323
Warren "Baby" Dodds—Drums	323
Dewey Jackson—Cornet and Trumpet	325
Jesse Johnson—St. Louis Producer/Promoter	327
George Murphy 'Pops" Foster—Bass	328
Walter Gabriel "Fats" Pichon—Piano	329
Sidney Desvigne—Trumpet	330
Alvin Elmore Acorn—Trumpet	331
Charles "Buddy" Bolden—Cornet & Trumpet	332
Joseph Streckfus Interviews on Jazz and Louis Armstrong	334
Music: Louis Armstrong—Fate Marable 1917 (Dated 11/04/1958)	334
Music	336
Music—Louis Armstrong—1920*	337
Boards of Directors and Officers of Streckfus and Related Companies	341
Streckfus Steamers, Incorporated Steamers Operations—1936 Through 1943	345
News Clippings	351
Released after Dive	351
Admiral Crew Saves Swimmer in River	352
Soldier Leaps off *Admiral*, Swims Ashore to Win $5	352
Deckhand Missing after Fall into River	353
Asks $3000 in Damages for Injuries Inflicted by Jitterbug Dancer	353
Man Jumps from Steamer *Admiral*	353
Body of Vet Sought After Dive Off Boat	354
Body Discovered in *Admiral* Paddle	354
Body Caught in Paddle Wheel	355

Table of Contents

Female Lifeguard Jumps from *Capitol*	355
Missed the Boat	356
The Streckfus Family	357
The Children of Commodore John Streckfus and Theresa Bartemeier Streckfus	357
The Family Tree of the Commodore—Captain John Streckfus	359
The Captains of Streckfus Steamers, Inc.	360
EPILOGUE	361
The Competitive Landscape	361
Operational Challenges	363
Passing the Torch, Reluctantly	364
John Curran Streckfus	364
Roy Michael Streckfus Jr.	364
Robert Bernard Streckfus Sr.	365
William Sauvage Streckfus	365
Taps for the *Admiral*	366
TIMELINE	369
AFTERWORD	373
ACKNOWLEDGMENTS	375
INDEX	377
ABOUT THE ARTHUR	387

AUTHOR'S PREFACE

My Streckfus family heritage is anchored to my entrepreneurial great grandfather, John Streckfus. From Rock Island, Illinois, the Commodore, of Bavarian descent, built a spectacular excursion steamboat business which thrived during the twentieth century.

Streckfus Steamers brought sightseeing, hot jazz music, and moonlight cruises to the American populace along the Mississippi and Ohio rivers. Along the way, Streckfus and his sons ambitiously renovated wooden and all-steel vessels, of which the palatial *President* and *Admiral* were the most famous.

The multi-storied vessels housed dancefloors the size of football fields. With great jazz musicians and dance bands that largely hailed from New Orleans and St. Louis, the Streckfus excursion fleet was hugely popular and provided summertime entertainment from St. Paul to St. Louis, and from Pittsburgh to New Orleans. Regrettably, popular interest in riverboats faded post-World War II and the Streckfus Steamer fleet was repossessed by Boatmen's Bank in 1980.

What remains on American rivers of the once proud excursion riverboat business is rather inauspicious today. Two faithfully-restored steamers do remain: In the Kentucky city of her name, the 1914-vintage *Belle of Louisville* operated seasonal excursions on the Ohio River. In New Orleans, the steamboat *Natchez* provide great harbor cruises year round from its berth at the Toulouse Street wharf, adjacent to Jackson Square.

When your travels next take you to Louisville or the Crescent City, please enjoy an afternoon on the river. Examine the engine rooms of the *Natchez* and *Belle of Louisville* and tour their pilot house. And, while the sternwheel spins a cascade at the stern, imagine the glory days of Streckfus Steamers, Inc.

~ Arthur L. Smith
September 2023

PREFACE

"Put it this way. Jazz is a good barometer of freedom . . . It has its beginnings. The United States of America spawned certain ideals of freedom and independence through which, eventually, jazz was evolved, and the music is so free that many people say it is the only unhampered, unhindered expression of complete freedom yet produced in this country."[2]

~ Duke Ellington

"When it comes to the origin of the word 'jazz,' it seems that each person simply believes what she or he wants to."[3]

~ Lewis Porter

You are free to make your own decision on the origins of jazz. There is a word, "jasm," that dates to the 1800s, at least, that is associated with vivaciousness and may be related to "jism," which means the same: spirit, energy, vitality, pep.

Most convincing from our perspective is that the period of early Marable-related musical work on Streckfus steamers introduced "jazz" to a wide swath of the population along the Upper and Lower Mississippi and Ohio rivers.

The Original Dixieland "Jass" Band's "Livery Stable Blues" (1917) is widely accepted as the first "jazz" record. Victor Talking Machine Co.'s

---

2 Geoffrey C. Ward and Ken Burns, *Jazz: A History of America's Music* (New York: Knopf, 2000), pg. vii; a quote by Duke Ellington.
3 Lewis Porter, 2-26-2018 WBGO.org

ad, promoting the record, stated, "Spell it Jass, Jas, Jaz, or Jazz—nothing can spoil a Jass band!"[4]

There are many theories as to the origination of the word "jazz." I prefer my own the most: The word comes from saying aloud "J" and "S," as in "*J.S.*," the riverboat that heralded its port arrivals with colorful, energetic music as though to say, "Here comes the *J.S.*"

From its beginnings on the Mississippi River, jazz quickly caught on from coast to coast and particularly to Chicago and abroad, being a quintessential ingredient in any depiction of the Roaring '20s.

"Jazz was just bursting to get out of New Orleans and swim upstream," stated Captain Clarke C. "Doc" Hawley, author of *The Excursion Boat Story: Moonlite at 8:30.*[5]

---

[4] Lewis Porter, 2-26-2018 WBGO.org
[5] As related by Clarke C. Hawley to the author.

INTRODUCTION—FITZGERALD JAZZ

Jazz. Born in the twentieth century, a huge cast of musicians, band leaders, and producers served as the midwives for its birth. Creative inspired growth of jazz is a wonderful and rich story. However, it (jazz) is not the central theme of this narrative.[6,7]

Jazz and the Big Smoke Canoe centers on the role that John Streckfus and his sons played in the epic early development of jazz that took place hand in hand with the rise of excursion steamboating on the Mississippi and Ohio.

F. Scott Fitzgerald (1896–1940) chronicled what the great author characterized as the "Jazz Years." What we lack from Fitzgerald is how best to pin down the "Jazz Years" to a specific stretch of American history. Were the Jazz Years the best of the Roaring '20s? Or was it that dark period of Prohibition and the Depression? Did the "Jazz Years" annex the economic recovery into, and after, World War II?

What is certain is that jazz did not end when Fitzgerald died unexpectedly on December 21, 1940.

Jazz is still alive, breathing, and kicking. This truly American musical art form is all around us: today. It's everywhere, yet difficult to define.

---

[6] Many, many others have attempted to define and chronicle what jazz is and how it came to be. Geoffrey C. Ward and Ken Burns authored a fabulous 490-page (500-photo) tome, *Jazz: A History of America's Music*. The written text accompanies Burns's 10-part PBS documentary series, "Jazz: A Film by Ken Burns." (We note, however, that riverboat jazz is only a minor subject in the documentary.)

[7] By far the most thorough and comprehensive research on the world of Mississippi River jazz and the riverboat musicians who performed was done by historian William Howland Kenney. Kenney's *Jazz on the River* (Chicago: University of Chicago Press, 2005) is a treasure.

PART I

Early History of the Mississippi River

"The Mississippi Valley continues the Inland Empire, a region which in its development has helped to make the United States a leading world power. Near St. Louis unite the three main branches—the Ohio, the Upper Mississippi, and Missouri—of the Mississippi River system, the finest network of inland waterways possessed by any country."[8]

---

8 Mildred L. Hartsough, Preface, *From Canoe to Steel Barge on the Upper Mississippi* (University of Minnesota Press, 1934), pg. xix.

A GREATLY CONDENSED HISTORY OF THE MISSISSIPPI[9, 10]

Native Americans roamed the Mississippi Valley for what is now believed to have been more than 10,000 years before the first onslaught of European exploration began roughly 500 years ago.

Life forms appear in the paleontological records in the mid-Cenozoic or Glacial (Ice Age) epoch. Archaeological artifacts suggest that the valley was home to mammoths, mastodons, giant sloths, and bison in the final epoch of the most recent Ice Age.[11]

The indigenous people left their mark—mounds—as evidence of continuous human habitation. Indian mounds endure and pay homage to the far-ranging host of tribes active throughout the Upper and Lower Mississippi. Their stone spearheads have been found in the fossils of prehistoric beasts near the headwaters of the Arkansas River (Osage Valley of Missouri).[12]

---

9 Paul Schneider, *Old Man River: The Mississippi River in North American History* (New York: Picador, 2014), pg. 9.

10 Norbury L. Wayman, *Life on the River: A Pictorial History of the Mississippi, the Missouri, and the Western River System* (Bonanza Books, a Division of Crown Publishers, Inc. 1971), pg. 2.

11 Hartsough, *From Canoe to Steel Barge*, pg. 13.

12 Wayman, *Life on the River*, pg. 2.

THE STRECKFUS RIVERBOAT DYNASTY

It may be pretentious to open this Mississippi riverboat story with pre-Columbian history. However, very sparse historical records exist of Native Americans' impact on the Mississippi Valley. Admittedly, the role of the indigenous tribes in the evolution of the great Mississippi Valley must remain understated.

The Midwestern rivers have native names: Mississippi—a spelling bee hurdle—is derived from the Algonquin *misi-ziipi* or "great waters" or "father of waters." Missouri is Sioux for "wooden canoe people" and Ohio comes from "oyo," which is Iroquois for "great river."

Walt Whitman wrote in 1904 in *An American Primer* that "Mississippi" was the most suitable nomenclature for the river:

> I was asking for something savage and luxuriant, and behold here are the aboriginal names. I see how they are being preserved. They are honest words—they give the true length, breadth, depth. They all fit. Mississippi! The word winds with chutes—it rolls a stream three thousand miles long.[13]

Mark Twain wrote in 1883 in *Life on the Mississippi*:[14]

> Considering the Missouri its main branch, it is the longest river in the world–four thousand three hundred miles. It seems safe to say that it is also the crookedest river in the world, since in one part of its journey it uses up one thousand three hundred miles to cover the same ground that the crow would fly over in six hundred and seventy-five.
>
> It discharges three times as much water as the St. Lawrence, twenty-five times as much as the Rhine, and three hundred and thirty-eight times as much as the Thames. No other river has so

---

[13] Walt Whitman, *An American Primer* (The Atlantic, April 1904 issue), pg. 18.
[14] Mark Twain, *Life on the Mississippi* (James R. Osgood & Co., 1883), pg. 21.

A Greatly Condensed History of the Mississippi

vast a drainage-basin: it draws its water supply from twenty-eight States and Territories; from Delaware, on the Atlantic seaboard, and from all the country between that and Idaho on the Pacific slope—a spread of forty-five degrees of longitude.

The Mississippi receives and carries to the Gulf water from fifty-four subordinate rivers that are navigable by steamboats, and from some hundreds that are navigable by flats and keels. The area of its drainage-basin is as great as the combined areas of England, Wales, Scotland, Ireland, France, Spain, Portugal, Germany, Austria, Italy, and Turkey; and almost all this wide region is fertile; the Mississippi valley, proper, is exceptionally so.

Scanned from inside cover of *The Excursion Boat Story: Moonlite at 8:30* with permission from Capt. Hawley.

THE NEW WORLD & THE RACE FOR ITS CONTROL

Most accounts of the earliest Mississippi Valley exploration and exploitation begin with the efforts by the Spaniards and the earliest French adventurers—all seeking that ephemeral, quick route to the fabulous riches of the Far East.

Waving the flag of his home country in 1519, Spanish conquistador and cartographer Alonso Álvarez de Pineda is said to have coined the great river "Rio de Santa Espiritu." About a decade later, Panfilo de Narvaez, a Spanish conquistador and soldier, traveled past the mouth of the river as well. In 1541, the explorer Hernando de Soto reached the Mississippi near Memphis, Tennessee, by land, traveling through the interior via Florida.

More than a century later, the priest Jacques Marquette and fur trader Louis Joliet documented the river from Wisconsin to its intersection with the Arkansas River. In 1682, René-Robert Cavelier, the Sieur de La Salle, documented the Mississippi to its mouth, claiming the entire Mississippi Valley, which he named "Louisiane," for France.

What led these wild adventurers from Europe to the New World? A quicker route to China initially, then the prospects of riches to be plundered.[15]

---

15 Herbert and Edward Quick, *Mississippi Steamboatin'* (New York: Henry Holt & Co., 1926), pg. xi.

Picture the thriving port of New Orleans circa 1750, truly an international harbor of commerce. Goods from the lands that then constituted Louisiane—from southern British Columbia and Saskatchewan to the Gulf of Mexico—traveled in keelboats and barges.

From the Crescent City (New Orleans), outbound hides, tallow, pork, lumber, and flour were packaged for the high seas and shipped to France and the West Indies. Northbound, barges and keelboats carried cotton, rice, sugar, indigo, and fabrics from the looms of Europe.

Family members of George Washington, the first president of what would become the United States, were among wealthy colonists of Virginia who formed the Ohio Company in 1748 to buy, then resell to British settlers, land in Ohio Country in what is western Pennsylvania today. Encountering resistance from the French and Native Americans, Virginia's governor sent Washington to negotiate.

Subsequent events resulted in the start of the French and Indian War, ultimately concluding in 1763 with a British victory, gaining westerly control of the Mississippi River. However, as Britain was nearly broke and the current inhabitants of Ohio Country were threatening war, Britain forbade its colonists from residing west of the Appalachian Mountains. The result? Britain won the land, but the Ohio Company was out of business.

Washington was well versed in the tumultuous power race among the leading European rulers. Since the New World was discovered, England, France, and Spain sought total domination of this land, its still-untold assets, and commerce. The bitter, age-old feuds of Europe, transplanted across the Atlantic onto North America, bred seemingly endless wars and conflicts with colonists. Each European initiative dragged in Native American tribes that were enlisted to support the side that made the biggest promises. Nobody thought much of the Indians' pre-existing ownership of this land.[16]

---

16 Wayman, *Life on the River*, pg. 4.

The New World & The Race for Its Control

When the would-be invaders from Europe first entered the Mississippi River Valley, many Indian tribes were present, each with its own unique dialect. The many extensions of the Algonquian family occupied both banks of the Mississippi above the junction with the Ohio. The Algonquians spread eastward into Ohio and northward into Michigan, Wisconsin, Minnesota, and Canada. To the west were the Sioux and the natives of the Great Plains including the Crow, Mandan, and Osage tribes. To the southeast of the confluence of the Ohio and Mississippi were the Muskogean tribal families. These were the Chickasaws, Creeks, Choctaws, and Natchez. Further south in the Lower Mississippi were the Caddo, Tunica, and Atakapa.

VERY EARLY HISTORY SINCE DE SOTO

Our history of the Mississippi Valley, when contrasted with 3,000-plus years of Eurasian activity and documentation, can conveniently be condensed into the roughly 500 years since de Soto. Of that half millennium, the first 300 years of expansion were relatively modest and geographically concentrated.

It was only from the birth of America with the Revolutionary War that westward expansion gained momentum. The existing arterial waterways had long aided the Native American culture. Now, they offered a remarkable avenue from which to expand and exploit the riches of the great rivers of the Mississippi Valley.

Hernando de Soto
Wikimedia Commons

Mildred Hartsough's *From Canoe to Steel Barge on the Upper Mississippi*, first published in 1932, does justice in chronicling the incredible development of the Upper (and Lower) Mississippi.

THE STRECKFUS RIVERBOAT DYNASTY

Let's start with Hernando de Soto. In 1541, under his command, 600 well-equipped soldiers set out for the New World. Starting in Florida, the de Soto expedition worked its way along the Gulf Coast, finding neither riches nor hospitality. Native tribes were treated poorly by the Spanish explorers and while bloody skirmishes were few, the ranks of the Spaniards were thinned by sickness and inadequate provisions. Likely the first explorer to reach the Mississippi, de Soto built watercraft to cross at Chickasaw Bluffs (Mississippi); La Salle later built a fort at that site.

After a fruitless year of search produced nothing of lasting value but rough-sketched maps of the Lower Mississippi delta, de Soto regrouped at the same Mississippi site to prepare to return to Mexico City. Stricken with fever, de Soto perished and was ignominiously buried in the mighty river, ostensibly to conceal from the local tribes the expedition leader's mortality. Explorer de Soto's expedition marked a historic first when a handful of survivors rode their manufactured craft to the mouth of the Mississippi.

Exploration by de Soto and earlier Spaniard expeditions by Cabeza de Vaca, Àlvarez de Pineda, and Panfilo de Narvaez generally pursued travel along the southeastern Gulf Coast area; these Spaniards had a common objective in seeking gold, great fame, and, with it, a passage to China.

"Those Spaniards and French . . . (who were seeking) . . . in these unknown lands (great wealth) were adventurers, explorers, exploiters, sometime missionaries, but not geographers."[17]

Fast forward 100 years: Remarkably, Spain had, by default and other preoccupation, surrendered its quest for New Spain to France. The more practical French took a totally different, commercial tack. Swooping down the St. Lawrence to the Great Lakes, French explorers established outpost settlements and made great efforts to befriend the powerful Iroquois nation. While early interaction and trading with the Iroquois was fruitful for the French explorers, these allegiances would come under great stress.

---

17 Hartsough, *From Canoe to Steel Barge*, pg. 4.

Very Early History Since de Soto

Bad blood among the French settlers and the Iroquois would spark a change of heart; northeastern tribal support swung to the British and crippled the French settlements. The early French successes quickly faded with time under the weight of British belligerence and great cockney firepower.

Meanwhile, a wild and colorful Frenchman, Jean Nicolet, reportedly reached the Mississippi through Lake Michigan via Green Bay in the 1650s. Another mysterious pair of French explorers, Radisson and Groseilliers,[18] combed the area in the 1650s as well. Radisson may well have stumbled across the Mississippi headwaters when he stated, "went into ye great river that . . . has two branches, the one towards the West, the other toward the South."[19]

Jean Nicolet
Wikimedia Commons

Nicolet, Radisson, and Groseilliers are hardly common protagonists in Upper Mississippi Valley folklore. But to their credit, the records suggest they placed first dibs on "New France" some 15 years earlier than the illustrious Jolliet and Marquette.

---

18 Hartsough, *From Canoe to Steel Barge*, pg. 7.
19 *Ibid.*

MARQUETTE AND JOLLIET— THE NEXT DISRUPTORS

In a note regarding "The Song of Three Friends," the poem's author, John G. Neihardt, wrote in 1918:[20]

The heroic spirit, as seen in heroic poetry, we are told, is the outcome of a society cut loose from its roots, of a time of migrations, of the shifting of populations. Such conditions are to be found during the time of the Spanish conquests of Central and South America; and they are to be found also in those wonderful years of our own West, when wandering bands of trappers were exploring the rivers and the mountains and the plains and the deserts from the British possessions to Mexico, and from the Missouri to the Pacific.

In 1665, a Jesuit priest, Father Allouez, from his camp on the western edge of Lake Superior had heard, as had others, of ". . . a great river name Messipi."[21] Early explorers of the Upper Mississippi were of a common mindset that the mighty river would track forever westward—from which the passage to China was assured.

Louis de Buade de Frontenac, who became governor general of New France in 1672, shared this view and sought confirmation from a new

---

20 John G. Neihardt, *Collected Poems of John G. Neihardt* (New York: The Macmillan Company, 1926), pg. 631.
21 Hartsough, *From Canoe to Steel Barge,* pg. 8.

expedition specifically formed to explore the Upper Mississippi. Enter Father Marquette, a seasoned explorer with impeccable credentials, including life at outposts where he had mastered some Indian dialects. In an unlikely marriage of talent, the devout Jesuit priest was joined by Louis Jolliet, a trapper, explorer, and man of the woods. Commissioned by Frontenac, Jolliet and Marquette outfitted in Montreal and prepared for what was to be an epic trek accompanied by five French-Indian canoe men steering two birchbark canoes.

Beginning May 17, 1673, from Michigan's Upper Peninsula, the party followed an established Wisconsin route, and the early days

Pere Marquette
Wikimedia Commons

of the journey went well. Marquette's missionary zeal combined with Jolliet's outdoorsman guile and experience to produce an improbable success. By July 16, the party had reached the mouth of the Arkansas River, beyond which point, seasonal factors, possibly hostile tribes, and the presence of Spaniards occupying the Gulf Coast justified a reversal of course.

Jolliet had methodically built his base of maps as the expedition moved south from the Great Lakes

Louis Jolliet
North Wind Picture Archives/Alamy Stock Photo

Marquette and Jolliet—The Next Disruptors

toward his perspective of an ultimate end in the Gulf of Mexico. These remarkable documents survive and clearly indicate all the key arteries of the mighty river: the Wisconsin, the Iowa, the Illinois, the Ohio, the Missouri, and the Arkansas.

"It was the part of Marquette and [Jolliet] . . . to travel a large part of the length of the river, to make possible a relatively accurate map of its course, and to eliminate definitely the belief that the [Mississippi] would supply the hoped-for route to China."[22]

Louis de Buade de Frontenac
Wikimedia Commons

Perhaps Frontenac was displeased when Jolliet delivered his maps and accounts of the journey. No riches from China were to be wrested from the Mississippi. However, the governor general was keen to see the value of this knowledge. Now France was in a position to claim and occupy the whole Mississippi Valley and to stake out the countryside and profitable fur trade west of the Great Lakes.

---

22 Hartsough, *From Canoe to Steel Barge,* pg. 8.

RENÉ-ROBERT CAVELIER, SIEUR DE LA SALLE— EXTRAORDINARY EXPLORER

Enter René-Robert Cavelier, Sieur de La Salle, who sailed to New France in 1666. If the seventeenth century was indeed the "Era of the Explorer" in North America, then La Salle stands very tall.

A man of extraordinary accomplishment, La Salle is often referred to as a priest. But although he entered the Jesuit order, he left before completing requirements. Having entered the order, however, he sailed to New France to join his brother, a Jesuit priest, and began to learn the native languages.

Upon his land grant was born what became the city of Lachine, which is now part of Montreal.

THE FIRST LA SALLE EXPEDITION

La Salle's financial success with selling tracts of what became Lachine funded his next career: explorer, trapper, and fur trader. He is said to have

A 19th-century engraving of Cavelier de La Salle
Wikimedia Commons

been a fascinating, persuasive, and ambitious character. In 1669, after some progress beyond the southern shore of Lake Ontario, La Salle's nine-canoe Ohio expedition faced hostilities among the Seneca and Algonquin, halting progress. Perhaps it was fortunate that La Salle could not proceed farther at this time—his health was jeopardized by a virulent fever.

Back in Montreal for a few years, the iconic La Salle became friends with Frontenac, who had arrived in 1672. It was here that the great explorer, lured by the prospect of taming the mysterious Mississippi River, conceived of a grand plan to create an empire in New France.

Chevalier Henri de Tonti
Wikimedia Commons

The fur trade business in the Great Lakes and environs was booming and represented a core base from which to operate. What La Salle needed was more men, sturdy forts, and lots of capital to combat the encroachment of Dutch and English foes.

By 1674, he had secured a royal grant to Fort Frontenac on the northern shore of Lake Ontario. At some point during his time in New France it is likely that he met the seasoned Jolliet, who undoubtedly would have shared his unique maps and knowledge of the Upper Mississippi.

La Salle returned to his native France where he displayed critical charm and persuasion. He was honored with letters of nobility, the title to Fort Cataraqui (later renamed Fort Frontenac), and, of greatest importance, a concession to expand the French fur trade into lands west and southwest. His lifelong friend and companion Chevalier Henri de

Tonti (also known as "Iron Hand" and "Thunder Arm"[23]) was enlisted as lieutenant.

In the ensuing years, La Salle devoted his energies to the building and defense of a host of French forts on the rivers and tributaries of the Great Lakes. He demonstrated extraordinary skill in communicating with the various Indian tribes. With Tonti, La Salle built Fort Conti in tribute to Tonti's patron, the prince of Conti, at the mouth of the Niagara Falls where the Iroquois had established portage.

LA SALLE CLAIMS "LA LOUISIANE"

Originally launched during the inhospitable winter of 1679, the famous Mississippi Expedition with 40 men led by La Salle and Tonti began poorly. After building a stockade and fort on the Illinois River near Peoria, La Salle returned to Fort Frontenac for provisions while trouble brewed with the natives. In his absence, his soldiers mutinied, exiled Tonti, and destroyed Fort Crevecoeur.

It took two years for the Mississippi expedition to regroup and rebuild necessities for their next leg of the journey. At the intersection of the Illinois and Mississippi, the band of explorers built canoes and traveled on to Memphis, where Fort Prudhomme, the first French fort in Tennessee, was erected. The next leg of travel down the Lower Mississippi moved expeditiously and, remarkably, without any tragic developments.

We credit La Salle for staking out Louisiane in the name of King Louis XIV. This was on April 9, 1682, when La Salle stood with his exploration party and local natives and erected a cross bearing the French coat of arms. In one audacious and flamboyant action, La Salle claimed the entire Mississippi Valley for his king and countrymen.

"On that day, the realm of France received on parchment a stupendous accession. The fertile plains of Texas, the vast basin of the Mississippi, from

---

23 http://www.historynaked.com/chevalier-henri-de-tonti-thunder-arm/

its frozen northern springs to the sultry borders of the Gulf; from the woody ridges of the Alleghanies to the bare peaks of the Rocky Mountains—a region of savannahs and forests, sun cracked deserts, and grassy plains, watered by a thousand rivers, ranged by a thousand warlike tribes, passed beneath the sceptre of the Sultan of Versailles, and all by virtue of a feeble human voice, inaudible at half a mile."[24]

With the Tricolor planted on the fertile soil of Louisiane, La Salle, along with Tonti and his band, made their way upstream and, by 1683, established a French presence at Fort Saint Louis on the Illinois River.

THE ILL-FATED TEXAS EXPEDITION

After a hero's welcome was bestowed in Quebec and Montreal, La Salle returned to Paris, also to the cheers of crowds. Not content to enjoy his wealth and noble appointment, he began plans for colonizing the Lower Mississippi. In the summer of 1684, a veritable armada of French ships carrying some 400 men and women set forth for the mouth of the Mississippi. Meanwhile, Cavalier's faithful one-armed partner, Tonti, was to follow the 1682 river expedition toward the goal of a rendezvous with La Salle's fleet at the Mississippi's mouth.

La Salle had demonstrated a fabulous entrepreneurial flair and vision and had bounced back from seemingly unrelenting adversity thus far. But it seems that the dealer in luck had plumb run out of wild cards for the young explorer.

La Salle's Texas expedition was an unmitigated disaster; after losing one ship to pirates in the West Indies, the fleet miscalculated its progress by 400 miles and sailed west beyond the mouth of the Mississippi. Now in Texas waters, one ship sank in the inlets of Matagorda Bay and another ran upon a reef further south near Victoria. No visible maps of the Gulf Coast existed, and for the next two years La Salle's would-be colonists wandered

---

24 Hartsough, *From Canoe to Steel Barge,* pg. 15 (quoting Parkman).

in marshes of the lower delta of Texas. In 1688, with provisions depleting and no reinforcements, skirmishes with warring local Karankawa Indians eventually eliminated the last of the French settlers. Disenchanted members of La Salle's crew had mutinied and killed Cavalier in an ambush one year earlier. Tonti's multi-year search for La Salle was to no avail: René-Robert Cavelier, Sieur de La Salle was dead at 43.

The French nobleman's claim to La Louisiane remained a powerful triumph with lasting historical significance. Over the next century, La Louisiane would be ceded to Spain and then returned to France. It would be 1803 (121 years later) before Napoleon and President Jefferson inked the Louisiana Purchase.

PART II

How the Mississippi River Was Tamed

CORPS OF ENGINEERS—COMMENTARY

In the early 1830s, the goal to vastly improving navigation on the major U.S. rivers was seized by the Corps of Engineers. Legislation in Washington at the time dictated that the Upper and Lower river basins provide a minimum nine-foot depth and minimum channel width of 400 feet. Architectural and engineering planning moved into full swing to construct a series of locks and dams and, behind them, a series of slack water pools. Work on the Upper Mississippi lock and dam system began immediately but was not fully completed until a century later (1930–1940).

Locks and dams on the Upper Mississippi are peculiar inventions which, while not built for flood control, provide an ingenious stairway to connect bidirectional river commerce from St. Paul to St. Louis. Dams on the Upper Mississippi hold back a set level of water to prevent shoaling of the tidal pools and to aid and support hydroelectric generation.

Locks operate with a set of gates—measured to permit access for riverboats, tugs, and barges of standard dimensions. The large Keokuk, Iowa, locks are 100 feet wide and, with gravity on their side, open (for downstream flow) and close (for upstream flow.)

The Corps has another responsibility: to hold river pools unchanged above Lock and Dam 15 at Rock Island, Illinois, to promote the conservation of wildlife.

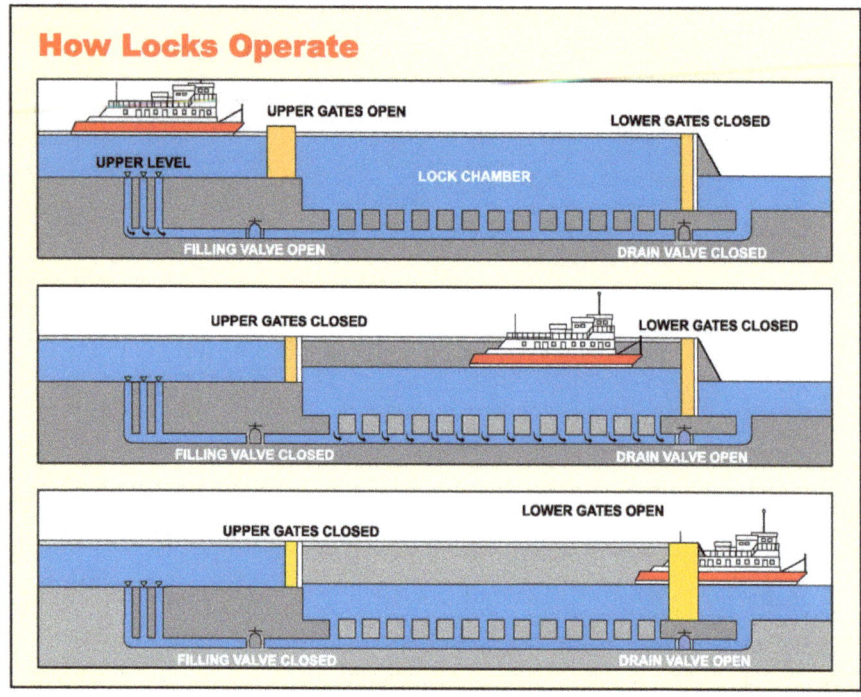

Diagram of lock operation
Source: The United States Army Corps of Engineers, Louisville District

LEVEES, LOCKS, AND DAMS

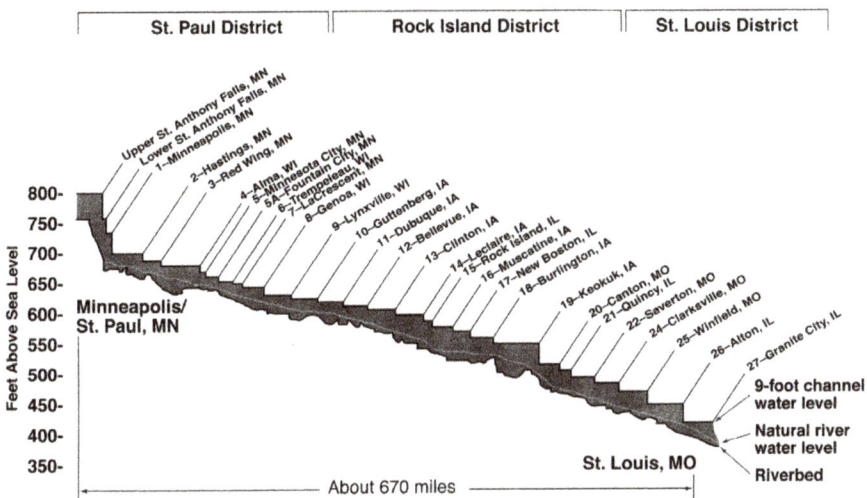

A "Stairway of Water" makes commercial navigation possible between Minneapolis and St. Louis (U.S. Army Corps of Engineers, St. Paul District)

The history of the commercial development of the upper and lower segments of the Mississippi and its host of tributaries is one of continuous efforts by humanity to gain control and impose its will on the great river. Mother Nature created a grand series of veins and arteries that gather billions of gallons of fresh water each day, albeit of a brown hue and flowing on a decidedly irregular course of travel. In due course, water from the extended reaches of Montana, Canada, and Pennsylvania commingle on a tumultuous epic trek that empties into the Gulf of Mexico at Venice, Louisiana.

River-sourced transportation is the lifeblood that sparked the development of the Mississippi Valley. It was accepted that successful navigation would constantly be challenged by snags, shoals, submerged rocks, and rapids. These customized locks and dams allowed river commerce to effectively climb or descend the Upper Mississippi, overcoming the powerful forces of the river's natural ebb and flow.

The strategic and integral role the Mississippi played in the Civil War greatly raised recognition by Congress of the Corps of Engineers. With time, the Corps was able to access funding to widen and deepen and, with maps, lighthouses, and channel markers, greatly improve the safety of the major waterways. Before the Corps pursued a thoughtful, engineering-centric approach to enhancing Mississippi Basin transportation, efforts were crude and haphazard to address channel falls and rapids. Native Americans provided the best answer to the explorers: just circumvent the obstruction with portage.

Henry Shreve, a giant of a man and the creative designer of the steamboat *Washington*, was also the king of the sawyer and snag removal business. (A sawyer is a group of trees embedded in the river bottom at a less than perpendicular angle and subject to the pressure of the current, appearing and disappearing at intervals and mimicking the motion of a saw at a sawmill. A snag refers to trees, branches, and other pieces of naturally occurring wood found sunken in rivers and streams; it is also known as coarse woody debris.) In 1816, Shreve successfully challenged the Fulton/Livingston riverway monopoly. Shreve also holds a key place in riverboat history for championing the use of "cutoffs," where a straight channel was carved through an S curve in the river, shortening, straightening it, and raising the volume of water.

In 1824, the Corps was given the assignment to secure the leading forms of navigation and safety in the Mississippi Valley. That same year, it received a $75,000 appropriation to clear the Ohio River and Lower

Mississippi and appointed Shreve superintendent and snagboat manager. The double-hulled snagboats—"Uncle Sam's Tooth Pullers"—did their job removing snags, sawyers, rafts, and debris, paving the way for New Orleans and St. Louis to emerge as transportation hubs on the Mississippi between 1820 and the Civil War.

One of Shreve's legendary accomplishments was his success in breaking up a 40-mile-long lumber blockage on the Red River, the same river that flows through Shreveport, Louisiana, named for the great man.

In 1879, the Mississippi River Commission was created with oversight regarding focused dredging to remove sandbars, general efforts at channel deepening, and riverbank protection.

A critical decision was assigning the Corps to maintain and operate the Upper Mississippi lock system and to dredge the Mississippi to a minimum nine-foot depth for its entirety.

UPPER MISSISSIPPI VS. LOWER MISSISSIPPI GEOGRAPHY

For the northern segment of the river (above and including St. Louis), 27 locks and two dams exist below the northernmost passage at the Upper Falls of Saint Anthony, just above St. Paul and Minneapolis, Minnesota. Picture a 42-story building. The river has an aggregate fall of more than 420 feet over this 670-mile stretch of the Mississippi.

For the considerably longer, 1,100 miles of the Lower Mississippi, the rate of descent slows measurably. As the starting point for the second half of the great river, the Corps sets the confluence of the Ohio and Mississippi rivers at Cairo, Illinois. Cairo is 290 feet above sea level[25]; for the last 450 miles, the riverbed is below sea level. Today's Lower Mississippi, abetted by a never-ending levee system of massive earthworks, is measured at 15 feet below sea level at Vicksburg and 170 feet below at New Orleans.[26]

---

25 John M. Barry, *Rising Tide: The Great Mississippi Flood of 1927 and How it Changed America* (New York: Simon & Schuster, 1998), pg. 37.
26 Barry, *Rising Tide*, pg. 39.

The straight-line measure of 600 miles from Cairo to the Gulf is more than the 1,000 of twisting, turning sinuous miles.

Although the average descent of the Lower Mississippi amounts to a mere three inches to the mile, the movement of the Father of Waters through that gentle slope can hardly be characterized as stagnant or sleepy. The Lower Mississippi volume of fresh water has been measured as 16,792 cubic meters per second; only slightly less than Canada's Saint Lawrence River, which flows into the Gulf of Saint Lawrence.

Remarkably, the Mississippi ranks No. 10 in terms of discharge among the largest rivers of the world, at about 17,000 cubic meters per second, while the Amazon holds the No. 1 title at some 209,000 per second.[27]

More facts:

"The valley of the Mississippi is 20% larger than China's Yellow River, double that of Africa's Nile and India's Ganges, fifteen times that of Europe's Rhine. Within it lies 41% of the continental United States, including all or part of thirty-one states. No river in Europe, no river in the Orient, no river in the ancient, civilized world compares with it. Only the Amazon and, barely, the Congo have a larger drainage base. Measured from the head of its tributary the Missouri River, as logical, starting point as any, the Mississippi is the longest river in the world, and it pulses like an artery of the American heartland."[28]

There are only 43 dams which regulate the flow of the Upper Mississippi from its origin at Lake Itasca. Surprisingly, there are no dams on the Middle and Lower Mississippi.

The first fourteen dams are located north of Minneapolis. They serve this headwaters region and provide for power generation and general recreation. Below, the remaining 29 dams serve the flow of all riverway traffic with a series of locks promoting commercial travel.

The Upper Mississippi has long been the location of thousands of wing dams or wing dikes, which channel (scour) the central course of the river

---

27 National Park Service website, Mississippi River Facts; https://www.nps.gov/miss/riverfacts.htm
28 Barry, *Rising Tide,* pg. 21.

while promoting conservation and preventing riverbank erosion. The lock and dam system was strengthened in the 1930s when the Corps concentrated its efforts on maintaining a nine-foot-deep channel to accommodate traffic, the preponderance of which was, and is, barge.

The Mississippi starts with a mere three-foot depth at its origin in Lake Itasca before it deepens to up to 12 feet at Minneapolis. At Lake Pepin, just south, it enjoys a depth of up to 30 feet.

Heading to St. Louis, the depth averages 30 feet. Joining the Missouri River there and, just south, the Ohio River at Cairo, its average depth begins to increase to up to 100 feet. Owing to regular dredging, the depth from Baton Rouge, Louisiana, to the Gulf can exceed 200 feet.

Bridges, anathema to the riverman, have been used to span the Mississippi since the 1850s. In earlier days, rudimentary bridges and fording shallows allowed the crossing of the uppermost Mississippi where the nascent river was more of a stream. And, as history recorded the legal battle between the Railroad Bridge Co. (represented by Abraham Lincoln) and the owners of the *Effie Afton*, clear course of right of way has long been contested.[29]

There are no fewer than 10 states from Minnesota to Louisiana that define or share a portion of their borders with the Mississippi. Along this north-south demarcation of the mighty river there are 43 significant bridges, among which many have been rebuilt and expanded over the years for auto, truck, and rail traffic. At the start of the journey downriver is the Stone Arch Bridge at Minneapolis; about midway in St. Louis are the Chain of Rocks and Eads bridges; and in greater New Orleans are the Huey P. Long and Crescent City Connection bridges.

---

29 Brian McGinty, *Lincoln's Greatest Case: The River, the Bridge, and the Making of America* (New York: Liveright, 2015); or a blog post by the Davenport Public Library: https://blogs.davenportlibrary.com/sc/2008/05/06/remembering-the-effie-afton/; or Botkin, *A Treasury*, pg. 139.

ABE AND THE FLATBOATS

There were several elements of flatboats that were advantageous, the most important of which were affordability and ease of acquisition. Abandoned debris was everywhere along the banks of the river—logs, wrecks, and lost pieces of lumber. These odds and ends could be lashed together and, quickly, a new craft was ready to travel—downstream, that is.

The Achilles' heel of flatboats is a rudimentary shortcoming: their lack of propulsion. Steerage was cumbersome and it greatly limited

A flatboat
The Project Gutenberg eBook, American Merchant Ships and Sailors, *by Willis J. Abbot, illustrated by Ray Brown, pg. 267*

their range of operations other than as ferry service to cross the river. Keelboats were perfected and dominated cargo transfer between 1750 and 1820, although flatboats existed well into the 1860s steamboat era.

Flatboats were an inexpensive means of traveling with the current of the great rivers and, as such, served as temporary quarters for men and women headed down the Ohio, Missouri, and Mississippi. Abe Lincoln built a flatboat raft near Springfield, Illinois, while working with this stepbrother. He rode the vessel to New Orleans where the cargo was sold and anything worth its salt was parted out, and finally, the timbers and planks became the foundation of a new structure.

It was by flatboat that Huck Finn and Jim traveled the Mississippi by night.

"Now you'd see a raft sliding by, away off yonder. . . . Once there was a thick fog, and the rafts and things what went by was beating tin pans so the steamboats wouldn't run over them. A scow of a raft went by so close we could hear them talking and cussing and laughing—heard them plain; but we couldn't see no sign of them; it made you feel crawly; it was like spirits carrying on . . . Jim said he believed it was spirits; but I says: "No, spirits wouldn't say, 'Dern this dern fog.'"[30]

---

30 Mark Twain, *The Adventures of Huckleberry Finn* (UK: Chatto & Windus/New York: Charles L. Webster and Company, 1885), pg. 171.

MIKE FINK, KEELBOATMAN

On the continuum of Mississippi water transportation into the nineteenth century, the bookends we know are the birchbark canoes and dugouts favored by the natives for centuries (and from 1500 to 1690 by explorers from de Soto to La Salle) and then the advent of the steam-powered showboats launched by Shreve and Fulton in the 1800s.

Native Americans making a dugout canoe, circa 1590
Wikimedia Commons

Birchbark Canoe
Courtesy of John Lindman, The Bark Canoe Store

Placed in the dead center of the sandwich of time between canoe and steamboat was the flatboat/keelboat period. One particularly key date was 1803, when Thomas Jefferson inked the Louisiana Purchase—a crucial turning point in history when America first began its juggernaut to dominate both the Upper and Lower Mississippi Valley.

The keelboat era belonged to Mike Fink and his colleagues. This era, from 1700 to 1820, was a rough-and-tumble period dominated by the rapid expansion of the relatively crude craft. From 1751 we have reports of keelboats ascending from the Lower Mississippi and, by 1810, some 400 keelboats were active on the Ohio. As late as 1817, commercial riverboat traffic between New Orleans and St. Louis, Louisville, Cincinnati, and Pittsburgh was dominated by a cadre of large keelboats and barges.

A keelboat
www.history.army.mil

Nicholas Roosevelt's *New Orleans* steamer, backed by Robert Fulton and Robert Livingston, may have notched the first successful steamboat cruise from Pittsburgh to New Orleans, but the keelboat fleet did not surrender easily.

Although the keelboat was a glorified raft, primarily propelled by deckhands with poles and ropes, it was vastly superior to rough flatboats. The presence of keel and rudder apparatus was often abetted by a sail and mast, although a favorable wind in the appropriate direction was a rarity.

It was a 70-foot keelboat that Lt. Zebulon Montgomery Pike employed as he journeyed north from St. Louis to the Falls of Saint Anthony at Minneapolis between 1805 and 1807. Under orders from General James Wilkinson, appointed by Jefferson as governor of the Louisiana Territory, Pike was to trace the Mississippi to its source and demonstrate to the fur traders and trappers that this was now American territory.[31]

Riverboatman Mike Fink, alias the Snapping Turtle, dominates the landscape of the keelboat era from 1750 to 1820. Larger than life in all dimensions, Fink was never one to underestimate his own talent and strength. He boasted, "I'm Mike Fink, king of the keelboatmen. I can

---

31 Schneider, *Old Man River,* pg. 239.

out-run, out-hop, out-jump, throw down, drag out, and lick any man in the country. I'm a Salt River roarer, a ring-tailed screamer; I love the wimming (wimmin) and I'm chock-full of fight!"[32]

Mike Fink
Wikimedia Commons

River folklore abounds of Fink's accomplishments as a marksman with impeccable accuracy and of his ability to consume a gallon of whiskey on a 24-hour bender and take on any foe. Fink climbed from ordinary keelboatman to head poleman, then steersman, and finally patroon, or master of the vessel. A rough, tough betting man, Fink was known to provoke hostilities among his competition.

"I've got the best crew and the fastest boat on any river, and if ary man says no, I'll be in his hair quicker than hell can scorch a feather."[33] Constantly raiding local farmers and townsfolk, Fink was forever afoul of the law. Fink's remarkable feats came to an end in 1823 when his last venture as a fur trader led to a double homicide, heavily lubricated by spirits, near the mouth of the Yellowstone River.

---

32 Hartsough, *From Canoe to Steel Barge*, pg. 38.
33 *Ibid.*, pg 34.

THE SHOWBOAT SAGA

After the glory days of keelboats had waned and before the 1900 appearance of purposed excursion steamers, were the "showboat" years. More floating theater than boat, showboats flourished during the relatively brief period from 1830 to 1865.

Far inferior to paddle wheel steamers, showboats were crude vessels of some 100 by 16 feet, usually lacking their own means of propulsion and resembling hastily constructed shacks built around a stage or stages. Here, second-rate actors were floated down river from one small port town to the next. The average offering was a melodrama with aspiring troupes reaching for applause from performances of *Hamlet* or *The Merchant of Venice*.

Gilbert R. Spalding's showboat
The Floating Palace
Wikimedia Commons

Some of the entertainment presented by showboats was unsavory. Meanwhile, there were legitimate operators like actor William Chapman and his family who offered clean thespian entertainment. However, showboating deteriorated when the 200-foot-long *Floating Circus Palace* emerged.

Showboating fell into disrepute in the 1850s and was abruptly, but mercifully, terminated by the Civil War. Ironically, the *Palace* met its demise when it was confiscated by Confederate troops in 1862 and turned into a hospital.

Mountebanks posing as showboat actors were known to bilk the public, compromising the reputations of legitimate operators and offering itinerant merchants a stage from which to flog "patent medicines" and elixirs surprisingly similar to pure whiskey. In the end, the showboat trade was undone by the motley array of gamblers, robbers, pirates, and prostitutes that infiltrated its ranks to prey on the unwary.

The *Cotton Blossom*
Courtesy of the Dave Thomson Collection at Steamboats.com

Interest in showboats had a brief revival in the 1920s on the heels of the publication of Edna Ferber's novel and subsequent Broadway musical and movies, all titled *Showboat*. One inaccuracy was repeated in the movie versions: the *Cotton Blossom* vessel in Farber's novel was actually a barge and not a self-propelled steamer.

CONSTRUCTION AND DESTRUCTION OF THE MISSISSIPPI ARTERY OF RIVERS

The Hudson River's enormous mile-wide width and up to 200-foot depth provided Robert Fulton a great canvas on which to design and operate his first steamer, the famous *Clermont* (as she came to be known), although formally named the *North River*. The nickname is for co-developer Robert R. Livingston's home, Clermont Manor, where the steamer would port during her journey to and from Albany and New York City.

The 1807 *Clermont* wasn't an obvious or spectacular success in the eye of the burgeoning water transportation industry. In fact, the few shoreline bystanders who witnessed the event on the lower Hudson were hardly in awe when Fulton's craft clumsily navigated from launch to dock without grave miscue or outright disaster.

Robert Fulton
Wikimedia Commons

Moving inland had created new obstacles: powerful (unpredictable) winds and tide. Sure, sail could work on the inland rivers—maybe for minutes, perhaps hours—but the future flow, depth, and direction of each river passage confounded captains. Sail was not the option.

A wild inventor, Fulton stood on the "shoulders of his predecessors": Many had experimented before, and major progress was notched. Fulton's steam apparatus, hardly ready for prime time in 1807, was the wave of the future.

In the early days of the nineteenth century, eastern steamboats differed markedly from their western counterparts: their deeper drafts provided ample cargo space, but the early models were underpowered mechanically for the more powerful river flows. Their ultimate shortcoming was not at all appreciated: the deep Hudson had welcomed Peter Minuit and his merry band of original traders who made the ultimate "million dollar" trade for Manhattan Island. (Minuit paid the Lenape Native Americans 60 guilders—approximately $1,329 US in 2023).

Beads, trinkets, and promises. Sad to think that the commerce with the Native Americans has been so lopsided for so long.

Fulton craft's deep-hull design made them unsuitable for the shallow, shifting western river bottoms.

Robert R. Livingston
Attributed to Gilbert Stuart
Wikimedia Commons

Peter Minuit
Wikimedia Commons

THE GLORY DAYS OF STEAMBOAT EXPANSION: 1820-1870

F ulton and Livingston's Hudson River creation—the *Clermont*—marked, in 1807, the epic, first commercially viable steamboat journey. Men of great legal and financial insight, Livingston and Fulton sought a monopoly on inland riverboat transportation. Only Louisiana acquiesced. The uncontested first steamboat on the Mississippi, the *New Orleans*, funded by Nicholas Roosevelt and built in Pittsburgh, docked in the city of the steamer's name in 1810.

The *Clermont*
Wikimedia Commons

Folklore has it that an old Negro, seeing the *New Orleans* pass through Natchez, remarked, "Ole Mississippi done met her master now."[34]

Had the Livingston monopoly continued, the rapid adoption of steamboat commerce might not have materialized. Thankfully, American innovation and free markets intervened.

---

34 Wayman, *Life on the River*, pg. 144.

THE STRECKFUS RIVERBOAT DYNASTY

Enter keelboatman, inventor, entrepreneur, and patriot, Henry M. Shreve. He's the fellow celebrated in the northern Louisiana city of Shreveport. Well familiar with inland rivers, and knowing that they're shallower than eastern rivers, Shreve doubted the Fulton/Livingston-design boat would work well on the Mississippi.

Shreve teamed with a partner in Pittsburgh and converted the small *Enterprise* to a new class of Mississippi steamboat—one that would outperform the existing eastern river steamers of Fulton design.

Henry M. Shreve
Wikimedia Commons

Shreve accompanied the *Enterprise* on an uneventful and successful maiden voyage from Pittsburgh to New Orleans. He defied the Fulton/Livingston monopoly by traveling the Lower Mississippi. Not unexpectedly, legal fireworks quickly enveloped the *Enterprise*; the vessel was seized by the courts. At the time, Shreve had a mission: to demand clarity from the Louisiana judiciary in a direct challenge to the legitimacy/legality of the Fulton/Livingston monopoly.

It should be noted that, in addition to pursuing the court case, Shreve found the energy to lend an important hand to General Andrew Jackson, whose troops were preparing for the British advance on the Port of New Orleans. Shreve, who was in New Orleans having delivered supplies to Jackson via the

The *Enterprise*
Wikimedia Commons

Enterprise, was in Chalmette, Louisiana, manning firearms in Jackson's defense in the Battle of New Orleans—the final skirmish in the War of

The Glory Days of Steamboat Expansion: 1820–1870

1812 and one that, paradoxically, had already been declared a victory before the decisive U.S. rout of the British, as the war had ended 18 days earlier.

The *Enterprise* had been a grand experiment. Now, Shreve set out to build his magnum opus: the *Washington*. Built on a flatbottom hull with a shallow draught, the *Washington* featured a novel concept: its boilers and pistons were placed on the deck and not below, in the hull. To meet the need for cargo storage and passenger staterooms, the *Washington* was built like a wedding cake, with stories above the hull.

Every great inventor must experience painful setbacks. For Shreve, the first sea trials of the *Washington* in 1816 were a disaster. A tragic boiler explosion caused the deaths of 13 *Washington* crew members. Shreve, though scalded himself, saw that necessary repairs and refinements to the vessel were implemented. He then guided the *Washington* to New Orleans, where it was welcomed with much fanfare and promptly seized again by the courts.

Livingston is reported to have addressed Henry Shreve: "You deserve well of your country, young man, but we shall be compelled to beat you if we can."[35]

The Fulton/Livingston monopoly was declared unconstitutional in 1816.

In 1817, the *Washington*, demonstrating proven engineering and ample boiler power to overcome strong Mississippi currents, made the round trip from Louisville to New Orleans in 41 days. (By the 1850s, steamers routinely completed each leg of this journey in five days.)

The *Washington*
Wikimedia Commons

The 1820s ushered in a period of remarkable growth in steamboating. Shreve's contraption was streamlined; innovative boiler and piston engineering was introduced; and steerage was much improved, including the introduction of the sidewheeler, a popular design.

---

35 Hartsough, *From Canoe to Steel Barge*, pg. 46.

By some accounts, there were 230 steamboats active in 1834, primarily on the Ohio River. At that pivotal time, some 3,000 keelboats and flatboats were also still competing for river commerce.

However, for the torrid westward and southward U.S. expansion, steamers were quickly becoming the water transportation mode of choice; in less than a decade, the number of active keelboats would dwindle to a mere handful (55) while shipyards were furiously turning out more and better steamers.[36]

"The accelerating effect of steamboats on the economy and population of the watershed can hardly be overstated. In the decades before the Civil War, the population west of the Appalachians grew at a rate three or four times that of the nation as a whole. There were a million people of all races in the watershed in 1810, a figure that grew sixfold by 1840.

"By the time the Civil War erupted, nearly half the population—15 million people—lived in the towns and cities that seemed to blossom out of nowhere along the rivers. Between 1810 and 1840, St. Louis grew from 1,600 to 77,000; Cincinnati, from 2,500 to 115,000; and New Orleans, from 17,000 to more than 116,000.

Mark Twain
Wikimedia Commons

"At the top of the river, Minneapolis went from a single U.S. Army fort at the falls of Saint Anthony to a town of nearly 6,000 by 1860."[37]

New and affordable access to markets reached inland as the golden era of new steamer construction itself transformed Pittsburgh, Cincinnati, Wheeling, and Louisville into centers of

---

36 Hartsough, *From Canoe to Steel Barge*, pg. 57.
37 Schneider, *Old Man River*, pg. 249.

The Glory Days of Steamboat Expansion: 1820–1870

iron manufacturing and machinery. On the Upper Mississippi, opulently outfitted steamers began to offer "the Fashionable Tour," which attracted wealthy tourists, including some contemporary authors of note.

Samuel Clemens hailed from Hannibal, Missouri. His chronicles of the history of the Mississippi River are legendary, as is his *The Adventures of Huckleberry Finn*, "the great American novel." Years after apprenticing and becoming a riverboat pilot (1857–1859), Mark Twain recounted his extraordinary experiences in the epic *Life on the Mississippi* (1883).

Born in 1835, Twain grew up to see the rise, and later the retrenchment, of the great Mississippi steamship era. Twain died in 1910, just as Streckfus Steamers Inc. founder John Streckfus was introducing the excursion steamer era.

Not all writers were as kind to the Mississippi as Mark Twain. In *Domestic Manners of the Americans*, Frances "Fanny" Trollope, described her 1828 adventure aboard the *Belvedere*: "Let no one who wishes to receive agreeable impressions of American manners, commence their travels in a Mississippi steam boat; for myself, it is with all sincerity I declare, that I would infinitely prefer sharing the apartment of a party of well conditioned pigs to the being confined to its cabin."

In *A Treasury of Mississippi River Folklore*, B.A. Botkin wrote:

> Over some of the sloughs and backwaters and swamps. . . . hangs a

Frances Trollope
by Auguste Hervieu
Wikimedia Commons

The *Belvedere*
Courtesy of the Dave Thomson Collection at Steamboats.com

fading memory and perhaps the ghost of an odor compounded of raw whisky and cheap perfume. . . . Lawless men have always flocked to the edge of things . . . the Mississippi itself was a boundary line . . . and men—and women—whom the law would lay its hand upon needed only to cross from one bank to the other in order to escape jurisdiction.

So there came into being the floating dance hall which was also a saloon and brothel. It might be just a pair of flatboats joined together. . . . Thieves, female harpies, and men who would do murder for a meed (sic) were aboard these floating dives. Their chosen victims were the rude raftsmen and lumberman who at winter's end had come out of the valleys of the six great timber rivers in response to the primal urges of lust and liquor.

With thicker settlement, the floating resorts, also called 'love boats,' disappeared. They never quite came back, but there was something rather like them during Prohibition; still moonshine is made in the sloughs and swampy woods behind some of the islands. Somehow stagnant water and righteous living never got along well together.[38]

Charles Dickens
by Margaret Gillies, 1843
Wikimedia Commons

Sharp-tongued Charles Dickens, who visited the Mississippi Valley in the 1840s, wrote in *American Notes for General Circulation*: "But what words shall describe the Mississippi, great father of rivers, who—praise be to Heaven—has no young children

---
38 B.A. Botkin, Editor, *A Treasury of Mississippi River Folklore* (New York: Crown Publishers, Inc., 1955), pg. 370.

like him!" He went on to describe it as "an enormous ditch . . . running liquid mud."

John James Audubon wrote of his 1843 journey in *The Missouri River Journals* that the steamer was "the very filthiest of all filthy old rat-traps I ever travelled in."

He further commented on his fellow passengers, "Our *compagnons de voyage*, about one hundred and fifty, were composed of Buckeyes, Wolverines, Suckers, Hoosiers, and gamblers, with drunkards of each and every denomination, their ladies and babies of the same nature, and specifically the dirtiest of the dirty."[39]

John James Audubon
by John Syme, 1826
Wikimedia Commons

Twain wrote in *Life on the Mississippi* that it is said there is a nutritiousness to the river's water and that those who drank it "could grow corn in his stomach if he wanted to." Meanwhile, he wrote that Ohio River water was too clear to be worthwhile.

He quoted a riverman: "You look at the graveyards; that tells the tale. Trees won't grow worth shucks in a Cincinnati graveyard, but in a [Saint] Louis graveyard they grow upwards of eight hundred foot high. It's all on account of the water the people drunk before they laid up. A Cincinnati corpse don't richen a soil any."[40]

Botkin wrote in *A Treasury of Mississippi River Folklore*:[41]

Captain Barney . . . every evening before supper lowers a tin bucket into the muddy river, and, when it is filled, drinks the thick brown

---

39 Schneider, *Old Man River*, pg. 256.
40 Twain, *Life on the Mississippi*, pg. 227.
41 Botkin, *A Treasury*, pg. 5.

fluid until every drop has vanished. "Keeps my health a-going good." He drawls lazily. "It's this here filtering and all the fancy fixings they do to the water that causes all of the sickness there is nowadays. Just takes all the strength out of it."

"Talk about filters," said a Cincinnatian. "Just drink a quart of Ohio River water, and stand out in the sun for five minutes, and you will find the water coming out of every pore, beautifully filtered, while your stomach becomes converted into a sandbag, and you can hear the gravel when you walk."

Missouri Woman traveler: "So charged with sand and mud, why is it supposed to be healthful?" She was silenced by the Captain's glare, "Because it scours out your bowels, Ma'am."

LINCOLN AND THE ROCK ISLAND RAILROAD BRIDGE LAWSUIT

Competition between the water transportation community and the powerful railroad industry came to a peak in the mid-1800s. Construction of the first railroad bridge to span the Mississippi, the Rock Island, Illinois, to Davenport, Iowa, crossing, began in 1853 and sparked a lasting wave of controversy. A year later, West Point graduate Jefferson Davis, then secretary of war under President Franklin Pierce, ordered that work on the bridge be halted.

Rock Island, whose rapids had been surveyed years earlier by another West Point graduate, Robert E. Lee, stood out as a prime bridge location. The rock island that gave the city its name offered a superb site on which to anchor a three-part span: a short bridge between Illinois and the island and, after a leg across the island, a longer bridge section to the Iowa shore.

In 1854, however, Secretary Davis wanted a bridge across the Mississippi in the South. A court order to stop construction at Rock Island failed, however, as the island had long been abandoned as a military base.

On April 22, 1856, there was a celebration when the first eight cars of passengers crossed the great river from Rock Island to Davenport by rail. With western railroad traffic now a reality, a new era of American expansion seemed at hand. Nonetheless, all was not well for the Rock Island Bridge: new suits challenging its right to passage were yet to come.

Two weeks after the bridge opened, the steamer *Effie Afton* had an unfortunate altercation with the bridge. It is unclear what caused the *Effie Afton* to veer off course after it had successfully passed under the new structure.

Inexplicably, the vessel lost power and crashed against a bridge pier/footing. The steamer caught on fire in minutes and sank shortly some half-mile downriver. Thankfully, all the *Effie Afton* passengers (excepting a herd of 300 cattle), were saved.

The owners immediately filed a lawsuit, contending that the bridge unlawfully interfered with river commerce. Interests on the Mississippi quickly lined up with the plaintiff.

Paul Schneider wrote in *Old Man River: The Mississippi River in North American History*, "What the powerful steamboat industry was after . . . was not just removing the Rock Island Bridge, but stopping all bridges across the Mississippi as a way of protecting their business from the burgeoning railroad industry. The case pitted the power of St. Louis and New Orleans against that of Chicago and New York: riverboats against railroads."[42]

The import of the case, *Hurd v. Rock Island Railroad Co.*, brought forth the best legal counsel for a trial in Chicago on Sept. 8, 1857. The railroad's interests were well served by a tall, gangly attorney from Illinois. Abraham Lincoln was corporate counsel for the Illinois Central and the Alton & Sangamon railroads. Moreover, Lincoln had a long history of defense of the Illinois Central and had lobbied for federal land grants of 2.5 million acres in the state of Illinois, benefiting the railroad.

In 1900, Ida M. Tarbell, in *The Life of Abraham Lincoln*, quoted Henry W. Blodgett, who was a law student during the trial and later became a federal judge: "I have always considered it as one of the ablest efforts I ever heard from Mr. Lincoln at the bar. His illustrations

---

42 Schneider, *Old Man River*, pg. 270.

were apt and forcible, his statements clear and logical, and his reasons in favor of the policy—and necessarily the right—to bridge the river, and thereby encourage the settlement and building up of the vast area of fertile country to the west of it, were broad and statesmanlike."[43]

Testimony of 18 witnesses to the fire and sinking of the *Effie Afton* were heard over the course of the 14-day trial.

In Blodgett's words, Lincoln's arguments stressed that "one man had as good a right to cross a river as another had to sail up or down it; that these were equal and mutual rights which must be exercised so as not to interfere with each other, like the right to cross a street or a highway and the right to pass along it."

Abraham Lincoln
by Joslin, 1857
Wikimedia Commons

As for crossing the river, "must it always be by canoe or ferryboat?"

Lincoln then drew a vivid picture of the future of the great West lying beyond the river. "The necessities of commerce demanded that the bridges across the river be a conceded right, which the steamboat interests ought not to be allowed to successfully resist, and thereby stay the progress of development and civilization in the region of the West."[44]

Lincoln was passionate and his arguments were persuasive—but not to the extent that there was a clear victory for the rails; the trial ended in a hung jury. Eventually, the case was settled by the U.S. Supreme Court, permitting the Rock Island (and other bridges) to remain, and settling the question for all time.

---

43 Botkin, *A Treasury*, pg. 139.
44 *Ibid.*

Swift railroad expansion across the Mississippi and its tributaries (often abetted by predatory pricing and other anti-competitive practices) ushered in the eventual death blow to the commercial packet steamer business.

EADS VS. HUMPHREYS—ENGINEERING FIREWORKS ON THE RIVER

The multitude of states benefiting from the Mississippi, Ohio, Missouri, and connecting waterways increasingly demanded federal attention. Meanwhile, unrelenting national growth and economic expansion were a powerful impetus compelling cooperation with Washington. Between 1842 and 1847, important conventions were held in Cincinnati, Memphis, and Chicago, bringing pressure on the Capitol to address obstacles to river navigation and flood control, and to improve access to the Gulf of Mexico, as unpredictable sandbars formed at its mouth.

At the time, James Buchanan Eads (1820–1887) and Andrew Atkinson Humphreys (1810–1883) waged a lifelong battle over how to best address the challenges of the Mississippi. Each was a distinguished and influential engineer; each disagreed on nearly everything related to the mighty river.

HUMPHREYS

Humphreys, whose grandfather and father each made significant contributions to the design and construction of U.S. warships (including the USS *Constitution*, "Old Ironsides"), was preordained to enter the U.S. Military Academy at West Point. After a brief stint in the battlefield, he became a civil engineer with the Army Corps of Engineers and began a decade of work on flood and riverbed control. The *Report Upon the Physics and Hydraulics of the Mississippi River*, which he co-authored and was published in 1861, was widely acclaimed.

Humphreys' work on surveys and engineering the Mississippi often clashed with that of others, specifically civil engineer Charles Ellet Jr. An appropriation of funds was approved by President Millard Fillmore and divided between Ellet and Humphreys; each was to lead his own independent study of the river and solutions, particularly to flooding. The men differed in their conclusions. "Ellet proposed a comprehensive approach to control floods, including improving levees, enlarging natural outlets, and adding artificial outlets and reservoirs."[45]

Andrew Atkinson Humphreys
*Brady-Handy Photograph Collection
Wikimedia Commons*

Meanwhile, "Humphreys continued to reject the engineering hypothesis that underlay the levees-only idea. He continued to warn that the closing of natural outlets would be disastrous. Yet he was recommending that levees, and levees only, be used to contain the Mississippi River and its floods. He had found a facile way to reconcile his conclusion with seemingly contradictory analysis and data."[46]

Later, Humphreys's engineering talent was tapped when planning was underway for the first transcontinental railroad. The onset of the Civil War led to his promotion to major and chief topographical engineer. His service in the Civil War was legendary, with meritorious combat action in

---

45 Barry, *Rising Tide*, pg. 45.
46 *Ibid.*

battles at Antietam, Fredericksburg, Chancellorsville, and Gettysburg. He was decorated and promoted repeatedly, rising to the rank of permanent brigadier general.

Ellet was killed while commanding a Union warship.

Post-bellum, Humphreys returned to the Corps and served as Chief of Engineers with oversight over several hundred officers and civilians working on crucial river and harbor work. However, James Buchanan Eads took Humphreys to task on many concepts and scientific assumptions.

Separately, Humphreys, who became a sworn enemy, professionally challenged Eads's engineering marvel, the Eads Bridge at St. Louis, doubting the safety of its two steel arches of 600 and 400 feet and urging its demolition.

Returning to the Mississippi, Eads and Humphreys next butted heads on a national quandary: The "last 100 miles" of the river delta. Who could deliver the best answer to keeping this vital commercial and defense corridor open through to the Gulf of Mexico?

EADS

James Buchanan Eads (named for a relative, future President James Buchanan[47]), unlike Humphreys, grew up in poverty in St. Louis. Employing self-taught academic proficiency in the sciences and civil engineering, Eads was a visionary, creative engineer. First, Eads invented and built salvage vessels uniquely suited to the Mississippi River's extreme currents and introduced a unique diving bell.

James Buchanan Eads
*Brady-Handy Photograph Collection
Wikimedia Commons*

---

47 Barry, *Rising Tide*, pg. 28.

The business prospered and his knack for clearing the river earned him the courtesy title of "Captain" from river pilots in recognition of his brave work deep in the dangerous water under his diving bell; Eads did a great deal of the diving himself.

The Civil War focused Eads's attention elsewhere. Consulted for his knowledge of the Mississippi, he was pressed into service immediately. His mission: design and construct ironclad warships in support of the Union effort.

In short order, he produced seven ironclads and converted a river steamer into the metal-reinforced *Essex*. Altogether, Eads produced 30 ironclads of increasing adaptability and range; these gunboats were instrumental in the Union successes at Fort Henry, Tennessee, and the Union attack on the important Confederate city of Mobile, Alabama.

An 1875 drawing of Eads Bridge
by Camille N. Drie
Wikimedia Commons

After the war, his novel arch Eads Bridge, constructed between 1867 and 1874, employed a cantilever design and was the first all-steel structure. With a center support resting on bedrock under the river, the two spans of the arched structure of 600 and 400 feet allowed steamer traffic to pass easily.

The Eads Bridge is still in use today, nearly 150 years later, and is designated a National Historic Landmark.

EADS AND HUMPHREYS COLLIDE

The continual silting up of the mouth of the Mississippi had been an ongoing dilemma since the Corps first struggled to cut a shipping lane through the sandbars in 1837. The jetties that were originally erected by the Corps were ill-designed and proved of little value.

Eads vs. Humphreys—Engineering Fireworks on the River

Humphreys, in his position as head of the Corps, had promised a shipping channel with a depth of 18 feet. He placed all his bets on two super-sized dredge barges, the first of which was the *Essayons*, built and put in action in 1868.

The results were abysmal: the dredges were underpowered and ineffective.[48]

Humphreys's officer in charge of the Corps' effort, Captain Charles Howell, was under great duress; he had resorted to blaming the shallow cut across the bar on sabotage by tugboats.

U.S. Army Corps of Engineers dredge boat Essayons in 1871, at work removing the bar at the mouth of the Southwest Pass on the Mississippi River.
Wikimedia Commons

The idea of a canal, first proposed in 1832, was resurrected and the Corps and New Orleans businesses gave it their blessing.

". . . The New Orleans Chamber of Commerce . . . reported that while it did not fear New Orleans' loss of position through the competition of railroads, serious danger to her future lay in the hampering of trade by the sand bars at the mouth of the river."[49]

Enter Eads, on the cusp of the opening of his grand bridge. He circumvented the Corps and other naysayers with an outrageous proposal: He would employ a series of wooden jetties that would channel the river and scour the bottom to a depth of 28 feet at a width of 350 feet.

Eads was so convinced and convincing, he offered to build the jetties at his own risk at a cost less than the canal proposal of $13 million.[50] Humphreys and the Corps waged a powerful campaign to discredit Eads and his engineering project.

---

48 Barry, *Rising Tide*, pg. 69.
49 Hartsough, *From Canoe to Steel Barge*, pg. 195.
50 Barry, *Rising Tide*, pgs. 71–75.

A national furor ensued, and it took an act of Congress for the "Eads Jetties" proposal to prevail in 1874. The jetties worked beautifully, and South Pass became the favored channel of choice into and out of the Gulf.

Eads did not give up after one victory. His work returned to the more expansive and challenging task of deepening the entire Mississippi.

". . . Eads proposed to invade the river, to build not levees back from the banks but jetties in the river channel. These would constrict the water year-round, even at low water, and apply a constant scouring of the bottom. He also called for cutoffs to create a far straighter and faster river. All this, he was certain, would significantly deepen the river."[51]

Eads' Jetties
Wikimedia Commons

---

51 Barry, *Rising Tide*, pg. 79.

PART III

The Streckfus Family

BALTHAZAR STRECKFUS

Johannes Streckfus was greatly troubled and in suspense as his bride, Catherine Geiger Streckfus, entered labor on April 30, 1821. He knew the risks a later-in-life pregnancy could present, and Catherine was with child at age 41.

Later that evening, he fought tears of joy and sorrow. First, he stood elated as he gathered his new son, Balthazar, in his arms; later, he grew despondent, holding Catherine's hand as her vital signs faded into the night. Catherine died the next day, leaving Balthazar and a brother, Michael, five, in his care.

Under Johannes's guidance, young Balthazar trained as a wagon-maker and blacksmith in their town, Laudenbach, Main-Spessart, Bavaria. Balthazar's courtship with the lovely Anna Marie Schaab, a fellow Bavarian also of straight Germanic descent, led to marriage in 1845. The couple, living in a hamlet of Munich, soon celebrated the birth of daughters, Barbara and Catherine.

These were unsettling political times in and around the Prussian empire, and the prospect of emigration to America was compelling to the 29-year-old Balthazar. The flight of emigrants to the U.S.—the Forty-Eighters—was responsible for the creations of a "German Belt," which, while concentrated in the Midwest, extended across the country from Pennsylvania to the Oregon coast. In recent years, an estimated 44 million Americans considered themselves of Germanic descent, roughly 14% of the U.S. population.

Protests, discontent, and uprisings had broken out in many European countries. At home in Bavaria, these were the days that constituted the German Revolutions between 1848 and 1849, which pitted middle-class liberal principles against the more radical reformists of the working class. At this time, Marx and Engels were active supporters of constitutional reform. While the revolutionary forces failed in unifying the German-speaking state, the discontent led to the German emigration boom that lasted from 1820 to World War I.

Balthazar must have been quite resourceful and convincing when he announced to Anna Marie that the family was to depart from Le Havre, France, on the *Mobile* for New York City on April 1, 1852.

The *Mobile* had a capacity of 960 and its Master was J.H. Tailox. The journey was to be 40 days. Horrendous weather and angry seas battered her across the Atlantic, causing her to veer off course and finally unload at the Port of New Orleans after 90 days at sea.

The Atlantic crossing was challenged by more than extreme weather. Life-threatening diphtheria, smallpox, and dysentery haunted the passengers, and at least one poor soul was lost overboard.

Balthazar, Anna Marie, Barbara (b. 1848) and Catherine (b. 1850) survived the treacherous journey. Remarkably, while at sea, the family welcomed a newest member: Anna Marie gave birth to a boy, Michael (b. 1852), named for his uncle still in Bavaria. Details of the voyage are according to a scrapbook kept by Margaret Ann Streckfus, a descendant of Michael, the boy born at sea. Separately, Gregg and Eve Boyle of Salina, Kansas, acquired an antique trunk at auction in 1982. They were hoping that it belonged to Gregg's ancestor, Balthazar's son Michael, and that Michael had moved to Saline County with his wife in 1878. After cleaning, they found the faint words "B. Streckfus uber Havre nach New Orleans" on the trunk, meaning "across Le Havre toward New Orleans." If it really is the Streckfus trunk and the words are correct, the story that they had been blown off course cannot be true.

Balthazar Streckfus

The weather in New Orleans—often warm and humid—did not suit the family, so they ascended the Mississippi River to settle on a parcel of land in Edgington, Illinois, 20 miles southwest of Rock Island. They farmed, even though Balthazar was a trained wagon-maker, not a farmer. While there, the family grew, as John (b. 1856), Mary (b. 1860), Anna (b. 1864) and Henry (b. 1866) were born.

Balthazar and son John delivered grain from their farm to Rock Island, which had been incorporated in 1837. They sent it out by any one of several of the regularly docking steamboats at this port across from Davenport, Iowa. In 1860, more than 700 rivercrafts tramped the Mississippi River.[52]

Balthazar Streckfus
Ancestry.com

> Native American Indians were fascinated by "the big smoke canoes" which loudly coughed, snorted and bravely paddled upstream against the strong currents of the wild Missouri, Ohio and Mississippi rivers.[53]

John, deeply fascinated with the river trade, stowed away by hiding in a corn sack. He was a mere six or eight years old when he experienced his first waterborne adventure. (In one family story he was six; in another, he was eight.) In her doctoral dissertation, Dolores Jane Meyer reports that

---

52 "Steamboat Graveyards Yield 'Time Capsules' to Salvagers," Jim Shur, Associated Press, July 7, 2002, *Los Angeles Times*.
53 Dolores Jane Meyer, "Excursion Steamboating on the Mississippi River with Streckfus Steamers, Inc.," Ann Arbor, Mich.: University Microfilms, 1976, c1968, pg. 88.

he stowed away on the steamboat *Gem City*. If correct, it is very romantic indeed because *Gem City* was owned by the Diamond Jo Steamboat Line, which John would purchase in 1911. Many sources, however, including Captain Fred Way's account, claim that *Gem City* was built in 1884 after John was an adult; another that *Gem City* was built in 1881 and burned in 1883. John was punished by his father for stowing away, but he did not lose his desire to be a steamboat man.[54] Famously, Balthazar was not amused, and young John was severely reprimanded. Nevertheless, the young man's water lust had been kindled and would burn bright in the coming years.

In 1868, the Streckfuses moved to Rock Island, Illinois, where Balthazar opened a profitable wagon-making and blacksmith shop attached to the home his sons Mike, Henry, and John built for the family at the corner of 9th and 4th. The trip into town from the farm in Edgington had become "just too much on a daily basis."[55]

By 1876, John, now 20 years old, owned a grocery store and mill jointly with a maternal cousin, Joseph Schaab. In 1880, he married Theresa Bartemeier of Davenport, Iowa.[56] Nine children followed. John Streckfus became known as "the Commodore," not as a military title–but an appropriate moniker. Certainly, it distinguished him from

**Capt. John Streckfus
"The Commodore"**
Arthur L. Smith's Personal Collection

---

54 Built to Last: Rock Island expands on its river roots, John Willard, *Quad-City Times*, July 17, 2001.
55 Rock Island, Illinois, Streckfus House, Balthazar Streckfus.
56 http://iagenweb.org/muscatine/biographies1911/bartemeier.htm

his son with the same name, and it fit him as the head of his renowned family. The Commodore died in St. Louis, Missouri, in 1925. By that time, he prided himself on many accomplishments of his steamboating business, and his obituary in the *Davenport Democrat and Leader* proclaimed him "the steamboat King."

Three generations of the family, beginning with the Commodore's own children, worked on various Streckfus boats. All the boys with the Streckfus surname became riverboat captains.

From a humble start on the very upper reaches of the Mississippi, John Streckfus and his sons and grandchildren built a magnificent business of palatial excursion steamcraft, affording millions of people millions of miles of travel pleasure on the Streckfus line of vessels for over a century.

On March 27, 1881, Balthazar passed away at age 59. He was an exceptional businessman who had succeeded in building a new life for his family in America. In addition to his primary work at the forge, he built a profitable block of homes and businesses in Rock Island. To express their gratitude, Balthazar's sons built a magnificent home in nearby Rock Island at 908 4th Avenue, a rock-solid brick testament to architecture (the house was built in 1867–1871). The Streckfus House stands today and is registered as a National Historical treasure.

The Streckfus House
908 4th Avenue, Rock Island, Illinois
Courtesy of Community & Economic Development Department City of Rock Island

It is also clear that Balthazar knew how to save and invest. Occam's razor holds that "entities should not be multiplied without necessity." An embellishment on pragmatism is that "parsimony is a virtue, particularly if practiced by an ancestor."

According to probate proceedings that were concluded on Aug. 13, 1881, Balthazar had accumulated significant assets. History offers little information on the distribution of his wealth. John Streckfus, who owned the grocery and mill by this time, was executor and likely applied his share of proceeds to buy his first boat.

THE *FREDDIE*, 1884

John Balthazar Streckfus's early fascination with the steamboats that paddled the Mississippi at Rock Island and Davenport had not diminished.[57] On land, he was reportedly bedeviled by chronic allergies exacerbated by his required constant exposure to grain dust.

By 1884, he owned the small sidewheeler *Freddie*, purchased from the government, and was president and general manager of his own Acme Packet Co., headquartered at Rock Island. It would have made sense that John's older brother, Michael, who was born at sea while the Streckfus family was crossing the Atlantic, would have been the son who chose to make his fortune on the water. Yet it was John. Michael did have an adventuresome spirit, though, and, when reaching his majority, he headed west to Kansas, where he put down roots in farming.

The dimensions of the *Freddie* and *Verne Swain* would pale in comparison with later excursion craft in the Streckfus riverboat dynasty with the *President* (1931) and the

The *Freddie*
Arthur L. Smith's Personal Collection

---

57 In his probate, the patriarch is referred to as John "B."; it seems realistic to conclude that he chose to shorten the cumbersome Balthazar.

Admiral (1940) ultimately becoming flagships. Freddie (length, 73 feet; beam, 16 feet; hold, 3 feet) could have been laid across the 90-foot beam of the *Admiral*, which entered service some 66 years later as the Mississippi's largest excursion steamer, on par with ocean-faring cruise lines.

Meanwhile, the sternwheeler *Verne Swain* (length, 122 feet; beam, 22.5 feet) would displace only a third of the *Admiral's* top lido deck when measured against its length. At 374 feet, the *Admiral* was a freshwater-based equivalent of an ocean liner.

John's experience in both farming and retail gave him keen business skills, but it also gave him a unique understanding of additional services needed by cargo customers—i.e., the Andalusia, Illinois, area farmers that included those in nearby Edgington, Illinois. Along with bringing Andalusian produce 10 miles north, he often transacted business with Rock Island merchants on behalf of his clients.

Selling their cargo for cash, he then acquired the laundry list of goods the farmers sought. Streckfus gave white-glove service and timely pickup and delivery. Consequently, ". . . farmers of the Andalusia vicinity beat a path to his boat."[58, 59]

With the *Freddie*, the Commodore, as John Streckfus came to be known, quickly established a thriving business. After a few years, Streckfus needed to upgrade and grow. The *Freddie* was sold back to the U.S. Engineers (later the Corps of Engineers) in 1889 when the *Verne Swain* took over the Streckfus route. The Streckfus family held great love and respect for the *Freddie* even after her name was changed to the *Mac*. The vessel was ultimately retired and dismantled for parts some half dozen years later.

---

[58] George W. Wickstrom, *The Town Crier* (Rock Island, Illinois: The J.W. Porter Company, 1948), pg. 21.
[59] Meyer, "Excursion Steamboating," pg. 88.

THE *VERNE SWAIN*, 1889

The *Verne Swain* was a sternwheel packet built by Capt. David M. Swain in 1886 in Stillwater, Minnesota. It was 122 feet with a 22½-foot beam—two thirds longer, about a third wider and nearly four times (134.7) the tonnage of the *Freddie*. By today's standards, the *Verne Swain I* was grossly underpowered, being driven by one 150-horsepower engine. Today it is not unusual to see a 35-foot offshore boat like a Mako or a Contender line sporting three 300-horsepower outboards. Surprisingly, this seemingly lean horsepower suited the *Verne Swain I* quite well. Under the Streckfus Line in the late 1880s the *Swain* had a well-deserved reputation as one of the fastest boats on the Upper Mississippi, clocking a torrid 18 miles per hour traveling with the current, and a still respectable 14 mph when headed upstream. We do concede that today's 900 hp (versus the Swain's 150) super-charged Contender can command a speed of more than 60 mph in choppy waters.

With demand for his services growing and having a larger cargo capacity, Streckfus expanded the daily run north to Fulton, Illinois, (east bank), and Clinton, Iowa, and Lyons, Iowa,[60] (west bank), stopping at both sides of the river along the way at Albany, Illinois; Camanche, Iowa; Cordova, Illinois; Princeton, Illinois; Port Byron, Illinois; Le Claire, Iowa;

---

60 Lyons has since merged into the city of Clinton.

and Hampton, Illinois, piloted by Capt. Zack Suitor initially and by Capt. Fuller Smith later.

The Commodore was most inventive: Upon arrival at 10:30 a.m. at Davenport, Iowa, he remained docked for four hours, counter to traditional packet routine. The new schedule allowed passengers to visit the department stores and various other businesses and have their purchased goods delivered to the *Verne Swain* before departure at 2:30 p.m.

The *Verne Swain* then stopped across the river at Rock Island at 3:00 p.m. before continuing her leapfrog return to Clinton, Iowa, and both Lyons and Fulton, Illinois, completing the day's itinerary at 8:30 p.m.

Through timely adherence to this challenging schedule, the *Verne Swain* developed a solid base of clients. Key loyal patrons were traveling salesmen whose enterprises were on hand. They benefited from developing business relationships across miles of ground by water daily yet still returned to their home ports each evening.

In 1893, Streckfus rebuilt the *Verne Swain* with two new boilers. After five successful years of tramping the Mississippi, he boldly experimented with serving the Ohio River as far north as Owensboro, Kentucky. The results were unacceptable, however; commerce on the Ohio proved insufficient to support the *Verne Swain*'s regimen.

The *Verne Swain*
Murphy Library Special Collections/ARC, University of Wisconsin–La Crosse.

Streckfus quickly admitted defeat and, in 1895, returned the *Verne Swain* to the Davenport/Rock Island-Clinton/Lyons/Fulton route on the Upper Mississippi.

VERNE SWAIN VS. JO LONG

Sensing a grand opportunity to establish a successful base of operation, a competitor emerged: Capt. Joseph Newt Long initiated service in 1896 with his eponymously named packet vessel, the *Jo Long*, and sparked a riverboat race that captivated townsfolk all along the banks of 35 miles of Mississippi waterway.

Streckfus immediately saw that the unique Clinton-to-Davenport trade he'd "owned" since 1889 was in jeopardy. That he had had little competition was due to the precipitous attrition in riverboats after the mid-19th century in the wake of the rise of rail, combined with the fact that riverboats have a short life expectancy—about 18 months, on average.[61]

An ad for the *Jo Long*, underneath an ad for the *Verne Swain*, in the *Clinton Morning Age* promoted:[62]

Ship your freight with us if you want prompt and efficient service.
A trip on this speedy steamer will be made a pleasant and memorable one.
Beautiful Scenery!
Passing through the great eighteen miles of rapids.
A sight forever to be remembered.

---

61 "Steamboat Graveyards Yield 'Time Capsules' to Salvagers," Jim Shur, Associated Press, July 7, 2002, *Los Angeles Times*.
62 *The Clinton Morning Age*, July 19, 1896.

THE STRECKFUS RIVERBOAT DYNASTY

A battle for market-share supremacy began with the oldest form of showboating: competitive racing. At the beginning of the 1896 season, the *Jo Long* initiated the contest by embarking head-to-head with the *Verne Swain*, leaving the dock at the same time and following the same itinerary to Davenport, including stops at each of the string of ports between.

But the two boats proved equally fast and agile, and the daily races invariably ended in a dead heat. Quickly, Streckfus decided to double the stakes and the cost of having a seat at the table: He purchased the sternwheel rafter the *City of Winona* in June.

The *City of Winona* was an attractive white sternwheel rafter that traced her origin to Youmans Brothers and Hodgins, the Winona, Minnesota, shipyard from which she emerged in 1882. The length of the *City of Winona* was 137 feet with a beam of 29 feet and a hold of four and six tenths.

The *City of Winona*
Courtesy of the Dave Thomson
Collection at Steamboats.com

Equipped with 305 horsepower engines, the *City of Winona* was much more strongly powered than the *Verne Swain*.

The strategy was to pit the *City of Winona* against the *Jo Long* for the downstream journey each morning. Meanwhile, the home port of the *Verne Swain* was relocated to Davenport, Iowa, and she was run upstream each day. Capt. Jo Long swiftly responded, chartering the *Douglass Boardman* to match the *Swain*'s new, reversed itinerary.

For the Upper Mississippi rivercraft season that summer, travelers were treated to not twice, not thrice, but four times more river-transit options. The four craft—*Verne Swain, Jo Long, City of Winona* and *Douglass Boardman*—each made a daily roundtrip, racing one another in spirited competition.

Verne Swain vs. Jo Long

Upping the high-water mark, Streckfus added a band of musicians to each of his vessels, entertaining passengers along the daily journey. Capt. Jo Long, not to be outdone, added bands to each of his.

The shootout between Long and Streckfus became the talk of the region and a form of "racing fever" spread among friends of the contestants.[63] The four boats now attracted even more customers to witness this contest for commercial leadership, and fares were dropped to 25 cents.

The epicenter was Le Claire, Iowa, where the vessels would cross paths each day, midstream. Capt. Long was a Le Claire man, born there in 1851, and a member of the local Masonic lodge. He was thus the fan favorite at this juncture. The contest became even more heated as the summer of 1896 progressed, and thousands of passengers and onlookers became captivated by these exciting steamboat races.

The recollections by Rock Island's Capt. George Hakes of these legendary shootouts between the *Jo Long* and the *City of Winona* were published in the *Rock Island Union*.

The *Verne Swain*
Murphy Library Special Collections/
ARC, University of Wisconsin–La Crosse.

The *Jo Long*
Murphy Library Special Collections/
ARC, University of Wisconsin–La Crosse.

"In the races Capt. Streckfus won by some clever maneuvering. He had the larger boat of the two and carried heavier cargoes. When he was heavily loaded with freight, he would get a start and when

---

63 Meyer, "Excursion Steamboating," pgs. 93–94.

the *Jo Long* would pull alongside and attempt to pass, by a clever bit of manipulating of his boat he would run close alongside. The *Long* was the lighter craft, and caught in the suction of the *City of Winona* would be unable to forge ahead and the two boats would run neck and neck."[64]

Captain Walter A. Blair, principal of the Council City Packet Company, worked out of Davenport and was witness to the racing drama. Blair commented, "The fact that with all the racing up and down every day, running the rapids up and down in all kinds of weather and with the crews and passengers greatly excited, [that] there was no accident to any of the boats, surely means there was a lot of good steamboating done on both sides."[65]

Regrettably for its enthusiasts, the Streckfus/Long steamboat contest ended abruptly in August 1896. Captain James Osborne, agent of the Streckfus and Diamond Jo lines in Davenport, was embroiled in a shouting match at the Diamond Jo warehouse with Capt. Long, who took the discussion to a significantly more serious level. As he held his pocketknife in Osborne's face, he leapt forward, stabbing the rival captain. Osborne's wound was investigated by the police and deemed not life-threatening.

Nonetheless, Long was arrested. The *Davenport Daily Times* reported on Dec. 5, 1896:[66]

LONG CASE ENDS
CAPT LONG FOUND GUILTY OF A MINOR OFFENSE.
The jury returns a verdict late this afternoon
guilty of assault to commit great bodily injury

---

64 Meyer, "Excursion Steamboating," pg. 94.
65 Blair, a friend of the Commodore, later worked on a Streckfus excursion steamer and penned "A Raft Pilot's Log," 1930, pg. 155.
66 Le Claire, Iowa, River Men—Obits and Other Info—Celtic Cousins

Verne Swain vs. Jo Long

Curiously, the *Davenport Weekly Democrat* placed the article about Long's subsequent sentencing on page 3, rather than page 1. Capt. Long, as well as Capt. Streckfus, had competed in print in the summer of 1896 too; their ads often appeared side by side. Streckfus managed to get his ads placed on top, though.[67]

The *Democrat* reported on Dec. 17, 1896:[68]

> Capt. J. N. Long was up before Judge Waterman Monday morning to receive his sentence for the crime of which he was found guilty by the jury at the recent trial. He was accompanied by his attorneys Messers. J. A. Hanley and E. E. Cook, they being practically the only ones in the court room at the time. After some preliminaries Judge Waterman stated that he would sentence Capt. Long to pay a fine of $100, so that the total amount to be paid by Capt. Long, aside from his attorney's fees, will be about $250. He was not prepared to make a settlement at the time, but the court allowed him time to get the money instead of committing him until paid, as is sometimes done.

Moving on, meanwhile, Long seemed to be getting ready for the next season. The *Davenport Daily Times* reported on Dec. 26, 1896:[69]

> Captain (Joseph) Newt Long was a caller at the *Times* office today and he was asked about the future of the steamboating business. He said that although the prospects [were] not the best for next season's trade, his new boat was never the less being built rapidly for entrance into the trade upon the opening of navigation next spring. The boat in question will be 185 feet long, 30 feet on the bottom and 38 feet on the deck. The old *Boardmen* machinery

---

67 *The Clinton Morning Age*, July 19, 1896.
68 Le Claire, Iowa, River Men—Obits and Other Info—Celtic Cousins
69 *Ibid.*

has been bored out and thoroughly overhauled. She will have two new fire box boiler[s] 24 feet long, capable of carrying 250 pounds of steam. Her cabin work is being done by a Mr. Ismak of Cincinnati who is an expert ship carpenter. The new boat will have a speed of fifteen miles an hour and will be well able to take of all the business and freight given her.

The captain also said that the cabin of the *Jo Long* is being remodeled and she will come out in the spring brightened with two coats of white lead and zinc. The natty little craft entered the trade on May 2nd, 1896, and ran 29 trips in that month, 30 in September, 30 in October and 7 in November, making 176 trips in all, there being but two trips lost in all that time, and each occasion being the result of an accident. This is a truly remarkable record.

But Long's reputation, thus his business, deteriorated badly and the escalated competition with Streckfus took a mortal commercial toll. Because he was financially weakened and unable to keep current on his charter fees on the *Douglass Boardman*, creditors seized both vessels, forcing him to withdraw entirely from the Clinton-to-Davenport trade.

Lesson: Don't let bravado cloud judgment and avoid any contest where you lack sufficient resources to stay the competitive course.

The *Davenport Democrat and Leader* reported on Feb. 25, 1910, that it had received news that Long passed away after a two-month illness in Seattle, Washington, where he had moved two years earlier, followed by his family a year later.

His obituary described Long as "for years one of the best known rivermen and steamboat owners on the Upper Mississippi."[70]

While serving as . . . master and pilot, Captain Long engaged in many an exciting race and invariably came out with flying colors.

---

70 Le Claire, Iowa, River Men—Obits and Other Info—Celtic Cousins

He was also regarded as one of the most skillful pilots and for years piloted the majority of the boats over the treacherous waters.

He was the owner of the steamer *Jo Long*, which for years plied in the packet trade, between Davenport and Clinton and which had the distinction of being the fastest boat in these . . . rapids between Davenport and Le Claire.

ACME PACKET VS. ANCHOR LINE

While Capt. Streckfus was battling with Capt. Long, Acme Packet was embroiled in an ongoing battle with Anchor Line Co., which had ruled the Lower Mississippi. Here, customers' taste for morality came into play just as it had in August 1896 when Capt. Long's favor ended upon drawing a knife.

The Streckfus family was devoutly Roman Catholic. This factored into the Streckfus brand of service. John Streckfus oriented his passengers' experience to that of "family friendly," with a commitment to safety and ethical behavior. Capt. Walter Wisherd, general passenger agent for Acme, commented to the press years later upon the birth of a Streckfus newbuild:

> We propose to cater to the very best class of people. There are many . . . who want to go out for an afternoon's excursion who have been fearful of the average excursion boat, because of their reputation. On this one . . . no gambling or disorder of any kind will be allowed.
>
> There will be a lady attendant, and ladies and children will have the same protection and care they would receive in their own homes.[71]

---

71 Meyer, "Excursion Steamboating," pg. 116.

Aboard steamers, there were murders and more. Iowa GenWeb Project has accounts in its river-stories section titled "Circus Gangs and Other Bad Men," "Recipe for Murder," "Murder on the Steamer *Muscatine*," and "Stabbing of James Holden."[72] The final story cites the *Daily Gazette*, Nov. 18, 1868:

THE KNIFE!

A MAN DISEMBOWELED IN A SALOON!

He is not Expected to Live!

A DESPERADO AND MURDERER ARRESTED!

The story begins, "Yesterday afternoon the steamer *Key City* landed a gang of as desperate-looking men as ever murdered in night time."[73]

"The Murder on the *Dubuque*" begins:

> A father lying dead by the side of his son each grasping cold revolvers in their hands while standing above them was Mate Dan Breen of the Diamond Jo Line was the awful sight which greeted the eyes of the passengers and employees of the boat as they rushed to the forward hatch on the main deck of the steamer *Dubuque* at noon today [July 10, 1902]. The double tragedy occurred just as the boat pulled away from the Davenport landing and was the result of a

---

72 "Stories of Life on the Rivers," Iowa GenWeb Project (iagenweb.org)
73 "The Stabbing of James Holden," Iowa GenWeb Project.

squabble which had been in progress for 15 minutes. The men were known as Christopher Leonidas and son, and went under the title of "The Roving Cowboys." They had been plying their trade of venders of hair restorer in Rock Island but had evidently met with little success for they still had five days for their license to run and had booked for passage up the river. They were apparently under the influence of liquor.[74]

Bullets were flying and the event was steeped in mayhem, according to a witness's testimony during the trial:[75]

John Selectman, colored porter on the boat and eyewitness of the shooting, was the next witness. He proved the stellar attraction of the inquest and kept the jury and crowd laughing. He detailed the trouble over the moving of the medicine men's baggage and remarked rather disconsolately that he was between two fires and really did not know who he was working for. The mate ordered him to do one thing and the medicine men ordered the other preceding. The medicine men held the trump cards in the shape of guns and whips and he rather guessed that they were the balance of power. When the shooting started John seems to have again been between two fires. He graphically described the triangle in the center of which he stood and how he squeezed his 200 odd pounds of meat up against the hatchway to escape the flying bullets. He was very uncertain as to the number of shots fired but said that it seemed like a dozen or more were going. He had come disgusted with the whole affair early in the game and told the mate that he would have nothing to do with the prisoner's baggage.

---

74 "The Murder on the *Dubuque*," Iowa GenWeb Project.
75 *Ibid.*

THE STRECKFUS RIVERBOAT DYNASTY

"Diamond Jo" Reynolds didn't serve alcohol on his boats and discouraged drinking and gambling, according to a captain's account published in 1931.[76]

> Of the many steamers that Diamond Jo had bought, he never lost one by fire, sinking, explosion or seizure. The line had a few sunken boats but they were always raised and repaired. . . . [H]e never lost one in the 40 odd years of operation. . . . The Diamond Jo sold all its property [in 1911] but retained the title under which it operated for almost 50 years with honor, credit and profit. . . .[77]

But the Anchor Line was incessantly beset by troubles. No doubt, a contributor to these not infrequent "accidents" was its notoriously substellar client base. Was it simply careless management or a lack of commitment to honest business practices that doomed the Anchor Line?

The Anchor Line was not always struggling. In its early years after its 1859 founding as the Memphis and St. Louis Packet Line, Anchor occupied a special niche in Mississippi commerce during the Civil War. Memphis and St. Louis steamers were devoted to supporting the Union military effort on the Mississippi north of the Confederate-held ports of Vicksburg, Mississippi, and Port Hudson, Louisiana.

After these Confederate strongholds were forced to surrender on July 4, 1863, the firm moved to greatly expand operations and claimed a new moniker: Anchor Line. Significant growth took place between 1880 and 1887 when seven sizable (275- by 45-foot) Anchor Line sidewheelers were custom designed and constructed at the Howard Shipbuilding yard in Jeffersonville, Indiana.[78]

While Anchor Line's boats were palatial, as well as sleek and agile on the water, their passengers were far from uniformly elegant. The company

---

76 *Quad-City Times*, Feb. 1, 1931. Captain Walter A. Blair.
77 *Quad-City Times*, Feb. 1, 1931.
78 This Howard complex subsequently gave birth to the *J.S.* in 1901.

did not screen its passenger roster to eliminate hucksters and card sharks. As a consequence, the history of Anchor Line excursion boats was filled with unsavory characters perpetrating trouble.

Of particular notoriety, the *Corwin H. Spencer* steamer allowed management-favored gambling. Fisticuffs and thievery were reportedly pervasive on board.[79] And the company was marred by frequent intersections with bad luck and calamities of various origins—from snags to fires to ice, and even to tornadoes—sending it from cradle to grave in 39 years.

In that time, 16 vessels flew the Anchor Line flag. Acts of God and accidents befell Anchor Line boats, even after the company's demise:[80]

Belle Memphis (I), 1866–1880, dismantled.

James Howard, 1870–1881, burned beyond repair, St. Louis, Missouri.

City of Vicksburg (I), 1870–1880, sunk by a river snag, Ashport, Tennessee.

Belle Memphis (II), 1880–1897, damaged beyond repair by snag, Chester, Illinois.

City of Providence, 1880–1910, destroyed by ice.

City of Vicksburg (II), 1881–1896, damaged by a tornado, St. Louis, Missouri; rebuilt as *Chalmette* (1896–1904), sank.

City of Cairo, 1881–1896, destroyed by a tornado, St. Louis, Missouri.

City of Baton Rouge, 1881–1890, sank, Hermitage, Louisiana; two casualties.

City of New Orleans, 1881–1898, dismantled; equipment used in the *City of Pittsburg* (1898–1902), destroyed by fire, Cairo, Illinois, 75 casualties.

Arkansas City, 1882–1896, destroyed by a tornado, St. Louis, Missouri.

City of St. Louis, 1883–1903, burned, Carondelet, Missouri.

---

79 Meyer, "Excursion Steamboating," Pgs. 73–74.
80 Wikipedia article on the Anchor Line.

City of Bayou Sara, 1884–1885, burned, New Madrid, Missouri; eight casualties.

City of Natchez, 1885–1886, burned, Cairo, Illinois.

City of Monroe, 1887–1896, damaged by a tornado, St. Louis, Missouri; renamed *Hill City* (1896–1900), sank; raised, renamed *Corwin H. Spencer* (1900–1905), destroyed by fire, St. Louis, Missouri.

City of Hickman, 1894–1896, sank, Memphis, Tennessee; machinery used in the *City of Cincinnati*.

Bluff City, 1896–1897, destroyed by fire, Chester, Illinois.

Flagging passenger ridership coupled with an extraordinary high incidence of loss of packet commercial goods was too much for the Anchor Line to bear, culminating with a tornado at the ports of St. Louis and East St. Louis that destroyed two of its boats and damaged two others. At least 255 people died in the 1896 St. Louis tornado. Management sold the last vessel in 1898.

THE *CITY OF WINONA*

With Capt. Jo Long's eponymous company ending shortly after the passing of his widow in 1895 and the demise of the Anchor Line in 1898, Streckfus was ideally positioned to dominate Upper Mississippi packet commerce.

City of Winona
Courtesy of the Dave Thomson Collection at Steamboats.com

During the 1896 summer season of riverboat heats against Capt. Joe Long, Streckfus had bought the *City of Winona*. The *City of Winona* (Winona, Minnesota), built in 1882, was owned by the Youmans Brothers and Hodgkins. The original *City of Winona* was a "rafter" and operated by the lumberjacks and several client lumber mills until acquired by John Streckfus in 1896.

Between the years 1896 and 1900, the *City of Winona* played a vital role as complement to the *Verne Swain*. During the steamboat competition between Captains Streckfus and Long, it was the addition of the *City of Winona* that boldly raised the stakes. The *City of Winona's* entrance into the Clinton to Davenport competition was to strengthen the grip of the Streckfus line on that important stretch of the Mississippi.

Then Capt. Jo Long, fighting for his riverboat life, in effect "doubled the stakes" by chartering the *Douglass Boardman* to work the same cities and freight yards as the two Streckfus vessels. In the spring of 1896 Long first challenged the *Verne Swain's* established business. The *Jo Long* entered the trade and quietly copied the *Verne Swain's* routes and schedules, competing aggressively for both freight cargo and human cargo. By June of that year, Capt. Streckfus moved strategically to add the *City of Winona*. Looking ahead, Streckfus made the *City of Winona* purchase to protect the franchise with duplicate travel (one south to north and the sister steamer, north to south) being offered along what became "the *Verne Swain* corridor."

At the end of the struggle, when Capt. Jo Long had lost both the *Jo Long* vessel and the chartered *Douglass Boardman* packet, Streckfus was victorious, though challenged. Railroad expansion was like an insidious plague which preyed every day on riverboat commerce. Streckfus began his quest to create the first palatial excursion craft from scratch, to be the *J.S.* He recognized that the encroachment of interurban electric trolleys and the expansion of railroads was whittling away at river commerce.

For steamboat enthusiasts along the Iowa–Illinois banks, the spirited races and daily four-boat, multi-port Streckfus-Long rivalry were now a thing of the past.

Streckfus continued to invest heavily in repairs and maintenance; reliability and safety were of top priority. George Waters of *The Waterways Journal* commented in the spring of 1899 that "the *Verne Swain* and *City*

The City of Winona

of Winona came off the blocks at Kahlke's Boatyard in Rock Island looking like sweet young ladies with brand new Easter bonnets."

Waters added that "their newly painted white upper works made them look 'fresh as daisies' and the red wheelbarrow wheel of the *Verne Swain* seemed to 'loom up like a hollyhock.' "[81]

However, Streckfus knew economic trends were poor and getting poorer. As a result, the *Verne Swain* had a partial summer season in 1899 as there was insufficient demand to support two boats and river conditions were bad—not historic flooding; rather, there had been consecutive years of historic low water during the winters of 1897–1898 and 1901–1902[82]—limiting her voyages.

The *City of Winona* was still active until an early winter truncated her season and both she and the *Verne Swain* were put into early hibernation.

Streckfus entered the new century with plans for a solid and profitable tour of seasonal duty for both of his vessels. Acme Packet agent James Osborne, "talking his book," stated optimistically, "There are many people who would prefer a river trip to one by rail. Traveling men tired of the dust and jarring will be glad of the chance to float in a comfortable boat."[83]

But the dismal 1899 season seemed robust in contrast to that of 1900. The *Verne Swain* had been an important contributor to the Commodore's success, but Streckfus wasn't sentimental: He sold her to the Dixon Brothers of Peoria, Illinois, in the fall of 1900.[84] The Dixon firm, in recognition of the *Verne Swain's* fast river performance, renamed her *Speed*.

For the next five years, the *City of Winona* was kept busy defending the hard-won Clinton-to-Davenport business. Because the river watermark improved during the 1902 season, she waged a successful operating campaign.

---

81 Meyer, "Excursion Steamboating," pg. 96.
82 Low Water Records for Mississippi River at St. Louis, Weather.gov
83 Meyer, "Excursion Steamboating," pg. 97.
84 *Ibid.*, pg 98.

THE STRECKFUS RIVERBOAT DYNASTY

For the winter, Streckfus decided to experiment with running the fast and sleek *City of Winona* from Cairo, Illinois, to Hickman, Kentucky. Streckfus was known for his calculated risk-taking. "Perhaps, he thought, the Cairo/Hickman sector of the Upper Mississippi would provide a better volume of freight and passengers."[85]

In reality, he found the volume of business to be anemic and accepted this for what it taught: a worthy idea, but nevertheless a fast failure.

Streckfus was savvy and pragmatic. The way he saw it, the packet-vessel era was drawing to an end. He had a vision for the future of his steamboat business. He wanted to move away from the freight business that had a secondary reliance on passengers. He was ready to enter the excursion steamboat business, the one niche of steamboating that was profitable and ripe for expansion.

He held a grand vision that his Acme Packet Co. could become more—a lot more: the kingpin of excursion rivercraft on the Mississippi. The Commodore expected his firm to expand and operate steamers on the Upper Mississippi and its tributaries all the way along the great river to the Gulf of Mexico.

---

85 Meyer, "Excursion Steamboating," pg. 100.

THE *J.S.*

It was the spring of 1901, and the E.J. Howard & Co. shipyard and shore were abuzz: The keel of the Streckfus steamer, the *J.S.*, was being fashioned. In continuous business since 1834 in Jeffersonville, Indiana, the Howard shipyard was experiencing a frenzy of boatbuilding action. Much of the Howard yard's work to date had been on the repair and retrofit of existing vessels, the bulk of which were packets.

However, Howard had won the beauty pageant, so to speak, and it—not one of the many competitors along the Mississippi and Ohio—was chosen by Streckfus to bring this fabulous new sternwheeler to life. The *J.S.* would be the first large-scale excursion steamer built for that purpose on the western rivers. Huge gilded letters would proudly announce her approach to each port.

Streckfus had been conserving his profits. This stash, coupled with the proceeds from the *Verne Swain* sale, provided the seed capital from which the *J.S.* sprang. Streckfus camped out in Jeffersonville, overseeing every aspect of the vessel's construction. He had personally designed her:

The *J.S.* Under Constructions
Murphy Library Special Collections/ ARC, University of Wisconsin-La Crosse.

THE STRECKFUS RIVERBOAT DYNASTY

175 feet in length with a 33-foot beam and 5½-foot hold. His creation, built from scratch, was unique—so much so that he carved his initials into the new steamer.

While the packets *Freddie, Verne Swain,* and *City of Winona* were scrappy competitors for freight and passengers on the Upper Mississippi, it was the *J.S.* sternwheeler that secured the Streckfus family legacy in excursion steamboating. Remarkably, the family business would, for the next 90 years, become the excursion steamboat leader, serving the major port cities along the Ohio and Mississippi rivers down to the magical port of New Orleans.

Building the first commercial enterprise of a new genre of riverboat—the built-for-purpose floating palace—allowed John Streckfus to unleash his creativity. Reporters from *The Waterways Journal* marveled at the "spare no expense" ingenious improvements and high-end features unique to the *J.S.* Powerful 576-horsepower engines propelled the stern drive of the fabulous vessel. One journalist noted that the *J.S.* was "the best-known steamer to ever ply the Upper Mississippi—besides being the boat most photographed."

Streckfus used the finest materials available and from the premier manufacturers of the day. Charles Hegewald Co. of New Albany, Indiana, was the source of the boilers and related equipment at the heart of the power plant. A novel mechanical cleaner operated on the boilers independently and allowed for continuous maintenance. Her engines were lever high-pressure with a California cut-off and "a steel doctor, steamship-up rigging, cast steel cross-heads and flanges with steel cylinder timbers."[86]

The working steam steering apparatus for navigating the *J.S.* came from the Crawley & Johnston firm in Cincinnati. Specifically cast for the *J.S.*, an enormous boat's bell that reportedly emanated a lovely silver tone was created by the E.W. Vanduzen Co., also of Cincinnati.

For the electric light plant, Streckfus turned to Carlisle & Finch, while he chose Chapman Electric Co. of Louisville, Kentucky, to install the ship's

---

86 Meyer, "Excursion Steamboating," pg. 106.

extensive lighting system. The sternwheeler was an electricity-revolution showpiece with 400 incandescents, a Lenz 6,000-candlepower headlight and some 2,000 capboom lights outlining the decks (a capboom is a light bulb with a cap or hood over it to protect the light from the elements. Capbooms are strung along pipes or railings).[87]

The *J.S.*
Source: Arthur L. Smith's Personal Collection

The Commodore was not humble or subtle when he illuminated the *J.S.*, his first-of-a-kind creation. The extra bulbs made the golden *J.S.* letters on either side of the pilot house beacons especially noticeable.

Symmetrical, sleek, and yet roomy, she spent 10 years calling on virtually every port of significance along the complete 2,000 miles of the Mississippi. While Streckfus did not abandon opportunities to move freight in her spacious hold, it was the excursion trade for which the vessel was designed.

---

87 Meyer, "Excursion Steamboating," pg. 106.

The J.S.
Courtesy of the Dave Thomson Collection at Steamboats.com

Overnight-passenger staterooms, traditionally found on a packet's second deck, were noticeably absent. Eschewing the traditional packet layout, Streckfus had purposely eliminated the deck devoted to sleeping quarters. The *J.S.* was—from Streckfus' novel design—an excursion steamer purposed not for overnight comfort, but for day-by-day customer sightseeing and entertainment.

Designed with a strong skeletal structure that eliminated the need for support columns, the second deck of the *J.S.* offered a magnificent, 100-foot by 27-foot dancefloor and a towering bandstand instead. Her four decks could accommodate up to 2,000 passengers.

Enclosing the ballroom were light, but strong, chestnut-framed windows of sliding glass; springs eased opening and closure. As the *J.S.* would experience weather extremes over her excursion season, the Commodore placed ventilators in the fore and aft with dedicated stringers to feed in hot and cold air.

Many years before Willis Carrier introduced air conditioning, the *J.S.* regulated temperatures on the dancefloor through opening and closing easily accessible registers on the stringers. From the cabin deck sitting

The J.S.

area, two large, curved stairways led to the texas—the top deck—that is traditionally open air with limited seating.

The *J.S.*
Source: Arthur L. Smith's Personal Collection

To facilitate the vessel's ease of access, the forecastle was a semi-circle. Thus, the iron landing stage, assisted by steam power, could reach the bank wherever the *J.S.* would stop to engage excursionists. This feature allowed her to land and embark with ease while other steamboats had to wait their turn to pull up very close to the bank to lower their landing stages.

The lower deck consisted of the crew's quarters—generally 25 regular hands—along with the kitchen, pantry, and refrigeration. Although the *J.S.* was not designed to attract the masses for overnight passage, the magnificent vessel did offer 10 elegant staterooms for invited guests. Located beside the captain's quarters on the texas, the staterooms offered steam heat, hot or cold air conditioning, a flush washstand, and a spacious observatory and social room enclosed in glass.[88]

The ship's construction cost was $13,450,[89] or about $440,000 today.[90]

---

88 Meyer, "Excursion Steamboating," pgs. 106–107.
89 WisconsinShipwrecks.org "*J.S.* (1901)."
90 CPI Inflation Calculator

MAIDEN VOYAGE—JUNE 29, 1901

The maiden voyage from the construction yard on the Ohio at Jeffersonville, Indiana, was to the *J.S.'s* virgin Acme Packet headquarters at Rock Island, Illinois. John Streckfus could not have been prouder; an exciting trip was ahead for the Streckfus family and their friends who were onboard. The *J.S.* was given receptions all along the route and visited by some of the most prominent steamboat men at every point at which she landed. All pronounced her "one of the most complete and modern steamboats."[91]

In addition to Streckfus, joining the maiden voyage were Mrs. Streckfus, their three daughters and two oldest sons, Joe and Roy; B. Winter of Rock Island; Col. and Mrs. James Donahue and William Peterson of Davenport; W.H. Lehmann of Des Moines; and Mr. and Mrs. Daniel Weiss and Mr. and Mrs. Chapmann of Louisville, Kentucky.

At Muscatine, Iowa, about 30 miles south of their destination, joining were Rock Island Mayor Frank B. Knox and Fred Hass, also of Rock Island, and E.M. Sharon, Hal Decker, S.W. Searle, and purser E.W. Baker, all of Davenport. At this time, Sharon presented Streckfus with a flag on behalf of the businessmen of Davenport.

---

91 Meyer, "Excursion Steamboating," pg. 108.

During the voyage, while at Cairo, Illinois, at the confluence of the Ohio and Mississippi rivers, one passenger wrote the following message to friends:

Steamer *J.S.* left Jeffersonville, Indiana at 6:15 P.M. Monday evening, stopping at New Albany, which port was left about 8 P.M. Made run from New Albany to Cairo, about 425 miles, without a stop in twenty-seven hours, which shows speed boat is capable of making. Capt. Streckfus has not pushed the boat to its full speed at any time. The machinery runs smoothly and there has not been the slightest hitch of any kind. Have never seen new engines perform their work more beautifully. Passed Evansville about 8:30 Tuesday morning. All the steamers in port there blew a steam salute in which most of the factory whistles joined and if the sound was not heard in the tri-cities it was because the wind was in the wrong direction. The *J.S.* was making about seventeen miles an hour when it passed Evansville and thousands gazed in wonder at the marvelous speed of this magnificent steamer.

The *J.S.*
Courtesy of the Dave Thomson Collection at Steamboats.com

The trip has been most delightful and Capt. and Mrs. Streckfus have proven themselves royal hosts. Our every wish is anticipated and if the rest of the trip is not full of pleasure and enjoyment it is or will be our own fault. Leaving Cairo, we do not expect to make a landing until we reach St. Louis.[92]

The *J.S.* made the 200-mile run from Cairo to St. Louis in excellent time for the day: 23 hours. On her arrival in St. Louis, she was given a

---

92 Meyer, "Excursion Steamboating," pgs. 109–110.

Maiden Voyage—June 29, 1901

reception and closely inspected by local steamboat men. Capt. Ed West assumed piloting on the Upper Mississippi at St. Louis, with George Earringer and Frank Temple as engineers.

Further on her inaugural cruise, there was a tremendous reception accorded the *J.S.* as she rode the Mississippi River currents into Davenport and Rock Island. The *Rock Island Argus* reported on June 29, 1901:

> Amid the booming of cannon and giant fire crackers, the waving of flags and cheers of the assembled crowds, Capt. Streckfus' new packet, the *J.S.* steamed proudly and gracefully into her home port this morning. Long had her coming been anticipated and the people of Rock Island and Davenport had been led to expect much of her. It is no exaggeration to say that every expectation was fully met.
>
> Out of courtesy to the people of Davenport, Capt. Streckfus, being a resident of Rock Island, turned the bow of his steamer toward that city first in tactful acknowledgment of the honors accorded him [there].
>
> On the [Davenport] side two cannon led the chorus, accompanied by steam whistles and a band, as a landing was effected. As soon as the boat touched shore the crowd surged aboard and it was over half an hour before the *J.S.* could be cleared for [disembarking to] the Illinois shore.
>
> On this side the Acme Packet Company's warehouse on the levee had been bedecked with flags and bunting and a great crowd stood in impatient expectation. A committee of businessmen headed by F.G. Young was there to give Capt. Streckfus the glad hand, and Bleuer's band was on hand by order of Mayor Knox. V. Dauber had his anvil stationed back of the Seventeenth Street depot and gave the captain a salute of ten shots as the steamer hove into view. When the boat swung to up the warehouse a wave of admiration swept over the throng and cheer after cheer broke out

spontaneously. Within a few minutes after the long steel bridge was dropped on the platform there were hundreds of people aboard, and every visible part of the boat was soon thoroughly inspected and pronounced good.

Streckfus originally planned to operate the *J.S.* in the Davenport–Clinton daylight trade along with the *City of Winona*. During the evening she would offer moonlight excursions.

He knew it was prudent to slowly ease his new vessel into the Upper Mississippi market. An early picture of the *J.S.* shows lettering across the texas stating that the boat was a Clinton, Davenport, Rock Island, and Fulton daily packet.

However, in the spring of 1902, Streckfus stated that he did not know when he would enter the *J.S.* in the local day trade.[93] In the evening, illuminated by bright lights and steeped in music, the *J.S.* was overwhelmed by the rollicking reception to which its "moonlight cruises" were greeted.

The Commodore was surprisingly frank—and perhaps naively boastful—when he stated that the *J.S.* would be withheld from working alongside the *City of Winona*. The local trade would be attended by the *City of Winona* alone. Streckfus violated a business principle to never reveal when business is good when he remarked to a local reporter: "[The] excursion business has proven so profitable that it may not pay me to take her off of [regular evening moonlight cruises]."[94]

---

93 Meyer, "Excursion Steamboating," pg. 112.
94 Meyer, "Excursion Steamboating," pg. 112.

A ROUGH PATCH FOR THE *J.S.*

The *J.S.*—by design, both wider and deeper than the *City of Winona*—was challenged by a daily run through the rapids between Clinton and Davenport. Moreover, in her inaugural season in July 1901, the new kid on the river encountered a violent storm and her wheelhouse suffered a major setback.

Apparently, the lead officer's signaling by bells was confused. Regrettably, the virgin steamer suffered moderate damage while tethered to the dock. Repairs were immediately undertaken and the *J.S.* then focused on large excursion ventures from all points along the river between St. Louis and St. Paul, Minnesota.

The end of her second season came prematurely in September 1902. Sailing from Red Wing, Minnesota, just south of St. Paul, and having just picked up passengers from Winona, Minnesota, the captain made a turn in the river to find three packet steamers hung up on sand bars.[95] The *J.S.* flexed her engine power and youth and went to work, freeing the other steamers.

She then headed upstream, but soon found herself pinned to a giant sandbar. The three other boats' captains went to reciprocate. But the *J.S.* persisted in clinging to the sandbar. The passengers were there for a night of generous food and drink provided by the *J.S.* crew with brilliant style and grace.

---

95 Meyer, "Excursion Steamboating," pg. 113.

ALL ABOARD FOR NEW ORLEANS, 1903

After her second successful excursion season working the Upper Mississippi's fast-growing port towns, the *J.S.* was overhauled at the Kahlke Brothers yard in Rock Island. Founded in 1868, Kahlke Brothers held a pristine reputation for quality, timely repairs, and restoration.

Owned and run by Hamburg natives John and Peter Kahlke, the shipyard thrived into the 1960s. (In 1924, the business was passed on to Peter's sons, Fred and Ed Kahlke.) Commodore Streckfus could appreciate excellent service at the yard as craftsmen worked night and day to make repairs quickly and return vessels to their respective excursion and commerce trades. Streckfus was well aware that the Kahlkes were celebrated experts when it came to broken shafts on sternwheel steamers.

An adventure lay ahead for the sternwheeler: a 1,500-mile journey downstream to outrun Old Man Winter. John Streckfus, whose parents and three oldest siblings first arrived in America at New Orleans, had not yet partaken of the Crescent City's international flavors and fragrances.

The *J.S.* Starboard View
Courtesy of the Dave Thomson Collection at Steamboats.com

In a bold step, he had the *J.S.* run excursions downriver. With not the slightest hesitation, the Streckfuses loaded their essential provisions onboard and set sail on September 30, 1903.

The planning had been underway for more than a year by Streckfus and his Acme Packet Co. executives—namely Capt. D.W. Wisherd and Streckfus's four sons and three daughters. Many a map of the winding Mississippi had been consulted for recordings of river depths and the location of challenging rocks and rapids.

Ample fuel and provisions had been loaded for what would be an epic, exhilarating one-month cruise. The company's advance men had been working with harbor masters at Vicksburg and Natchez, Mississippi, and Baton Rouge and Donaldsonville, Louisiana, arranging *J.S.* stops at each en route.

The beautiful *J.S.* was a momentous hit among the thousands who observed her gradual descent along the mighty river. Why the *J.S.* did not make a call at the port of St. Louis remains a mystery.

It was 8:30 a.m., October 29, 1903, when she paddled—calliope roaring—into the New Orleans harbor, drawing a din of horns and whistles among the tugs, ferries, and other rivercraft there to welcome her arrival. Indeed, the *J.S.*'s inaugural arrival in NOLA (a local near-acronym for New Orleans) in 1903 was among several firsts that year that marked a sea change in the trajectory of history: Marconi's first wireless communication between the U.S. and Europe, the first U.S. coast-to-coast automobile journey, and the Wright brothers' revolutionary first flight at Kill Devil Hills, North Carolina.

Waiting that morning onshore were some 250 delegates from the Mississippi River Improvement and Levee Association, fresh from their convention and eager to experience the elegance of an excursion on the *J.S.*

Major assets of the Streckfus Line were its "advance men," who spread the word of steamers' upcoming travel agenda and signed groups for special outings. Solely due to Acme's advance corps' success, the *J.S.* wasted no time in becoming a popular attraction as, on the same day as her arrival, she welcomed the 250 convention attendees for her inaugural NOLA excursion.

All Aboard for New Orleans, 1903

The *J.S.*
Murphy Library Special Collections/ARC, University of Wisconsin–La Crosse.

After a two-day break for provisioning and enjoyment of the Halloween holiday, the *J.S.* launched into her regular excursion schedule on November 1, hosting exceptional crowds whose excitement had been building with anticipation, whetted by the advance corps.

Voyages were offered at 2:00 p.m. and 8:00 p.m., each a 40-mile roundtrip; 50 cents for adults (about $17 in 2023) and 25 cents for children. From the dock at the terminus of Canal Street, which forms the western border of the French Quarter and eastern border of the central business district, the *J.S.* ventured downriver to the Stanton Plantation south of Algiers; reversed to Southport, north of the Garden District, upriver; and returned to the French Quarter.

Marketing documents chronicle that this was her most popular route. New Orleans is a city of great historical interest, and sights along the *J.S.*'s river tour included the Chalmette battlefields and monuments to the War of 1812, when the pirate brothers Jean and Pierre Lafitte stood side by side with then General Andrew Jackson in one of the great U.S. victories against the British.

The countryside along the levees boasts acres of beautiful orange and pecan groves. Night and day, the port was abuzz with ocean freighters loading and unloading along the miles of docks.

Because Streckfus was committed to seeing that "family friendly" was practiced at all times, he operated the *J.S.* with strict regulations and rules, which his officers and his four sons enforced at all times. Daughters Lily, Anna, and May worked alongside the crew as concessioners and pursers/cashiers.

Source: Arthur L. Smith's Personal Collection

Further to the safety of guests and crew, transactions on Streckfus boats were cashless. Additionally, the sight of cash on the boat would have implied that there was gambling, which was prohibited on Streckfus ships. Captains Alan L. Bates and Clarke C. Hawley wrote of this "Streckfus way" in *The Excursion Boat Story: Moonlite at 8:30*:[96]

> For many decades, . . . no one handled money on [Streckfus vessels] unless he was related by blood or marriage to the family. No one! Ever! It was impossible for a passenger to spend cash at the bar, dining room, or the gift shop. Scrip tickets were sold . . . by members of the family ensconced in little cages like bank tellers. . . . [B]y keeping money from all others, the honesty of the crew was guaranteed; and the customers often bought more tickets than they needed, making a source of income from goods never delivered. No scrip redemption booth was available when rides ended.

---

96 Bates and Hawley, *Moonlite at 8:30*, pg. 155.

All Aboard for New Orleans, 1903

It is no secret that scrip has profit-margin benefits to those issuing it; some scrip will never be redeemed. Another benefit to the ship's issuer is that guests often made plans for another excursion to put their unredeemed scrip to use.

What's more, scrip made for a better guest experience. Streckfus ships hosted thousands aboard at a time. Scrip did away with the need for making change and Streckfus prices were simple and standardized. Excursionists were aboard to have fun and not stand in long lines for those ahead who would have been waiting for change.

Streckfus ships began serving alcohol in later years, but at alternating hours to discourage inebriation. Scrip expedited the hourly rush of transactions.

It was meticulous attention to detail for safety, cleanliness, and order that allowed the *J.S.*—and the whole Streckfus fleet of excursion steamers before and that followed—to rise above the inland river competition.

Streckfus had taken a major commercial risk in bringing the *J.S.* 1,000 miles south, but it was a gamble that proved exceptional. In December of 1903, the *J.S.* served as the official lead vessel in welcoming the Louisiana Historical Society for its celebrated harborside naval review.

As it does today, New Orleans hosted numerous conventions in the early 1900s. Delegates were taken by the beauty and grace of the *J.S.* and, day and night, harbor excursions were fully subscribed.

The *J.S.* had a successful first winter in New Orleans. In early February, she began preparations for her return north for the summer. Streckfus and his family experienced their first Mardi Gras on February 16, 1904, and the ringing voices proclaiming: "Throw me somethin', Mister!" (a tradition of throwing trinkets and treats to Mardi Gras revelers) prior to their departure for home in Rock Island.

Streckfus pointed his eponymous vessel upstream. In Port Byron, Illinois, a journalist wrote:

> It is a matter of pride to the people of this locality that the *J.S.*, while not quite two years old, has won for herself a reputation

which is not held by many other boats in fresh water navigation. The big boat is the pride of the steamboat world.

She is as well known in the neighborhood of Red Wing, Minnesota, and in the vicinity of the Gulf of Mexico, as she is to those who have seen her so often in her home port. . . . Last year, the boat traveled more than 100,000 miles, and will probably exceed that this year."[97]

The fact that excursion crowds had thronged to the *J.S.* for the 1903–1904 winter season brought new competition for New Orleans passengers from the *Island Queen* and by the *City of Providence*, a survivor of the Anchor Line.

But New Orleans remained faithful to the clean-cut and polished gingerbread *J.S.* No doubt it was its wholesome appeal that attracted Crescent City families. As *The Waterways Journal* noted, the *J.S.* would have "no gambling or skin games on the boat; nor ex-police officers to drag suckers [who had lost their money] back to the wheelhouse to threaten to throw them overboard if they reported their losses."[98]

---

[97] Meyer, "Excursion Steamboating," pg. 118.
[98] *Ibid.*, pg. 119.

HOUDINI, THE *J.S.*, AND THE MUDDY MISSISSIPPI, 1907

Harry Houdini built a remarkable career as a master illusionist, magician, and stunt performer over a 52-year lifetime that was truncated by a ruptured appendix. It was on November 17, 1907, when Houdini, then 33, crossed paths with Commodore Streckfus and his excursion steamer *J.S.* at the port of New Orleans.

Accounts from *The Picayune* noted that the brilliant showman arrived with fanfare by automobile at the foot of Canal Street. A large crowd had gathered around the *J.S.* to witness a Houdini escape act spectacle.

Known as "Harry Handcuff Houdini," the artist had moved

Harry Houdini sitting atop a cotton bale at the foot of Canal Street in New Orleans. The steamboat *J.S.* is at the wharf.
With permission from the Keith Norrington Collection at Steamboats.com

from vaudeville to performing stunts and fabulous escape acts in Europe and across the U.S. His repertoire had blossomed to include escapes from ropes slung from skyscrapers, releases from straitjackets under water, and extrication from being chained upside down under water.

This was a dark, rainy day along the Mississippi, but Houdini was determined to complete his sensational performance. He emerged from the automobile and climbed aboard the bow of the *J.S.* already weighed down by heavy chains and with steel handcuffs clasped behind his back. An accomplice completed preparation for the feat by attaching prison-made constraint shackles to Houdini's feet.

Thus clad, Houdini made a gesture to the crowd and dived headfirst off the bow as a heavy downpour began. There was an extended period where the crowd, mostly silent, began to shuffle their feet as their anxiety rose. After minutes had passed—Houdini was said to have a 180-second lung capacity—a single fist emerged from the muddy water; moments later, Houdini's head became visible.

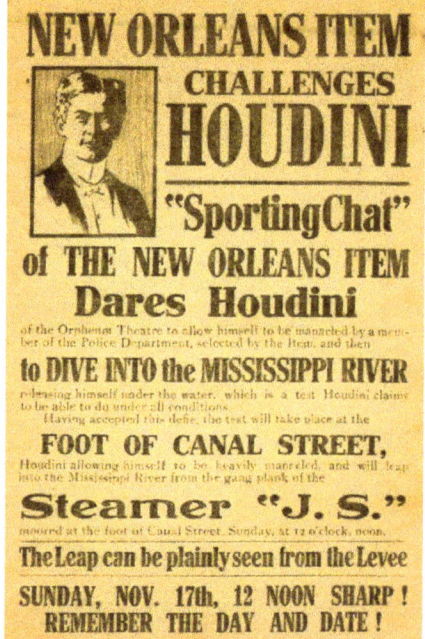

Advertising poster for Houdini's river stunt
With permission from the Keith Norrington Collection at Steamboats.com

Shaking water from his hair, the king of handcuffs threw his assorted cuffs and irons onto the main deck of the *J.S.* steamer and then swam, with strong sweeping strokes, to a small floating platform. From the platform, Houdini returned to shore.

It took some years, but Houdini did return to New Orleans for a week of performances in 1916. However, the cold, muddy waters of the Mississippi did not figure in the least in this later visit to the Crescent City.

Houdini, the J.S., and the Muddy Mississippi, 1907

Supporting his rationale to perform on dry land in 1916, Houdini stated to what was by then known as *The Times-Picayune*: "That's an awful river, the worst I have ever been in. Ugh! But it was cold! And the [farther] down I went the colder and darker it became. I said to myself then: 'If the trick doesn't work, I'm done for this time.' And even while I was working hurriedly and with all my skill to get the chains off, I felt the strong current forcing me I don't know where."

Houdini reportedly confided in the reporter that he was so fearful of the Mississippi that he had revised his will the night before. "I'll get in the water someday, my trick will fail, and then 'Good night!'" he said.[99, 100]

Houdini returned to perform in New Orleans in 1916, but all his stunts were performed on land.

---

99 *The Waterways Journal*, December 13, 2021, Keith Norrington. Source: Norrington WWJ 12-13-21.

100 https://www.nola.com/entertainment_life/houdini-escaped-from-straitjacket-high-above-canal-street/article_d4e30667-ba49-5779-8790-4d00b0fe07d9.html

THE *J.S.*'S FIERY DEMISE, JUNE 25, 1910

The *J.S.* skipped what would have been her annual New Orleans winter in 1905–1906 because a round of yellow fever (one of many since 1817) gripped the city and local environs the summer of 1905. Dr. Quitman Kohnke, health officer for New Orleans, reported that "Never before was so large a battle successfully fought against yellow fever as in New Orleans in 1905 and never before was so marked a victory won in the face of such dire predictions of defeat."[101]

Kohnke outlined how the fatality rate was fewer than 500 that summer; in some years, deaths in New Orleans alone would number as many as 8,000. He could only hope at the time that the new battle tactics—learned from the defeat of yellow fever in Cuba and Panama by Cuba's Dr. Carlos Juan Finlay and U.S. Army Major and surgeon Dr. Walter Reed[102]—would have a lasting effect.

The new tack did: The epidemic of 1905 was New Orleans' last after nearly a century of rounds that had earned the city the nickname "the Necropolis of the South." The Louisiana State Medical Society—and virologists and epidemiologists worldwide—celebrated a yellow-fever-epidemic-free

---

[101] The Yellow Fever Epidemic of 1905 in New Orleans. Dr. Quitman Kohnke, Covington, Louisiana. An Illustrated Address. Dr. Kohnke was Health Officer of New Orleans from September 1898 to September 1906.

[102] "Major Walter Reed and the Eradication of Yellow Fever," Army Historical Foundation

century in 2005, citing the 1905 eruption as "the last epidemic in the history of New Orleans *and* the United States."[103]

For the *J.S.*, subsequent seasons both north and south went well, and she enjoyed great commercial success, with a minor exception of weather extremes in August 1904.[104]

The *J.S.* put her firefighting skills to work in August 1906 when coming upon a burning bridge over Catfish Creek south of Dubuque, Iowa. The Burlington, Iowa, newspaper, *The Hawk Eye*, reported on the incident: ". . . [T]here were no means of extinguishing the flames when the steamer *J.S.* came up the river and swung in at the bridge. The fire hose of the *J.S.* immediately put into play and the fire was soon under control."[105]

This brush with uncontrolled flames would prove to be a strength of the vessel, as Streckfus would witness some five years later. If one were preparing the script for a disaster film, Bad Axe Island, north of Dubuque, would be a fitting location. A somber setting from which serious trouble would spring, it was 200 uninhabited acres of thick scrub and gray, soggy earth where the Bad Axe River emptied into the mighty Mississippi. It was here that the *J.S.* was to find her resting place.

Fire was always a threat to the steamboat trade: coal- and wood-stoked high-pressure boilers, themselves riding on tender wooden hulls, made for poor bedfellows. On the peaceful evening of June 25, 1910, uncontrollable flames brought an abrupt end to the *J.S.*, which had—with great irony—an impeccable record for fire safety and preparedness.

It was certainly not on the *J.S.*'s itinerary that night to find sanctuary in the northern shallows at the head of Bad Axe Island and burn to the water's edge in a kind of no-man's-land at the invisible boundary that separates Iowa and Minnesota.

---

103 Tomlinson W, Hodgson RS. Centennial year of yellow fever eradication in New Orleans and the United States, 1905–2005. J La State Med Soc. 2005 Jul–Aug;157(4): 216-7. PMID: 16250373.
104 Meyer, "Excursion Steamboating," pgs. 119–120. A storm in August 1904 swept *J.S.* against the Illinois bank near Andalusia. The *J.S.* was not damaged in the storm.
105 Meyer, "Excursion Steamboating," pg. 120.

The J.S.'s Fiery Demise, June 25, 1910

June 25, 1910. A clear, moonlit cruise under a waning gibbous moon at 93%.[106] 1,185 passengers—nearly capacity. Fresh air, a jazz band, and dancing. The boat was returning to Lansing, Iowa, from a roundtrip excursion of roughly 100 miles to La Crosse, Wisconsin, and back. As was their custom, the entire Streckfus clan—Mrs. Streckfus, four sons, and two daughters—were onboard. It was fitting that John Streckfus was standing at the bridge at this critical time.

At roughly 10:00 p.m., multiple shouts indicated a disturbance below. Then, the ship's mechanical fire alarm was sounded: FIRE ON BOARD! ". . . [A] a young boy [had] notified a crew member that smoke was coming through the planks of the hold."[107]

Streckfus, his family, and the *J.S.* crew of 25 bolted into action. Each assumed the role he or she had rehearsed many times in fire drills. At the first notice of smoke, Streckfus had ordered the pilot, George Nichols, to make quick to the most suitable firm ground.

> After attempting to extinguish the fire, it was decided to evacuate the passengers to Bad Axe Island. So, Capt. George Nichols nosed the vessel close to the island. A man confined to the ship's jail in the hold supposedly set the fire. The boats *North Star* and *Harriet* towed the *J.S.* out into the river to make it easier to put out the fire, but to no avail. The vessel burnt to the waterline. The *J.S.* was then towed to the Wisconsin side of the river and beached about two mile[s] north of Victory, Wisconsin. Rescued passengers were ferried to Genoa, Stoddard, and De Soto, Wisconsin by numerous boats.[108]

The jailed passenger, John Plein, had initiated the drama—the result of an apparent overconsumption of alcohol earlier in the evening while among the passengers. In 1910, Streckfus did not yet sell alcoholic beverages on

---

106 https://www.calendar-12.com/moon_calendar/1910/june
107 WisconsinShipwrecks.org "*J.S.* (1901)."
108 *Ibid.*

his boats, although this was well before Prohibition. Acme policy was that while it did not provide liquor or beer service, passengers could provide their own alcohol, BYOB. It seems Plein came well-stocked.

Passenger safety always came first. Streckfus was devout in his attention to vessel preparation each and every day his ships sailed. No small detail could be overlooked, including an ample stock of life jackets, ready ropes, overboard safety rings, and clear and open access to the gangway or landing stage.

Every matter that could jeopardize Acme customers' health and well-being was critical to Streckfus, his family, and the *J.S.* crew. This included regularly tended ashtrays. Later, Streckfus implemented a rule that the only smoking allowed was the "Stogie" cigar, which extinguished itself when left unattended.

Plein, a farmer from Lansing, Iowa, met his match with Capt. John Streckfus. To control unruly passengers, petty thieves, and general miscreants, the hold of the *J.S.* included a brig that found regular use.

Streckfus had approached Plein, who responded with abusive language and threatened fisticuffs. The Commodore attempted to calm the belligerent farmer, whose legs were unsteady, although there was no noticeable pitch or roll of the ship.

A week shy of his 54th birthday, John Streckfus was still a very powerful seaman—one with a reputation in combat for toughness and deft use of his fists. In 1895, he had been in a particularly noteworthy altercation with one of his deckhands, reportedly in defense of his position as Captain. The deckhand sued Streckfus; the court dismissed the suit. Separately, an assault and battery charge was dropped.[109]

In Plein's condition, no herculean effort was needed to subdue him. Instead, Streckfus called upon his eldest sons, Joe and Roy, to escort Plein to the brig. The hope was that Plein would sleep it off by voyage-end.[110]

---

109 William Howland Kenney, *Jazz on the River*, pg. 18.
110 Kenney, *Jazz*, pg. 18.

The J.S.'s Fiery Demise, June 25, 1910

It was not yet July, and Streckfus was anticipating a solid season of tramping the Upper Mississippi. Tonight's Iowa and Michigan excursionists were well-heeled customers taking in the sights, the pleasant cool breezes, self-serve libations, and dance. As it was relatively early in the evening, a young Fate Marable (he would become a legendary jazz musician), and his band were treating the crowd to some favorite musical numbers.

Marable was interviewed later about his approach to dealing with the evidence of smoke and fire encroaching upon the bandstand and dancefloor. He was strict with his band members on how they comported themselves. He was quoted:

> In the event of evidence of a major impending danger, such as fire, my band members were trained to remain composed. Quite literally, without missing a beat, they were to [remain] calm and focused—without any hesitation bringing their skill and talent to their specific instrument's contribution to each featured piece. It was essential that the band gradually dissipate and patiently move toward the established exits. An abrupt and hasty departure by the band could not occur. Instead, order and calm among any crowd was essential at such moments. I required my musicians—one by one—to slowly retreat from the bandstand until I was the sole performer coaxing sweet music from my piano.

This night—Marable's last performance on the *J.S.*—found Fate and his band, the Jazz-O-Sans, truly up to the challenge. Crowds are notoriously difficult to control without force and to convince to move peacefully and safely to available exits.

Marable and Streckfus both knew that a wild stampede of excursionists must be avoided. As they had practiced before, Marable's musicians slowly disbanded while the Streckfus managers and crew herded the crowd toward the bow of the vessel.

"Fire!

A warning came from the stokers' room, where it is said flames had burst from the hold and flamed up on each side of the fireman. Pilot Nichols, one of the heroes of the incident, sent word to the captain that he would hold his post until the boat was landed. The next instant the big fire bell on the upper deck boomed forth. Pilot Nichols began to execute a quick turn to put her bow upstream making for Bad Axe Island . . ."[111]

With the first whiff of smoke minutes earlier, Streckfus had chosen a swift and immediate objective: ground the vessel on Bad Axe Island. There was no time for an attempt to moor or to practice a soft landing; instead, the *J.S.* engines were throttled at a strong pace to hold the burning vessel against the island bank. The steamer was run aground with a thud.

Once the *J.S.* was firmly affixed to Bad Axe, the crew pivoted the stage located on the bow and aimed for the highest ground. With quick and decisive action, the stage was lowered and passengers made an orderly descent to firm ground. In this way, the precious passenger cargo of the *J.S.* was safely put ashore before the flames in the hold started to consume the main structure.

Imagine the scene that night. A few impatient passengers jumped over the guardrails of the *J.S.* to safety on the island, but some 1,100 filed off the burning vessel in somber regimen to stand on the shore. Here, Streckfus's two daughters were among the witnesses who saw the *J.S.* become engulfed in massive flames as she burned to the river's edge.

It was reported that Anna (27) and May (26) stood stoically on the Bad Axe Island shore, while lamenting the loss of the prized dresses and finery that had been bought in Europe that spring. May had just returned from visiting Lily, who had married in 1906 and lived in New York; her trunk was aboard with all her clothes and new hats from that trip. The

---

111 The *La Crosse Tribune*, Sunday, July 29, 1934.

The J.S.'s Fiery Demise, June 25, 1910

family Streckfus not only worked on but also lived on the boat during the excursion season.[112]

The loss of the *J.S.* was complete. Only a few life jackets remained as painful souvenirs of that tragic night; photos reveal that charred kindling was among the only remnants visible at daylight. To be sure, Streckfus would make an effort to salvage what was left.

But on balance, this undertaking proved fruitless. Bad Axe Island lived up to its name and surrendered scant assets of reclamation value. Even the ship's bell, although recovered by divers, had been melted by the intense heat into a large brass paperweight.

While not ascertainable, was it arson that sparked the fire in the hull of the *J.S.*? It is not improbable to consider that it was Plein who carelessly tossed a lighted smoke in the brig—possibly in an ill-fated attempt to escape. Plein remains a mysterious player in the saga.

Wreckage from *J.S.*
Murphy Library Special Collections/ ARC, University of Wisconsin–La Crosse.

Streckfus and Jack Page, the boat's watchman, were interviewed. Both testified that Plein had been set free from incarceration when the fire began. However, what can be the explanation of Plein's tragic death that night? His body and that of Emma Randall were eventually pulled from the wreckage.

> The official report concerning the two casualties was sent by Steamboat Inspectors, George B. Knapp and James I. Cary, to the Inspector General of the Department of Commerce and Labor, Washington D.C. They stated that a Mrs. Emma Randall, of New Albin, Iowa was drowned as she jumped overboard from the upper deck before

---

112 Meyer, "Excursion Steamboating," pg. 124.

the boat reached the shore, her death being caused by the boat swinging over her in rounding into the landing. The woman had hysterically attempted to jump from the boat two times before she finally broke away from the restraints of her friends and plunged to her death. The body of the other passenger, John Plein of Lansing, Iowa was later recovered by a diver from the sunken hull of the *J.S.*[113]

The inspectors heard many commendations of Capt. Streckfus and his actions which led to the remarkable safe landing of the *J.S.* that summer night on the Mississippi.

The *Harriet*
Murphy Library Special Collections/
ARC, University of Wisconsin–La Crosse.

The *North Star*
Murphy Library Special Collections/
ARC, University of Wisconsin–La Crosse.

Two packets, the *North Star* and the *Harriet*, had been moored in close proximity and their masters quickly came to ferry the *J.S.* passengers to safety. Her fiery end deserves note for the efficiency of her handling after discovery. All historical accounts of the event credit the nearly flawless disembarkation of some 1,000 passengers to clear thinking and calm execution by the Streckfus crew and officers.

A blemish to the incident was reported in the *La Crosse Dispatch* (Tribune):

---

113 Meyer, "Excursion Steamboating,' pgs. 121-122, citing Merrick, *Steamboats and Steamboatmen of the Upper Mississippi*, Vol IV.

The J.S.'s Fiery Demise, June 25, 1910

There is much resentment along the river of the ghoulish conduct of unknown persons who indulged in wholesale robbery at the expense of the stranded excursionists. Sunday morning six valises were found upon the shore, many of them cut to ribbons, and all looted of their contents.[114]

From St. Paul, Minnesota, to New Orleans, the *J.S.* was in her ninth season of plying the Ohio and Mississippi rivers. Indeed, she was the subject of every camera lens and a favorite recreation for river folks along the rivers' banks.

She was the first Mississippi purely-for-excursion vessel. She provided an introduction—a sweet intoxication, really—to the many pleasures of a Streckfus river cruise: the best jazz, an elegant ballroom dancefloor, and a genteel comfort that was provided by the entire Streckfus family.

The *W.W.*
Courtesy of the Dave Thomson Collection at Steamboats.com

The cards dealt by history often deliver painful, life-changing outcomes. From humble packets that focused on farm-to-town-to-farm trade, John Streckfus had forged a thriving excursion business and mastered the Mississippi's winding 2,000 miles of "wander" to the Gulf of Mexico. In a few short hours, the *J.S.* would be reduced to ashes and Streckfus would be challenged to recover and plot a new future for his riverboat career.

---

114 The *La Crosse Dispatch* (Tribune) Special Feature, Sunday, July 29, 1934.

CITY OF WINONA TO W.W.

Thankfully, Streckfus still operated the *City of Winona*. While the *J.S.* was showboating up and down the Mississippi for nine years, she had continued packet service in the Upper Mississippi. In 1904, she was working her traditional route. But this was to be her last hurrah before a transformational stop in Kentucky the next year.

She arrived at a boatyard in Paducah, Kentucky, in the spring of 1905 as a packet. By summer, she emerged as the *W.W.*, a glamorous excursion vessel named in recognition of Walter Wisherd, a business associate and close friend of Streckfus. The renaming of the *Winona* came as a surprise to Walter Wisherd. "When I was getting ready to book and advertise [the new vessel] her for excursions on the Upper Mississippi River, I asked Streckfus what he was going to name her and he replied brusquely, 'It's none of your business; you will find out soon enough.' I didn't know what to advertise until one day I was coming down over the levee and I saw a big *W.W.* over the pilot house. I knew what it was. She was nicknamed by the people of the river as "Watch and Wait," the "Weary Willy" and similar names of derision."[115] Rebuilt and rechristened, the *W.W.* was the first of Streckfus's "excursion conversions." [*Author's note*:

---

115 *Captain D.W. Wisherd Memoir*, Interviewed by John Knoepfle, University of Springfield, Illinois. 1955.

As Streckfus and Wisherd, at the time, forbade alcohol consumption on the new excursion vessel, the *W.W.* also was famously known at the "Water Wagon."]

The *J.S.* had proven the excursion-boat theme had appeal, attracting a growing clientele of riverboat dancers and sightseers. The *W.W.*, with a dancefloor capacity of 1,000, was ready for her coming out.

But safety came first: A late arrival of life preservers in Paducah delayed the party. She was a grand steamer that spent half of her life with the Streckfus fleet: first as a packet; then as an excursion steamer.

After June 25, 1910, she was all the Streckfuses had. The *W.W.* became the Streckfus excursion palace of 1911, and she worked a challenging schedule, originating trips out of Davenport and Rock Island that made a hairpin reversal at Muscatine, Iowa, before returning home.

The *W.W.*
Courtesy of the Dave Thomson Collection at Steamboats.com

A representative excursion offered in July 1911 departed Davenport at 2:30 p.m. and Rock Island at 3:00 p.m., touched land in Muscatine at 5:30 p.m., and pulled the gangway at 7:00 p.m. The next two and a half hours were devoted to the romantic "midnight cruise" with up to a thousand dancers "cutting the rug" on the *W.W.*'s elegant dancefloor.

City of Winona to W.W.

Courtesy of the Dave Thomson Collection at Steamboats.com

One fan of the vessel reported, "The *W.W.* bubbled with great music, wonderful refreshments and all the conveniences of home with clean cool fresh air added."[116]

Brutal competition with rail had forced Acme Packet to abandon the Davenport and Clinton trade.

---

116 Meyer, "Excursion Steamboating," pg. 102.

HERE COMES THE JAZZ

"... [L]ots of people made a good living working on the boats of the Streckfus Line."

—Louis Armstrong, 1954[117]

The excursion-vessel success of the Streckfus clan owes much to the hundreds of exceptional musicians who entertained their riverboats' customers. Their grand music came to be called "jazz" and folklore holds that the term is derived from exclamations upon hearing the *J.S.*'s beautiful, unmistakable calliope, remarking, "Here comes Jay-S."

The Streckfus landing whistle was part of the Diamond Jo legacy. It was one long, two short, one long, written on the keyboard as "▁▁▁ ▁ ▁ ▁▁▁."

Exceptional musicians and their exceptional music went hand in

The Commodore and friends
The Verne Streckfus Collection

---

117 Louis Armstrong, *Satchmo: My Life in New Orleans* (1954) pg. 146.

THE STRECKFUS RIVERBOAT DYNASTY

hand on Streckfus boats. John Streckfus had a musical background himself and played fiddle. He saw to it that his children had a musical upbringing as well.[118]

The Commodore first introduced his *J.S.* patrons to mellow sounds in 1901 and top-quality bands and orchestras were central features of every Streckfus vessel to ply the Mississippi and the Ohio.

> Of all the forms of entertainment on Streckfus steamboats, by far the finest has been that of music. From the days when Lily Streckfus beat out a tune on the calliope aboard the first *J.S.*, through the jazz era with Fate Marable and Louis Armstrong [later] on the *Sidney*, to modern day big-name bands on the *Admiral*, Streckfus excursion boats have carried music up the Mississippi.[119]

With no exceptions, John Streckfus continually sought out the best musicians he could locate and, in 1901, he introduced a talented Negro trio of mandolin, guitar, and banjo. Signed for the entire season while working the Upper Mississippi, the trio featured a banjo impresario rated the best in the U.S. by *The Waterways Journal*.[120]

When the *J.S.* headed south to New Orleans in 1903, the Hertzog orchestra was the season's entertainment, featuring the acclaimed Carl Hertzog on violin. On the trip to New Orleans and while docked in the Crescent City, the orchestra delighted *J.S.* passengers with the waltz and two-step.

Excursionists were treated to custom dance lessons; living onboard the *J.S.* for the season, the Merriams, a brother-sister team, offered lessons to all.

After success with outstanding bands that were led, respectively, by a banjoist and a violinist, Streckfus hired the legendary Black pianist Charlie

---

118 Chevan, David (1989). "Riverboat Music from St. Louis and the Streckfus Steamboat Line." Black Music Research Journal. 9 (2): 160. doi:10.2307/779421. JSTOR 779421
119 Meyer, "Excursion Steamboating," pg. 255–256.
120 *Ibid.*, pg. 256, citing *The Waterways Journal*, May 25, 1901.

Mills in 1903. Mills headed a highly sought-after quartet of White musicians on trumpet, violin, and drums.

A native of Quincy, Illinois, Charles Wenzel Mills's career on the Streckfus steamboats was four seasons as he sought further musical study on the East Coast to challenge his talent. Graduating from music school in Pennsylvania in 1909, he found work in New York City. There, his experience and recognition blossomed. He later joined a tour in Europe where he performed for Prince Arthur of Connaught in 1913.[121]

The Versatile Three
(Charlie Mills center)
Courtesy of Discogs.com

Another of Mills's notable accomplishments was sharing the calliope keys with Lily Streckfus, the Commodore's daughter—no small feat, as the steam calliope is extremely loud, extremely hot, and extremely wet. In time, John Streckfus put son Joe in charge of music on the boat.[122]

By the early 1900s, the calliope or "steam piano" had become the true musical calling card of excursion boats on the Mississippi. Invented and patented in 1855, the calliope had been adopted by showman P.T. Barnum to advertise the arrival of the circus. Powered by steam, the device was a bare-bones steel keyboard that fed to a collection of pipes or horns.

Always located on the vessel's top deck, the calliope is an instrument which must be heard to be appreciated. However, being too close to the action is not recommended: The volume and pitch of the calliope is a shriek, if not downright deafening.

---
121 "Quincy musician performs before British royalty in 1913," MaryLouMontgomery.com
122 Chevan, David (1989). "Riverboat Music from St. Louis and the Streckfus Steamboat Line." Black Music Research Journal. 9 (2): 160. doi:10.2307/779421. JSTOR 779421

A calliope is a series of more-or-less tuned whistles controlled by a small piano keyboard. The early calliope whistle valves were directly coupled to the keys by wires or rods; even with balanced poppet valves, they required much manual strength to operate them. Later developments of electrical solenoids to activate the valves enabled keyboards to be tapped instead of hammered, which relieved the players of much physical toil. There are no other controls; volume is at one level and that is LOUD.[123]

The calliope was the ultimate waterside advertising medium. While posters, flyers, and excitement created by the "advance man" could alert river towns that the *J.S.* was en route, it was the music of the calliope that would entice families to leave their homes and venture waterside to experience Streckfus-styled river sightseeing, music, and dance.

Of the calliope, Joe Streckfus himself wrote in 1958:

> There are at the present time but three large steam calliopes, or steam pianos, that were formerly heard in circus parades, excursion steamers, and river showboats on the Mississippi and Ohio rivers.
>
> These calliopes have brass steam whistles which can be turned by raising or lowering the bell—have balanced valves admitting the steam to whistle as brass keys are pressed down. The keyboard is like a piano, is played like a piano—takes practice and strong fingers to press down keys—just two and one-third octaves.
>
> There are but three large 32 whistle steam calliopes on steamboats today—one on the SS *Admiral* in St. Louis, one on the SS *President* in New Orleans and one on the SS *Avalon*.
>
> Calliopes are made to order by George Nichols of Cincinnati, OH and Evans & Co. at Evansville, IN.

---

[123] Bates & Hawley, *Moonlite at 8:30*, pg. 53.

Here Comes the Jazz

Steam from boilers is reduced by regulating valves to desired pressure and to maintain steady steam pressure in order to fill all whistles when played. (Calliopes) . . . can be heard from one- and one-half miles or more.

Don't you remember following the calliope that was at the end of the circus parade?

Fate Marable, Charlie Mills and Dick Little were experts in playing all the late popular pieces as well as the old favorites: "My Old Kentucky Home," "[I've Got] Rings on My Fingers," "Glow Worm," "There's No Place Like Home," "Bye Bye Blues," "So Long Mary" and "Good Night Ladies."[124]

---

124 Joe Streckfus paper written on November 4, 1958. From the Streckfus family records.

FATE MARABLE

With Mills's departure for Europe, Streckfus hired Fate Marable to lead music on the *J.S.*—and, yes, that included playing the calliope with Lily. Pardon the pun, but it must have been fate that brought together the Commodore and the 17-year-old biracial pianist.

Marable was something of a prodigy in his hometown of Paducah, Kentucky, where he had demonstrated remarkable musical skills at the piano—a talent nurtured by his mother, a music instructor. Lizzie Marable, largely a solo breadwinner, had orchestrated a comfortable living for Fate and his two brothers and three sisters. However, it certainly demanded her supreme energy to nurture her son's natural musical abilities to play classical piano and read—and write—music.

Down by the river, John Streckfus knew that his next hire would have big shoes to fill. Mills had developed a loyal following among regular passengers on the *J.S.* The year was 1907. The *J.S.* was plying the waters between New Orleans and St. Paul—tramping from town to town.

It is somewhat of a mystery how the Streckfuses became connected with the teenage Marable; we must surmise that the Commodore and his 20-year-old son Joe, who had assumed responsibility for music on the boats by this time, were following leads from riverboat contacts.

We can imagine the all-points-bulletin Streckfus had circulated: "Opening for Primo Entertainer on excursion steamer—Seeking virtuoso piano player, band leader. And—on top of it all—calliope impresario?"

Some reports credit Charlie Mills with making the introduction. The Commodore and Joe reportedly met Marable on the docks in Paducah, where the young man informed them that he was "between engagements and seeking employ as a pianist." In actuality, Marable was temporarily engaged in the shoeshine trade.[125]

Marable was to blossom onboard the Streckfus line and "his became the longest and most influential career in riverboat jazz."[126]

Fate Marable playing the Calliope on the *St. Paul*
Murphy Library Special Collections/ ARC, University of Wisconsin–La Crosse.

[With] his "uncanny talent for uncovering great musicians" and his dominant influence on the selection of musicians for his orchestras, Marable played a central role in directing a major musical stream in the Great Migration. He used his position as a leader of the best black dance bands on the leading excursion boats on the Mississippi and Ohio rivers to personally recruit ambitious musicians who were looking for ways to explore the more northerly reaches of the Mississippi valley [. . .].[127]

Although Marable and his talents came highly recommended, the Commodore and Joe demanded a rehearsal of sorts and wanted Fate to take a lesson from Charlie Mills on the calliope. The *J.S.* had been outfitted with one of the best, albeit crude, steam "whoopers." If he was hired,

---

125 Meyer, "Excursion Steamboating," pg. 257.
126 William Howland Kenney, *Jazz on the River*, pg. 40.
127 Kenney, *Jazz*, pg. 40.

Fate Marable

Marable would be required to tame the wild calliope and offer a stream *of steam* of great ragtime music as the *J.S.* cruised from port to port.

Marable knew he would have no trouble playing and conducting music for the dancing and listening public every night. Mastering the calliope would be another story, though. This was not to be done without appropriate armature, he knew.

Marable donned gloves to absorb the extraordinary heat of the steel keys, plus top-of-the-line foul-weather gear to shield himself from the unpredictable bursts of steam, and ear plugs to protect his hearing.

Fate Marable at the Calliope
Hogan Jazz Archive, Special Collections, Howard-Tilton Memorial Library. Tulane University

With the young man appropriately outfitted, Capt. John proceeded on a two-hour walk around Paducah while Fate experimented with the hot keyboard. Well into his walk, the Commodore's ears were treated to recognizable ragtime tunes.

Marable knew the job was his. "Capt. John triumphantly told his son [Roy, his second son, with whom he had taken a walk] that 'he knew Fate could do it with a little push.' "[128]

Charlie Mills had been a fine calliope player; this young kid Marable was even better!

Any student of the history of jazz will discover that Fate Marable was one of its true architects: Chapter One of every treatise on jazz begins with the pianist and conductor from Paducah, Kentucky. The legendary band leader was there for the discovery, incubation, and nourishment of this revolution in music.

Marable made the Streckfus brand of steamers synonymous with great "hot jazz." His bond with the Streckfus brothers began in 1907 and endured

---

[128] Meyer, "Excursion Steamboating," pg. 258.

a million miles of travel on the supersized waterways of the Ohio and Mississippi. He and the large cast of musicians he assembled gave performances on at least six Streckfus boats in his 33 years of roaming "steamer country" in its heyday, introducing millions to this exciting new sound.

Marable plays a central casting role in riverboat music in the early years of jazz. Marable "had been the premier musician in riverboat jazz. Louis Armstrong . . . had been this idiom's greatest improviser."[129]

> "The Streckfus Line encouraged the spread of jazz music. Captain Joe Streckfus, with hearty support from his father, John, the Commodore, was much taken with this New Orleans music. As an experiment, he sent a popular NOLA jazz band up the Mississippi on the *Sidney* in 1916.
>
> This was not the first time Streckfus Steamers has introduced Jazz music along the expanse of the Upper and Lower Mississippi and again Fate C. Marable 'stirred the drink.' The original *J.S.* had roamed as far south as New Orleans in the 1902-1910 period and excursion customers had been treated to their novel tunes and way of creative expression. Marable was the dominant fixture—the Streckfus Steamer jazz music legend—among a crowd of the 'jazz immortals.'
>
> On that special 1916 cruise, the New Orleans ensemble was in direct competition with a conservative 'fox-trot' orchestra which held the favored position on the dance floor bandstand. The legendary pianist, Fate Marable, stationed his musicians on the hurricane roof and forward of the texas. A swarm of passengers left the dance floor for the out-of-door musical treat of jazz."
>
> In 1907, Fate C. Marable had signed on the *J.S.* fully 11 years before Louis Armstrong joined his troupe of the time, the Jaz-O-Sans. [Passage modified from *Moonlite at 8:30*, Hawley, pg. 58]

---

[129] Joe Streckfus paper, written on November 4, 1958. Streckfus family records.

Fate Marable

Authors Note: Fate Marable was the musician who dominated the emerging riverboat jazz world. A fixture on the many vessels which composed the Streckfus Line of four decades, the great pianist tightly managed his ensembles. The composition of the Marable jazz bands was fluid as top musicians were recruited but often moved on from gig to gig, boat to boat and city to city. Marable was the conductor who ruled over the Streckfus Steamer musical empire. Marable-led ensembles were many and (in now chronological order) included the following:

Metropolitan Jazz-E-Sans Orchestra
The Jazz Syncopators
The Society Syncopators
The Jazz Maniacs or Fate Marable's Jazz Maniacs
Jazz-O-Sans
Marable's Capitol Revue
Marable's Waltz Revue
Cotton Pickers Orchestra
New Orleans Harmonists (on the *Saint Paul*)
The Harlem Steppers

PART IV

Packets to Excursion:
Wood to Steel

EXPANSION, 1911–

The Commodore had a vision of a fleet of excursion vessels that would carry the Streckfus name to every major port on the Mississippi and Ohio rivers. The ambitious gamble to build the grand excursion vessel had been a huge success with daily trips offering sights, hot riverboat sounds, and dance.

In doing so, the *J.S.* opened a new form of wholesome entertainment in the form of a unique family-oriented riverboat experience all along the Mississippi. For years, Streckfus had operated his headquarters from Rock Island, across from Davenport, at the border of Iowa and Illinois.

On Aug. 18, 1910, within eight weeks of the *J.S.*'s demise, the Streckfus Steamboat Line Co. was organized. The articles of incorporation:

> To purchase and own the requisite steamboats and other boats and barges, wharf boats, freight houses, machinery, tools and other necessary things and property to do a general transportation business in the carriage of freight and passengers and excursions, on the Mississippi and Ohio rivers and their tributaries.[130]

The venture had a capitalization of $250,000 (about $7.9 million in 2023). The corporate officers were Capt. John B. "The Commodore"

---

130 Meyer, "Excursion Steamboating," pg. 127.

Streckfus, 54, and two sons: Capt. Joseph Leo Streckfus, 24, and Capt. Roy Michael Streckfus, 23.[131] Younger sons John Nicholas, 19, and Verne Walter, 16, had yet to reach their majority but would, in due course, become integral to the enterprise as Streckfus Steamboat Line captains.[132]

Streckfus and his eldest sons made it a point to state "excursions" in the new company's articles of incorporation. Having demonstrated the success of the *J.S.* and the *City of Winona/W.W.*, the new tack for the Streckfuses was to make day sightseeing and night moonlighting their primary focus. Domination of the American river-excursion business was their pursuit.

The charter was for a duration of 99 years. Remarkably, the Streckfus line did approach 100 years of existence—surviving two World Wars, the Great Depression, and the skyrocketing rise in availability and affordability of rail, auto, and air transportation. Plus, the advent of free at-home entertainment: the television.

Excursion Steamer *W.W. Moonlight* on the Mississippi
Source: Arthur L. Smith's Personal Collection

When founded, the Streckfus line had 14 stockholders and a small asset base consisting of the excursion-conversion steamer *W.W.*, the barge *Acme*, and a partial interest in a Rock Island, Illinois, warehouse. The capital stock was $138,473, the preponderance of which was cash ($106,250) partially sourced from the insurance proceeds from the *J.S.*

The proceeds amounted to only 25% of the $100,000 of fresh capital demanded by shipyards for another Streckfus newbuild. Yet more daunting was the intermediate-term downtime. Commodore Streckfus reckoned it would require, at the least, two years of construction to build from scratch a replica of the magnificent *J.S.*

---

131 Roy Michael Streckfus was the author's grandfather.
132 In addition to John and Theresa Streckfus's four sons and three daughters, they had two more daughters. Theresa Agnes was born in 1894 and died before her first birthday, and Nina Agnes was born in 1897 and died in 1907 at age ten.

Expansion, 1911–

He turned to the "family and friends" means of raising capital, from his devout following of farmers, businessmen, and bankers from his years of service since 1884 in running the *Freddie, Verne Swain, City of Winona/ W.W.,* and the *J.S.* The Streckfus crew had brought nearly 100% of the passengers and crew to safety when fire had raged on the *J.S.*: Streckfus had a bankable track record.

> River business as a whole being in steady decline, investment in a steamboat company was not considered a good investment by the bankers, merchants or public. And because a lien for wages, supplies and repairs to steams came first, no first mortgage bonds could be placed on any vessel. This situation made it very difficult at that time to finance a steamboat business; bank loans could not be had; first mortgage bonds could not be issued. However, Capt. John Streckfus, with his four sons and three daughters, all experienced in the steamboat business, [were] looked upon by the public as the most logical persons to continue on in the steamboat business, [enabling] Capt. John Streckfus to sell enough common stock in his new proposed company to raise the necessary capital to purchase [more] steamers.[133]

Ahead was a 100-year journey that would bring excursion steamers to millions along the full expanse of the Mississippi and Ohio rivers from St. Paul and Pittsburgh to New Orleans.

The Commodore had already broken new ground with the single-purpose-built "Palatial Excursion Steamer" *J.S.* targeted to "sightseers and excursionists." Unlike the traditional packet steamers, the *J.S.* was absent sleeping berths; its focus was no longer freight shipping and storage.

The success of the *J.S.* was well known along the Rock Island-to-St. Louis corridor and potential investors were intrigued by the Commodore's

---

[133] Annie Amantea Blum, *The Steamer Admiral and Streckfus Steamers: A Personal View* (Corona, NY: 49th Avenue Press. 2012), From the words of Captain Joseph Streckfus, pg. 78.

grit in his more than two decades of running a popular, timely, and safe enterprise.

In the *Muscatine* [Iowa] *Journal* on Aug. 11, 1910—a scant seven weeks after the *J.S.'s* loss—the Commodore outlined his vision for the new Streckfus venture: "[The enterprise] will own a number of fireproof steel steamers, which will ply between St. Paul and the Gulf."[134]

Streckfus recognized that riverboat commerce was taking it on the chin from the railroads, which were out to crush competition. These were the days when deep Wall Street and Scottish pockets were financing the expansion of arteries of rail from coast to coast. The commercial-packet river trade was under unrelenting cutthroat competition.

Unrestricted by anti-monopoly laws or regulations, many railroads were de facto federally protected monopolies. By virtue of that they were granted the land and minerals—the rail magnates preyed upon the unorganized and far-flung fleet of packets that roamed the nation's rivers. The board game Monopoly was invented in 1903; none of the player tokens or real estate was—or, to this day, is—a commercial ship.[135]

By 1910, rails like the Missouri and Pacific had laid hundreds of miles of track along both banks of the Upper Mississippi. Rail empires thrived on predatory pricing, particularly rock-bottom rates during summer when river trade was most active. Conversely, rail prices soared in winter when customers could not take their business to boats, which were virtually shut in by ice.

Just two months prior to the end of the *J.S.*, the celebrated riverboat pilot and author Samuel Langhorne Clemens passed away in April 1910. Known outside the river-pilot trade as Mark Twain, Clemens had returned to the Mississippi in 1882 after a 21-year absence, chronicling his visit in a

---

134 *Muscatine* [Iowa] *Journal*, Aug. 11, 1910.
135 https://en.wikipedia.org/wiki/Monopoly_(game). The game was invented by the daughter of a newspaper publisher to demonstrate the dire economic consequences of permitting monopolies. A battleship and a race car token are still used today; these are the only two player tokens from the original game.

Expansion, 1911–

collection of stories, *Life on the Mississippi*, that includes having witnessed the rise and demise of the greatest Mississippi steamboat days.

Writing from his hotel room in St. Louis, Clemens wrote: "The most notable absence observable in the billiard-room, was the absence of the river man. . . . I saw there none of the swell airs and graces, and ostentatious displays of money, and pompous squanderings of it, which used to distinguish the steamboat crowd from the dry-land crowd in the bygone days. . . . But I suspected that the ranks were thin now, and the steamboatmen no longer an aristocracy."[136]

Continuing, he remarked of his tour of the river:

But the change of changes was on the 'levee.' This time, a departure from the rule. Half a dozen sound-asleep steamboats where I used to see a solid mile of wide-awake ones! This was melancholy, this was woeful. The absence of the pervading and jocund steamboatman from the billiard-saloon was explained. He was absent because he is no more. His occupation is gone, his power has passed away, he is absorbed into the common herd, he grinds at the mill, a shorn Samson and inconspicuous. Half a dozen lifeless steamboats, a mile of empty wharves, a negro fatigued with whiskey stretched asleep, in a wide and soundless vacancy, where the serried hosts of commerce used to contend! Here was desolation, indeed.

The towboat and the railroad had done their work, and done it well and completely. The mighty [railroad] bridge, stretching along over our heads, had done its share in the slaughter and spoliation.

[. . .] Mississippi steamboating was born about 1812; at the end of thirty years, it had grown to mighty proportions; and in less than thirty more, it was dead! A strangely short life for so majestic a creature. Of course it is not absolutely dead, neither is a crippled octogenarian who could once jump twenty-two feet on

---

136 Mark Twain, *Life on the Mississippi* (1883) Chapter 22, "I Return to My Muttons."

level ground; but as contrasted with what it was in its prime vigor, Mississippi steamboating may be called dead.[137]

St. Louis in 1858 had been as follows, as described by Dolores Jane Meyer in her 1967 dissertation "Excursion Steamboating on the Mississippi with Streckfus Steamers, Inc.":

> America's fast-growing population and healthy trade and enterprise made St. Louis—long before it was known as "the gateway to the West"—a thriving metropolis and the greatest steamboat center on the Mississippi. In 1858 St. Louis stood as the undisputed leader and home port of sixty regular packet boats and forty more "tramp" vessels which were operating on the Missouri River.[138]

By 1900, however, only 6% of grain shipments out of St. Louis were by river. After 1900, the decline in Upper Mississippi steam commerce accelerated.

John Streckfus had first become fascinated with riverboats as a child; by 1884, at 28, he had a boat of his own, the *Freddie*. By then, based on Samuel Clemens's 1882 observation, the business was already going the way of all flesh.

Time had never been on Streckfus's side. But by 1910, he had already eked out 26 years of profit. Riverboating had been his whole career to date.

And time was still not on his side; rather, the clock was accelerating. The Commodore recognized he must move with haste to protect the family trade and attend to the loyal clients he had won during the preceding 26 years.

News swirled through the riverboat eddies that a complete steamship fleet was on the block. In pursuit, Streckfus traveled to St. Paul, where he

---

137 Mark Twain, *Life on the Mississippi* (1883) Chapter 22, "I Return to My Muttons."
138 Meyer, "Excursion Steamboating," pg. 25

Expansion, 1911–

began negotiations with Capt. John Killeen, president of the Diamond Jo Line.[139]

Next, the Commodore traveled to the Windy City to meet with Killeen's boss, Jay Morton. Chicago-based Morton had gained ownership of the Diamond Jo Line in 1895 from the estate of his late sister, Mary, widow of Joseph "Diamond Jo" Reynolds. The couple had no heirs.

Morton was a seasoned hardline businessman with nary an ounce of interest in steamboats or the Mississippi. He had reportedly never set foot on any of the Diamond Jo vessels. Two dreadful seasons in 1909 and 1910 of extremely low water levels had thoroughly stressed Morton's resolve for the business.

Streckfus learned from traffic manager I.P. Lusk that repeated offers to sell one or two steamers piecemeal got an emphatic "thumbs down" from the Chicago office. What Morton sought from Streckfus was to assume title to the complete Diamond Jo fleet and the company's 16 warehouses in Iowa, Illinois, Missouri, and Wisconsin, as well as a boat yard, some barges, and assorted real estate.

Morton gave John Streckfus time to survey the far-flung Diamond Jo enterprise and offered a two-month option to fashion an "all or nothing" offer.

What had brought the Diamond Jo Line to its knees? As 1910 waned, the Upper Mississippi River was experiencing another round of extraordinarily severe and persistently depressed water levels. Streckfus wrote in his notes that his own plans in the summer of 1910 for a new enterprise had met with "the lowest level of water in which to maneuver the steamships in recent history."[140]

At St. Louis, the Mississippi was recorded at a historic low of -1.60 feet on Jan. 12, 1909, and a record -1.45 feet on Dec. 16, 1910.[141]

---

139 *Quad-City Times*, Feb. 1, 1931.
140 Source: Streckfus Steamers family records.
141 https://water.weather.gov/ahps2/water.php?wfo=lsx&gage=eadm7

The four vessels owned by Diamond Jo had remained tethered on sandbars close to shore for most of two full seasons of normal commercial activity. A soft industrial economy and intense competition from the railroads piled on, leaving the Diamond Jo Line near bankruptcy.

Commodore Streckfus saw opportunity, but he also saw a Line that had been long neglected. Each year, the wooden fleet was decaying and starved for the minimal maintenance capital required to keep the engines and machinery running at top performance.

We can envision the Commodore standing at the head of the table at the family's Rock Island home at 908 4th Avenue. His wife and their children are bowed in prayer. He rises and speaks:

> You must understand how difficult is our current situation. The fire destroyed a great steamship but, with God's grace, few lives were lost. The economy of the river is harsh and we have neither the time nor capital to rebuild the *J.S.* We have secured an option from Mr. Morton to own the Diamond Jo fleet of four packets and attendant assets. We need to pull together, move fast and work the heck out of these two sidewheelers and two sternwheelers. Our family must function as an extremely strong team of tough German descent. Immediate plans need to get underway to convert all of the Diamond Jo vessels to a future excursion life. There will be no wooden hulls now. Fireproof, steel vessels will become our future. The entire family will relocate to St. Louis, the fleet's primary harbor. We will hire many quality hands—men of strength and integrity. Our family will be spread across all the waters of the Mississippi. We will expand south to New Orleans and northeast to Pittsburgh. Our family will persevere and prosper.

Perhaps it was intentional that Streckfus didn't close a deal for the Diamond Jo Line until after New Year's Day in 1911. Winter is always the most dismal revenue season for Upper Mississippi boats. This particular

Expansion, 1911–

winter, the Mississippi fell at St. Louis, for example, to a record -1.90 feet on Jan. 5, 1911.[142]

In effect, the Upper Mississippi had been reduced to puddles.

That the Diamond Jo Line had been unprofitable for some time and low water was restricting commerce certainly were cards Streckfus held when negotiating. Streckfus closed a deal on February 3, 1911.

It was structured as a "highly speculative" and "highly leveraged" transaction. Morton agreed to sell the complete Diamond Jo asset base for roughly $150,000, of which $75,000 was cash at closing and the balance was a seller's note—at 6% interest with principal amortization over four years.

Formal portrait of the Streckfus Family. Left to right (1st row): John N. Streckfus; Commodore John Streckfus; Verne W. Streckfus; Theresa Bartemeier Streckfus (wife of Commodore John); May Streckfus. Left to right (2nd row): Roy M. Streckfus; Anna Streckfus Manthey; Joseph L. Streckfus; Lilly Streckfus Manning
Arthur L. Smith Family Collection, circa 1908–1910

---

142 https://water.weather.gov/ahps2/water.php?wfo=lsx&gage=eadm7

In addition to the four passenger and freight steamers—the *Saint Paul*, *Quincy*, *Dubuque*, and *Sidney*—Streckfus acquired the Diamond Jo headquarters wharf boat in St. Louis, two wooden and one steel barge, 15 wooden warehouses, two steel warehouses, and two lots of real estate.

The next challenge was the daunting "How to manage it all?"

The family followed the fleet, moving home and headquarters in 1911 to St. Louis, where the Diamond Jo Line assets were concentrated. Each successful excursion conversion would expand the reach of Streckfus Steamboat Line and strengthen its geographical influence and commercial might.

Daughters Lily (now 30), Anna (28) and May (26) worked as concessioners and pursers.[143] Sons Joseph (now 24), Roy (23), John (20) and Verne (16) worked as officers and enforcers of the Streckfus brand of family-friendly passenger experience.

> It took years of above-board treatment and kid glove service for the Streckfus steamer fleet to build its deservedly fine family-friendly reputation. To be frank, the growing excursion business was loosely regulated and the era of gamblers, women of the night and vagabonds was hardly fiction. One example was the [Anchor Line's] *Corwin H. Spencer* which had acquired an unsavory reputation. The *Spencer*'s certain dark notoriety stemmed from many years of loose and shoddy oversight by its owners and management. Like many excursion vessel competitors, the *Spencer* was notorious for lax controls and management-flaunted gambling on board.[144]

---

[143] The Streckfus daughters may have chosen to not be captains, rather than excluded from the option. Women were allowed to be river pilots at the time. The first woman river pilot was Blanche Douglass Leathers, who received her master's license in 1894.

[144] Meyer, "Excursion Steamboating," pg. 117.

Expansion, 1911–

Taking in the Diamond Jo Line steamers, Streckfus also still had the *W.W.*, which continued to provide excursions between Rock Island and Muscatine, Iowa. Records show that the *W.W.* was on a daily summer schedule, leaving Davenport at 2:30 p.m. and Rock Island at 3:00 and arriving at Muscatine at 5:30. After a leisurely 90 minutes docked in Muscatine, the excursion craft would return to her home port by 10:30 p.m.

The *Rock Island Argus* reported:

An excursionist could keep cool on this trip as the *W.W.* had plenty of room for those who did not wish to dance, but also had an elegant dancefloor for those that enjoyed the amusement. The *W.W.* offered great music, cool refreshments and . . . all the conveniences of home with fresh air added.[145]

As the transaction with Morton was consummated in February 1911, Streckfus had some latitude in preparations for the upcoming season. He and his sons wasted no time in readying the new Diamond Jo fleet for commerce.

–Sidewheeler *Quincy* (became the *J.S. Deluxe*, 1919), 265 feet long, four decks, rooms for 300 passengers and 120 crew. Capt. Maurice Killeen was named to her helm.

Quincy
Courtesy of the Dave Thomson
Collection at Steamboats.com

J.S. Deluxe
Courtesy of the Dave Thomson
Collection at Steamboats.com

---

145 The *Rock Island Argus*, July 19, 1911.

Dubuque
Courtesy of the Dave Thomson
Collection at Steamboats.com

Capitol
Courtesy of the Dave Thomson
Collection at Steamboats.com

—Sternwheeler *Dubuque* (built in 1897 from the hull of the *Pittsburgh*[146] became the *Capitol*, 1920), 257 feet long, four decks, rooms for 225 passengers and 100 crew. Capt. William Burke was named to her helm.

Sidney
Courtesy of the Dave Thomson
Collection at Steamboats.com

Washington
Courtesy of the Dave Thomson
Collection at Steamboats.com

—Sternwheeler *Sidney* (became the *Washington*, 1921), 221 feet long, four decks, rooms for 175 passengers and 100 crew. Capt. John Streckfus took her helm.[147]

—Sidewheeler *Saint Paul* (built in 1883; received an entirely new hull in 1903;[148] became the *Senator*, 1940), 277 feet long, four decks, rooms for

---

146 *Quad-City Times*, Feb. 1, 1931.
147 The *Daily Times*, March 6, 1911.
148 *Quad-City Times*, Feb. 1, 1931.

Expansion, 1911–

Saint Paul
Courtesy of the Dave Thomson
Collection at Steamboats.com

Senator
Courtesy of the Dave Thomson
Collection at Steamboats.com

320 passengers and 120 crew. Taking the helm was Capt. Con McGee,[149] who graduated from deckhand to captain under Capt. John Killeen.

Capt. John Killeen, president of the Diamond Jo line, retired from the river after the sale[150] and took over the Dubuque Boat & Boiler Co., turning it into "one of the most successful steel boat builders of the West."[151] Capt. Walter A. Blair wrote in 1931:

> John Killeen as a young mate rigged and fitted out Diamond [Jo]'s first steamer, the little *Lansing* in 1862, and also the much larger *Diamond Jo* in 1863 and excepting a few seasons as master of the *Imperial* when she was owned by John Robson of Winona, John Killeen was continuously in the line as master, [vice president]/superintendent and [general manager]/president until it was sold out in 1911. Capt. Killeen was known, admired and respected by the best people who traveled on steamers of the Diamond Jo line and all of them now living will be glad to know that he is still living and occasionally walks down to the landing to see how we are carrying on.[152, 153]

---

149 *Quad-City Times*, Feb. 1, 1931.
150 *Ibid.*
151 "Killeen, last great steamboat captain," *Quad-City Times*, June 21, 2004.
152 *Quad-City Times*, Feb. 1, 1931.
153 John Killeen passed away in 1938; he was 94. "Killeen, last great steamboat captain," *Quad-City Times*, June 21, 2004.

THE EXCURSION CONVERSION BONANZA

The *J.S.* was the brainchild of the Commodore. He had personally overseen her design, construction, and operations.

In 1915, the Commodore was 60 years old, and Joe, Roy, John, and Verne were in their twenties. It was time to get serious. The four brothers embarked on an ongoing series of renovations and conversions to steamboats that carried Streckfus Steamers on a wonderful ride for the next 30 years.

The Streckfuses immediately began investing to "excursionize" the *Sidney* with the complete removal of her packet staterooms and a conversion to more sightseeing berths plus the buildout of her dancefloor, bandstand, food-preparation facilities, and rest areas.

In her packet life, she outfitted for roughly 200 passengers and 100 crew. After all obstructing columns were removed from the mezzanine, the *Sidney* boasted one of the finest dancefloors on America's rivers: some 160 by 30 feet—nearly 5,000 uninterrupted square feet.

A ring of brightly upholstered seats outlined the dancefloor, giving exuberant guests time to catch their breath, and ran the complete length and breadth of the deck.

After the retrofit, the *Sidney* boasted a passenger capacity of 1,800. Joe Streckfus said:

> St. Louisans loved the *Saint Paul*, our only packet to excursion conversion that was not renamed. The new *Saint Paul* was launched in 1917—our fourth excursion vessel after the *J.S.*, the *W.W.* and the *Sidney*.
>
> In 1919, we saw that the market was receptive to another excursion vessel in St. Louis. We did not waste time and immediately put the *Quincy* on blocks in the shipyard to begin a total renovation to become the *J.S. Deluxe*.
>
> The palatial *J.S. Deluxe* was, by design, a much more elegant—and expensive—excursion conversion. It was our thinking at the

time to gear the workhorse *Saint Paul* to general harbor sightseeing traffic and concentrate the extremely beautiful and well-appointed *J.S. Deluxe* to a less-price-conscious clientele. The "Upscale Girl" was a giant hit in the St. Louis harbor.[154]

The *Quincy*, *Dubuque*, and *Saint Paul* were subjected to an intensive, thorough review of all mechanical, operational, and safety features. The Commodore and his four sons had a ton of work ahead as the three vessels had been idle and ignored, lacking regular maintenance for some time.

Pending conversion eventually to excursion, the *Quincy*, *Dubuque*, and *Saint Paul* were readied for regular packet duty between St. Louis/St. Paul and St. Louis/Burlington, Iowa. After the Streckfus team performed sea trials and fire and safety drills on each of the three boats, they were put in the charges of their captains, officers, and crew.

The general malaise in the river economy played into the Commodore's hand as he and his sons were able to interview and perform background checks on a host of prospective employees, some of whom were holdovers from the Diamond Jo days.

Source: Arthur L. Smith's Personal Collection

The years 1911 through 1916 were a time of innovation. While the *Sidney* and *W.W.* were focused on excursion operations solely (the *W.W.* upstream around Rock Island and the *Sidney* in New Orleans), the three packets worked their routes with gusto.

To keep the fleet moving for the first five years, the Streckfus family scrambled to find believers with a strong background on the river and with deep-seated confidence in Capt. John Streckfus and his bold plans. What the Commodore needed most were fresh sources of capital.

---

154 The reminiscences of Captain Joe Streckfus.

THE STRECKFUS RIVERBOAT DYNASTY

In the context of extreme duress in river commerce in general, seeking new funds for a steamboat company, albeit at a very attractive cost of entry, met with scant investment interest. These were unique times that were marked by the birth of the industrial revolution.

Henry Ford had patented his first automotive transmission (1911); the first Indianapolis 500 auto race had been run (1911); and the Supreme Court had flexed its muscle with the Sherman Antitrust Act (1890), which initiated a breakup of monopolies.

Streckfus brought determination and a strong will, but also ingenuity: He left no realistic commercial opportunity unexploited between St. Louis and St. Paul. For example, with the *Saint Paul* and the *Quincy* working the St. Louis-to-St. Paul route, Streckfus experimented with cooperation with the railroads with an enhanced offering to passengers.

In a deal struck with the I&I electric railway company that operated between Davenport and Clinton, passengers could take the *Saint Paul* or the *Quincy* morning excursion upriver and return to their homes in the afternoon via rail.[155] This proved popular among passengers; meanwhile, the steamboats could continue north.

Source: Arthur L. Smith's Personal Collection

In 1916, another innovation Streckfus devised was to issue rail tickets to anyplace in the United States, over any railroad. He suggested to the railroad operators that he and "they were both losing money on pleasure seekers who might have a week or two of vacation and could not lose time by making an exclusive water trip. Thus, combined water-rail trips were offered to tourists."[156]

---

155 Meyer, "Excursion Steamboating," pg. 128.
156 *Ibid.*, pg. 129.

Expansion, 1911–

Opportunities to enhance freight volumes and margins were not to be overlooked either.

The lack of good terminal facilities at most of the river cities hindered their business as it was challenging to load and unload at these central points. In order to attract incremental freight business, Streckfus arranged to give an insured bill of lading on all shipments over [his] Line in 1915. In 1916, Streckfus extended terms for hauling freight to and from the levee to uptown company warehouses. An insurance policy was issued from the warehouse to the final destination. This convenience helped to bring considerably more [freight] business to the Line.[157]

Streckfus sought to keep all the vessels as active as possible at all times, weather and water allowing. Benefiting from the autumn harvest, the *W.W.* and a chartered small packet, the *Nashville*, shipped barrels of apples each fall.

Excursion Boat "W.W." on Mississippi River
Source: Arthur L. Smith's Personal Collection

Over nearly 20 years, the *City of Winona/W.W.* served the Commodore and the Streckfus family exceptionally well. Again, Streckfus wasn't sentimental; he sold her in 1915. The *W.W.*'s next chapter was not kind; she left the Mississippi for the Ohio and, several years later, she sank while escorting a tow of barges downstream. She was not salvageable.

---

157 Meyer, "Excursion Steamboating," pg. 130.

TITANIC 1912, EASTLAND 1915

Bad news traveled at lightning speed from Chicago to Streckfus headquarters in St. Louis. The Commodore and his sons were in shock to learn of the SS *Eastland's* accident in 1915, when the news of the inexplicable and horrendous sinking of the RMS *Titanic* was still fresh in the minds of both seamen and passengers. Fatal accidents on excursion vessels were extremely rare. The *Eastland's* was bone-chilling.

The *Titanic*'s end had come in 2,000 feet of icy water on April 14, 1912. In contrast, the SS *Eastland*'s surrealistic accident took place in a mere 20 feet of water. On July 24, 1915, on the Chicago River, the *Eastland* lost ballast and rolled over. To this day, she holds the infamous record for the greatest loss of life from a single maritime disaster on the Great Lakes.

At capacity with 2,572 excited picnic-bound passengers, the "Speed Queen of the Great Lakes" had not yet left her moorings when she began to list portside. Notwithstanding efforts by *Eastland* crew to fill ballast tanks, she refused to respond. Hastened by a mad rush of passengers to the canal side, away from the wharf, the *Eastland* lurched, shuddered, and turned over on her side.

The grim count of crushed or drowned women, children, and men was tallied some days later: The *Eastland* disaster had abruptly and tragically ended the lives of 844 passengers and crew.

Western Electric Co., a major Chicago industrial company, had chartered the *Eastland* and four other Great Lakes passenger ships—the

THE STRECKFUS RIVERBOAT DYNASTY

Rochester, Petoskey, Theodore Roosevelt, and *Racine*—to take employees and their families to an annual picnic in Michigan City, Indiana.

The *Eastland* boarding began at 6:30 a.m. The crowds, many composed of Czech immigrants who worked at the Western Electric plant at Cicero, Illinois, anxiously awaited access on the corner of Clark and LaSalle. When the gangplank was opened, the crowd, in high spirits, swarmed aboard; the vessel had reached capacity by 7:10 a.m. when Passenger No. 2,572 was counted.

Witnesses reported that many passengers immediately gained the ship's interior, seeking warmth from a cool, moist morning. Hardly had families found seating and parked their picnic baskets when, around 7:15 a.m., the *Eastland* first pitched to port.

In apparent efforts to right the vessel, certain areas of the hull were flooded. However, these efforts—some of which were later deemed inappropriate decisions—may have hastened trouble: At 7:28 a.m. the SS *Eastland*, like a harpooned whale expelling a dying breath, rolled over and sank to the Chicago River bottom.

Below decks, her passengers were in panic as pianos, furniture, and a wall of people were violently thrust into the cool water; whole families were crushed by the wall of debris.

The *Kenosha*, a vessel tethered nearby, was brought alongside the *Eastland*, allowing passengers to leap to safety. In the river, many heroes dived into the ship to bring out the living—and the deceased. The bodies were too many to count, and temporary morgues were established to identify victims—some 220 of whom were Czech. Western Electric Company established a fund of $100,000 to aid survivors of the Eastland's deceased. George Halas Sr., NFL Chicago Bears owner and football legend, luckily "missed the boat," arriving too late to join friends, who survived by escaping through portholes onboard the *Eastland* that tragic morning.

The cause of the "sinking" was never fully ascertained. The accident was horrible—but it was not a "shipwreck." Certainly, it was known that the ship's design was narrow and top-heavy. The *Eastland* was righted on

Aug. 14, 1915, and recommissioned by the Illinois Naval Reserve as the USS *Wilmette*. The vessel was active during World War I and World War II in various capacities, primarily as a training vessel. She was decommissioned in 1945 and sold for scrap in 1947.[158]

The unimaginable loss of life on the *Titanic* in 1912—more than 1,500 passengers and crew died—had prompted adoption of the U.S. Seamen's Act of 1915, signed into law on March 14 by President Woodrow Wilson.

The new law required the installation of additional lifeboats and survival gear; these increments to the top decks surely exacerbated the natural top-heaviness of the *Eastland*. The passenger maximum had already been restricted to 2,600 when legitimate concerns for the vessel's seaworthiness were voiced.

While the Seamen's Act did not apply to river craft, Streckfus always pursued all preventative means possible. In his more than 30 years on the river, the Commodore religiously strived to assure the safety of all those aboard his boats. He ordered each of his craft be tested for possessing any weakness similar to that of the *Eastland*.

> The Streckfus boats were always maintained with rigid detail to exceed every safety standard that was enforced by steamboat inspectors. In the wake of the horrific capsizing of the *Eastland* in Chicago in 1915, Capt. Joseph Streckfus voluntarily implemented rigid inspections for all Streckfus vessels including the "Whaleback Steamer" test. All Streckfus steamboats—*Saint Paul, Quincy, Dubuque, Sidney*, and *W.W.*—were subjected to the Whaleback test. Each vessel required the placement on either side of the boat of the number of sandbags that equaled the maximum passenger capacity. At the time, each bag of sand was filled to equal 140 pounds, estimated to be comparable to the average weight of a passenger. With alternate placement of these "sandbag passengers"

---

158 Naval History and Heritage Command. https://www.history.navy.mil/research/histories/ship-histories/danfs/w/wilmette.html

on first the port, and then starboard, sides of each boat, the whaleback test was administered. Each of the Streckfus [boats] was then required to exhibit clean maneuverability in ebb and flow currents of the Mississippi. These safety challenges were part and parcel to the Streckfus program that avoided significant loss of life for its passengers in some 100 years of excursion steamboating on the riverways.[159]

---

159 Meyer, "Excursion Steamboating," pg. 130.

WORLD WAR I

The advent of World War I proved exceptionally trying as excursion and freight/passenger volumes contracted significantly. Joe Streckfus wrote: "Savings in banks were frozen for the summer months. Railroads were taken over by the Government, and our combination railroad-excursion business was cancelled. Streckfus [Steamboat Line] was forced to lay up all but two of its boats."[160]

However, Mother Nature intervened in a calamity that ultimately benefited the Streckfus Line. During the winter of 1917–1918, the competition was leveled by a force majeure of nature: an ice crush. An extraordinarily deep freeze in the St. Louis harbor virtually destroyed the entire excursion fleet of Eagle Packet Co.

Out of this unusual river phenomenon, Streckfus vessels were even more popular and excursion fares proved resilient. It created an opportunity to increase fares, according to Joe Streckfus:[161]

> We opened the season in St. Louis with [the new *Saint Paul*] on Decoration Day 1918, setting forth a new policy in the excursion

---
160 Blum, *The Steamer Admiral*, pg. 79.
161 *Ibid.*

trade of operating at a higher fare and giving better service. [We] ... enjoyed a successful season, enabling the company to pay the cost of remodeling and [still] show a net profit.[162]

---

162 Blum, *The Steamer Admiral*, pg. 79.

THE *DUBUQUE* BECOMES THE *CAPITOL*

Each of the quartet of the Diamond Jo Line of packet steamers purchased by John Streckfus offered a story of her own. The *Dubuque*, often cited for her inaugural launch in 1896, was built upon the hull of the *Pittsburgh* (1879), which had been demolished by the 1896 St. Louis tornado. Of all the boats at St. Louis at that time, nine were sunk and 15 were badly damaged.[163]

In 1901, the Diamond Jo's *Dubuque* had the misfortune of encountering an unforgiving and immovable tree stump while motoring about six miles south of Keithsburg, Illinois.[164] The result was a 142-foot gash ripped across her hull; that incision quickly doomed her.

It was reported that within just 30 seconds, she sank in roughly eight feet of brown, swirling Mississippi current. Thankfully, the bulk of the craft was still intact and rested on the sandy bottom such that only the lower deck was covered in water of two to four feet.

The rapidity of the Diamond Jo vessel's plunge to the river bottom was, in effect, a godsend; there was no time for panic and the safety of the 46 passengers was never jeopardized.

---

163 *Quad-City Times*, Feb. 1, 1931.
164 *Ibid.*

THE STRECKFUS RIVERBOAT DYNASTY

It was time for the ingenuity and energy of Capt. John Killeen, vice president of the line at the time, to save the submerged *Dubuque*.[165] Killen was of old country stock, born in Ireland in 1844, auspiciously coinciding with the onset of the Great Famine in which "within five years, a million Irish were dead while half a million had arrived in America to start a new life."[166]

Among those making their way to America, Killeen was orphaned at the age of nine and joined the riverboat business at New Orleans before the Civil War, working his way upriver to Davenport/Rock Island by 1892 and eventually becoming a shareholder and president of the Diamond Jo line.[167]

After considerable planning, Killeen devised a series of steps for recovery in which the craft was gradually pumped out and improvised patches and repairs to her hull were completed.

The result: The *Dubuque* was slowly lifted off the bottom as river water was exchanged for air. Then, with her boilers still operative, she freely floated and moved under her own power.

The Steamer *Dubuque*
Arthur L. Smith's Personal Collection

Excursion Steamer "*Capitol*,"
St. Louis, MO.-118
Arthur L. Smith's Personal Collection

Now, her cargo of freight was recovered and moved to safety in her namesake port in Iowa, where permanent repairs would be implemented. This entire salvage effort was managed by Capt. Killeen in a very impressive 38 days.

---

165 *Quad-City Times*, April 29, 1907.
166 Irish-Catholic Immigration to America. https://www.loc.gov/classroom-materials/immigration/irish/irish-catholic-immigration-to-america/
167 *Quad-City Times*, "Killeen, last great steamboat captain," June 21, 2004.

The Dubuque Becomes the Capitol

In the early months of 1920, the *Dubuque* underwent her excursion-vessel transformation to become one of the Streckfus family's most cherished steamers: the *Capitol*, featuring a grand dome on top like that of the nation's Capitol building, and commencing patriotic-themed nomenclature for future conversions and additions to the Streckfus fleet.

The *Capitol* Conversion
The Verne Streckfus Collection

It featured a bright white hull, white stanchions, and a delicate white gingerbread pattern of filigree with a sky blue tint that accented certain trim. Sky blue graced the 14 steel lifeboats. The Streckfus adoption of blue for the lifeboats became its visual trademark, a stark change from the traditional acorn brown.

From the interior boiler-deck entrance, magnificent enclosed dual mahogany stairways introduced passengers to the dancefloor deck, as eight beautiful carved white columns greeted them. These columns supported a huge glowing dome, another tribute to the Washington, D.C., landmark.

Here, on the edge of the giant ballroom, a rainbow of colored silk ribbons radiated below the dome. A highlight of the *Capitol*'s impressive dance deck was the plush green leather seating encircling the room. Here, spectators could take in the radiating jazz and be entertained by up to 2,200 fellow guests, some already on the couches from dancefloor fatigue.

The *Capitol*
The Verne Streckfus Collection

The Streckfus brothers and their father were trendsetters on the Mississippi with regard to the adoption of modern and creative concepts for their fleet of steamboats. The dancefloor was a modern mecca of contrasting, indirect illumination—a tribute to the elegant Capitol Theater in Manhattan that opened in 1919.

In a 1965 interview, Capt. Roy Streckfus recalled how the lighting was such a draw: "It was captivating; the continuously changing feature of red, green, blue and amber lights seemed to mesmerize the large crowds, which were a fixture on [the] *Capitol*'s dancefloor."[168]

The Verne Streckfus Collection

The *Capitol* (1923)
Murphy Library Special Collections/ARC, University of Wisconsin–La Crosse.

Also, an immediate hit among her patrons was her modern cafeteria, patterned after the Childs brothers' successful Childs Restaurant chain that was launched in New York City in 1889.[169]

---

168 Streckfus Magazine.
169 Childs Restaurants. https://en.wikipedia.org/wiki/Childs_Restaurants

The Dubuque Becomes the Capitol

For the next 25 years, thousands of fun-seekers basked in the brilliant and glamorous hues that flooded the *Capitol*'s third-level ballroom.

The *Capitol* replaced the *Sidney* in the Crescent City in 1921 when the *Sidney* was renovated and moved north to the Ohio River. New Orleans welcomed the *J.S.* in 1903, the *Sidney* in 1911, the *Capitol* in 1921, and the *President* in 1942 (until she was retired in 2000).

The *Capitol* was the Streckfus family's favorite wooden steamer and, for her long and colorful years on the water, was one of the most popular to work the full expanse of the Mississippi, with Capt. Roy Streckfus spending many years at her helm.[170]

As a result of Joseph and Roy's travels on Eastern U.S. rivers, they applied new ideas they'd observed to the *Capitol's* renovation. She became an ambassador of the Streckfus brand, a showpiece that incorporated the latest and greatest entertainment features of the day.

History has been kind to the *Capitol*; it is no doubt true that she was the most beloved and photographed of all the Streckfuses' old-time steamers. If traveling along the Mississippi or Ohio, one will likely find framed photographs of her and memorabilia in museums and shops in any river town.[171]

Excursion Steamer *Capitol* on the Mississippi
Arthur L. Smith's Personal Collection

Roy M. Streckfus and, later, his son, John Curran Streckfus,[172] captained the *Capitol* for virtually all her years. Capt. Roy had a gleam in his eye when he recounted the separate ports the *Capitol* would visit each tramping season. He could recite these ports of call by rote in his sleep: 35 altogether.[173]

---

170 As told to the author, grandson of Captain Roy Streckfus.
171 Meyer, "Excursion Steamboating," pg. 145.
172 Roy M. Streckfus was the author's grandfather; John Curran Streckfus, the author's uncle.
173 Based on the author's own experience.

Notwithstanding that excursion trips were available daily on the St. Louis-domiciled *J.S. Deluxe* steamer, tickets for the *Capitol*'s two annual visits to the Gateway City were highly sought. Another draw was the accompanying "race" between the *J.S. Deluxe* and the *Capitol* between the St. Louis harbor and St. Genevieve, Missouri. Tickets sold out five days in advance of the *Capitol*'s Labor Day stop in St. Louis at the end of her Upper Mississippi season in 1923.[174]

The *Capitol* at night
The Verne Streckfus Collection

---

174 Meyer, "Excursion Steamboating," pg. 146.

THE *QUINCY* TESTS THE ST. LOUIS TO NEW ORLEANS LONG-HAUL MARKET

This *Quincy* was the fourth steamer to bear the port of Quincy's name. She was a sidewheeler created in 1896 from the principal structure and key operating equipment of the *Gem City*, which Diamond Jo had bought in 1891 from William F. Davidson.[175] Under the Diamond Jo flag, the *Quincy* bounced back from a near tragic encounter with a tree snag, which caused her to sink rapidly in the summer of 1906.[176]

On a voyage near Trempealeau, Wisconsin, the *Quincy* hit a reef and, with the river at a low ebb, swerved to the shore where a large limb protruded into the river, unceremoniously ripping a massive hole in her hull.

Fortunately, if there could be fortune in such a disastrous situation, the bow held on to the shore while impaled. Her stern sunk rapidly in roughly 25 feet of water. Blessed by the firm contact with

The *Quincy*—Diamond Jo Line
Murphy Library Special Collections/ ARC, University of Wisconsin–La Crosse.

---

175 *Quad-City Times*, Feb. 1, 1931.
176 *Ibid.*, April 29, 1907.

shore, the *Quincy's* ultimate survival was not in great jeopardy. The captain and crew were able to safely escort the packet vessel's passengers—all comfortably high and dry on the upper deck—onto land with nary a problem.

Diamond Jo's Captain, John Killeen,[177] stepped into the situation and oversaw the process of patching the hull, then righting her before she moved on her own power to the shipyard for permanent repair.

After joining the Streckfus fleet, the *Quincy's* summertime Upper Mississippi packet service accommodated up to 300 passengers. Meals and berth from Davenport/Rock Island/Moline to St. Louis one way was $12.

But low water had her moored to shore in St. Louis all spring and summer. No movement is no revenue is no profit. Streckfus could not long support the *Quincy* as an unproductive asset.

Sensing opportunity, the Commodore and his sons changed course—literally: south to the Crescent City. Offering extended overnight passage hadn't been practiced since the old Anchor Line discontinued its St. Louis–New Orleans round-trip trade in 1896.

While the Wright brothers had demonstrated flight in 1903, this was 1911. It was not until 1914 that Tony Jannus offered what is considered the first commercial air travel—St. Petersburg, Florida, to Tampa, Florida, over Tampa Bay.[178] On the Mississippi, the Streckfus

Arthur L. Smith's Personal Collection

Line proposed that, while offering freight service, the *Quincy* would concentrate efforts on the passenger trade between St. Louis and New Orleans, with a roundtrip fare of $60 ($1,900 in 2023) and an 18-day journey.

She was clocked at 18 to 20 miles per hour downstream and eight to 12 miles per hour upstream. While expectations were high within the

---

177 *Quad-City Times*, April 29, 1907.
178 Wikipedia article on Tony Jannus.

The Quincy Tests the St. Louis to New Orleans Long-Haul Market

Streckfus organization, public interest failed to manifest; the inaugural journey comprised only 35 passengers, most of whom were there for the roundtrip.

Notwithstanding that the *Quincy* attracted a reasonable hold of freight at 25 to 60 cents per pound, the long-haul offering was discontinued after only a handful of months.

History does hold a place card for the *Quincy* as the last sidewheel steamer to successfully log the 900-mile trip. Today, American Cruise Lines offers a twenty-two-day Mighty Mississippi roundtrip for $15,935 per person, *prix compris* food, beverage, and berth. Granted, the Line does offer numerous stops along its myriad itineraries, covering the river from New Orleans to St. Paul.[179]

It was a painful lesson: The ambitious *Quincy* long-distance St. Louis–New Orleans offering was a failure; but it was a fast mistake. Ready to move ahead and never content with uneven river-handling performance, the Streckfuses seized the winter of 1913–1914 to make a major overhaul of the *Quincy*'s rudder system—moving to three from one.

This novel engineering vastly improved her dexterity. Like her sister sidewheeler *Saint Paul*, her paddlewheels already possessed a superior design—at the extreme rear of the vessel, about four-fifths her length and described as "engineered like a duck's legs."[180]

---

179 As per the American Cruise Lines website, accessed on April 10, 2023.
180 Meyer, "Excursion Steamboating," pg. 152.

THE 1921 SENSATION—THE GARDEN STEAMER
J.S. DELUXE

For the next five years, the *Quincy* turned her attention northward and worked the traditional St. Louis–St. Paul summer-packet route. In the winter of 1919–1920, it was her turn to cast off her humble past and commercial focus: She was radically altered to become the new "pride of the Streckfus fleet": the *J.S. Deluxe.*

The *J.S. Deluxe* became popularly known as the "Garden Steamer" due to the summer garden theme that enriched her interior décor. The St. Louis department store Scruggs, Vandervoort & Barney had been given instructions to duplicate the atmosphere of the finest gardens.

Accordingly, the ceilings of each deck were completely canopied with draped cloth of large green and white stripes. Sun drapes of the same material edged the sides of the decks. An indirect lighting system with 5,000 lamps and 75 light domes made of silken cloth added to the overall beauty, while palms and flower boxes completed the picture.

Oil paintings of beautiful scenes from along the Upper Mississippi were paneled in the interior-cabin decorations. These paintings were the work of Antonio Bianchi of Rome. The main deck was outfitted with circular summer rugs and wicker chairs that were painted blue, with black arms and tapestry cushions.

On the third deck, genuine Heywood-Wakefield ocean-steamer chairs lined the railings, while the dining deck boasted "fancifully painted Windsor chairs in yellow, with black edges."[181]

This colorful steamer provided a dancefloor of more than 8,000 square feet, surrounded by "scores of rocking chairs" for guests' comfort.[182] The *J.S. Deluxe* program advertised "ocean steamer service on the Mississippi."

The *Waterways Journal* wrote the following praise of *J.S. Deluxe* on Sept. 3, 1921:

The *J.S. Deluxe*
Murphy Library Special Collections/ ARC, University of Wisconsin–La Crosse.

> Experts who have been on board the *East St. Louis, Homer Smith, Island Queen, Capitol, Washington, America,* and *Majestic* declare that there has never been a boat to compare with the *J.S. [Deluxe]*, particularly the effect given the passenger as he steps aboard and walks down the main deck. Fountains, Japanese lanterns, canopies, rocking chairs, and steamer chairs combine to produce a sensation nothing short of fairyland.[183]

It was further declared that never in the history of steamboating at St. Louis had a steamer caused the sensation the *J.S. Deluxe* did in the 1921 season. With this special new service, the "best people in the city" were willing to ride on the steamer at $2 for a day's trip.[184]

---

181 From a passenger pamphlet of the *J.S. Deluxe* from the 1921 Season, retained by May Streckfus.
182 From a passenger pamphlet of the *J.S. Deluxe* from the 1921 Season, retained by May Streckfus.
183 From *The Waterways Journal*, September 3, 1921.
184 Meyer, "Excursion Steamboating," pg. 155.

THE *SAINT PAUL* BECOMES THE *SENATOR*

The *Saint Paul* was commissioned by William F. Davidson's St. Louis and St. Paul Packet Co. in 1883 and operated locally until acquired by the Diamond Jo Line. In 1903, she was rebuilt in Dubuque to company (Killeen's) specifications at 276.6 feet in length with a 37-foot beam and a rather deep hold of 6.4 feet.

A sidewheel packet at inception, the renovated *Saint Paul* sported two enormous 26-foot-diameter paddlewheels in the nether length of the vessel. The engineers/architects purposely located them at this unusually aft location as this positioning significantly aided her speed.

Mississippi River Steamer
Arthur L. Smith's Personal Collection

In 1917, she enjoyed a Streckfus facelift and was transformed into a spectacular excursion vessel, sporting the same moniker. It is illustrative to review the *Saint Paul's* travel itinerary between 1911 and 1916. Largely catering to passenger travel between the principal Missouri port and Minneapolis, she offered meals and a sleeping berth for the fare of $28.50 (slightly less, $25, to/from Rock Island), arriving in about four days.[185]

---

185 Meyer, "Excursion Steamboating," pg. 158.

This was relatively luxurious travel for the day—equivalent to $903 in 2023—and sought by those travelers seeking the "genteel" way of touring the great Mississippi.

The accommodations were spacious for 200, and each passenger was allotted up to 150 lbs. of baggage. (Unlike today's restrictions on luggage in air travel, size was not limited in any way.) In many ways, this generous convention is behind the pictures of old that depict red caps struggling to load a huge trunk alongside the tourist class.

Just a few months into new ownership, the *Saint Paul* attracted a capacity crowd on July 28, 1911, presenting a challenge for the Streckfus clan to meet unexpectedly strong demand. But river waters were not placid for the inaugural journey of the *Saint Paul*. Just 10 miles from her St. Louis departure, the vessel was effectively disemboweled by a snag hidden just below the waterline.[186]

Sidewheeler *Saint Paul* with Sternwheeler *Dubuque*
Courtesy of the Dave Thomson Collection at Steamboats.com

Fortunately, the calamity was quickly contained as she sank slowly into a comfortable five feet of muddy Mississippi water, while all passengers remained calm. Owing to the immediate safety response of the crew, the passengers were attended to while salvage preparations were undertaken to refloat the vessel.

Back on her natural even keel, she was diverted to Keokuk, Iowa, for immediate repairs. After a brief delay, she continued north to Minnesota with the bulk of her passengers. They completed the voyage with few complaints and with great respect for the *Saint Paul* crew—and a few exciting memories of the power of the Mississippi.

In 1917, still primarily operating as a packet, the *Saint Paul* carried limited excursions between Alton, Illinois, and the Jefferson Barracks

---

186 Meyer, "Excursion Steamboating," pg. 158.

The Saint Paul Becomes the Senator

Military Post of St. Louis. In 1918, she emerged as a floating jazz palace, the pride of the Streckfus fleet. She was described in a promotion in the *St. Louis Republic* as offering:

> 500 rocking chairs, 2,000 upholstered seats, 2,500 comfortable chairs, three soda fountains, an electric corn popper, electric band [J.C. Deagan "Una-Fon"], 100 electric fans, 5,000 electric lights, and a $10,000 steam calliope. Her dreamland dancefloor measures 200 feet long by 40 feet wide without a post—and entertains 1,500 couples dancing comfortably with open space on all sides, light and airy.[187]

The 1918 Decoration Day maiden *Saint Paul* voyage—a round trip to Jefferson Barracks—was a reasonable 50 cents for adults and two bits for children.[188, 189] Free parking at Washington Avenue Wharfs was advertised, indicating the growth in automobile use.[190]

In the *Saint Paul's* first excursion-only year, she made some 225 consecutive trips—often two per day, including a moonlight cruise[191]—and brought river excitement to an estimated 1 million men, women, and children.

In 1918, one memorable evening cruise turned into an overnight affair. Traveling about

Saint Paul after her 1917 facelift
Murphy Library Special Collections/ARC, University of Wisconsin–La Crosse.

---

187 Meyer, "Excursion Steamboating," pg. 160 from *The St. Louis Republic*, May 26, 1918, June 4, 1918.
188 *St. Louis Post-Dispatch*, May 27, 1918.
189 *Ibid.*, June 8, 1921. This ad shows the 1921 fare was between 50 cents and $1 depending on day and time of day.
190 *Ibid.*
191 *Ibid.*

three miles north of the Chain of Rocks Bridge in St. Louis, the *Saint Paul* was buffeted by a powerful windstorm and pushed onto a sandbar. Unable to dislodge from the sand, patrons proceeded to dance away the evening before bedding down with cots and blankets provided by crew.

The vessel was freed from the sandbar in the morning and the several hundred couples who had enjoyed an extended dance party and unexpected sleepover were safely deposited back at Washington Avenue.

The *Saint Paul* in St. Louis
Arthur L. Smith's Personal Collection

After her moonlit excursion on Labor Day, the excursion version of the *Saint Paul* left St. Louis for a tour of the Upper Mississippi's ports in early autumn. Prepared and winterized, she anchored for the ice season at Davenport harbor.

In 1921, the dancefloor was updated with hardwood maple to complement fashionable lighting fixtures and colorful interior decorations. The inaugural 1921 excursion was a special event, sponsored by the students of St. Louis University. And, like many cherished events of that summer, it featured the famous and beloved Fate Marable's Metropolitan Jaz-E-Saz Orchestra.[192]

Arthur L. Smith's Personal Collection

It wasn't until the winter of 1933–1934 that she required a major, $30,000 overhaul and hull-rebuilding in the shipyards of Paducah, Kentucky.

Then, in the summer of 1937, the Streckfus brothers determined that despite difficult economic times, it was time to explore the excursion

---

192 Meyer, "Excursion Steamboating," pg. 162 from *The Waterways Journal*, May 21, 1921.

The Saint Paul Becomes the Senator

trade up the expanse of the Ohio River. After making her way north, the *Saint Paul* established her home port in the Steel City, Pittsburgh. On the upper Ohio, she concentrated on tramping-oriented excursions from 1938 to 1939.

Mississippi River history attests: the *Saint Paul* worked diligently and continuously from acquisition in 1911 to the autumn of 1940—truly one of the finest flagship sidewheelers ever to fly the Streckfus flag.

THE *SENATOR*, 1940–1953

At winter's end, the *Saint Paul* emerged from a Paducah shipyard as the stately *Senator*. With only minor tweaks and updates, she had been expanded to a capacity of 2,700 excursionists. The Streckfuses intended the *Senator's* future to be anchored on ample profitable work for the seven-month Ohio River summer season from April 1 to November 1.

A year later, World War II rocked the United States of America. Pearl Harbor was attacked by the Japanese on December 7, 1941. A few days later, the U.S. declared war on Germany. The *Senator* could not operate in 1942 at all; the calling of wartime service abroad had decimated the riverports of available crew.

The *Senator* (1939)
Courtesy of the Dave Thomson Collection at Steamboats.com

The *Senator* (Packet/Excursion/Training boat, 1940–1953)
Murphy Library Special Collections/ARC, University of Wisconsin–La Crosse.

The *Senator* was not to sit idle in a time of need, however. In the summer of 1942, she was put on six-month charter to the U.S. Coast Guard and moved to St. Louis for duty, serving as a receiving and training vessel.

Her dancefloor became the sleeping quarters for more than 300 recruits. Featured prominently in the *Senator*'s ballroom were signs that cautioned "No Jitter-Bug Dancing Permitted." These warnings were a great source of amusement to the enlisted men and their officers.

As the charter expired November 1, 1942, the *Senator* returned her contingent to the base at Grafton, Illinois, and resumed Streckfus control. The next decade was a sharp contrast to the excitement of the ship's first 60 years.

She was moored under Eads Bridge, a road and rail crossing from St. Louis to East St. Louis, for her last ten years. A fixture on the river for decades, the *Senator* was gradually relieved of her beauty: her excursion lights, furnishings, and gingerbread exterior were parted out day by day.

Now functioning purely as a machine shop and warehouse for materials for other Streckfus steamers, the *Senator*'s central nerve center of boilers, pistons, and sidewheels were no longer needed.

Finally, in 1953, her remains—she, no longer having a pulse, which had roared at thunderous, joyous decibels in her day—were towed by the Streckfus-operated tug, *Suzie Hazard*, to the steamboat graveyard near Jefferson Barracks.

All that remained of this grand river lady was her wooden hull, which was reluctantly surrendered to a watery grave. Good times must come to an end.

At certain points in time in the late 1920s into the early 1940s, wooden-hulled Streckfus excursion craft—the *Sidney, J.S. Deluxe, Capitol,* and *Senator*—were calling on cities and towns the length of the Mississippi and Ohio rivers, with occasional detours onto the Missouri, Tennessee, Cumberland, and Green rivers.

The Senator, 1940–1953

Painful decisions had to be made each year as some of the most successful and beloved members of the Streckfus fleet had to be retired, dismantled, and, as a general matter of course after salvage, sunk at a final port of call: the estimated 200-mile-long boat graveyard that stretches along the Mississippi from St. Louis south to Cairo, Illinois.[193]

---

193 "Steamboat Graveyards Yield 'Time Capsules' to Salvagers," Jim Shur, Associated Press, July 7, 2002, *Los Angeles Times*.

DIAMOND JO FLEET RETIRED WITH GRACE

Eventually, all the wooden-hulled Streckfus fleet acquired from the Diamond Jo Line were extinct. The Streckfuses well recognized the overarching importance of safety on the river for patrons and employees. It was inevitable that they migrated to safer, less flammable, and more durable steel-hulled vessels.

Of retiring the *Capitol* in 1945, Capt. Roy Streckfus said it was hard work to puncture her bottom. "Born" in 1897 from the 1879-built hull of the Diamond Jo Line's tornado-ravaged *Pittsburgh*, her hull was still intact and in truly remarkable shape after hundreds of thousands of miles on the water and 66 years of meritorious service.[194] The steamer was not worn out; she was pushed aside by advancement in general nautical engineering and by safer and more durable materials.[195]

Before and after the *J.S.* fire, the many vessels Commodore Streckfus himself, and then his sons as well, owned and captained for more than a century boasted an exceptional track record. There were encounters with sandbars and the occasional snag, but the Streckfus fleet suffered only two casualties in its entire run—one, the suspected perpetrator of the *J.S.* fire;

---

194 Roy Michael Streckfus interview.
195 "The '*Capitol*' eventually became the steamboat with the longest record of service on the Mississippi." *Encyclopedia Dubuque*.

the other, the passenger who prematurely jumped from the boat, while all others safely walked off.

This great fortune to avoid misfortune came about from a trait Commodore Streckfus required of his family and business partners: strict adherence to safety first and doing it right the first time—and the second and third time too.

NEW BLOOD—THE *CINCINNATI*: STEEL & OIL

The *Cincinnati*, sister craft of the second *Island Queen*,[196] was built by a Philadelphia steamship operator in 1925 using a novel steel hull and steel wheel housings. Her original structure featured a unique two tiers of 350 staterooms, which catered to upscale tourists making the journey between Cincinnati and Louisville—a 125-mile overnight jaunt.

At 300 feet with a 90-foot beam, the *Cincinnati*'s formal design included cabin deck balconies extending the entire length of the upper deck. Each stateroom on the deck side of the vessel featured outer balconies with spectacular river views.

The *Cincinnati*
Murphy Library Special Collections/ ARC, University of Wisconsin–La Crosse.

The Great Depression then commenced. These were not the best of times for high-end tourism. The Cincinnati Packet Co. struggled mightily with the passenger trade and,

---

196 The first *Island Queen* was decommissioned after being severely burned in 1922 when several steamboats in Cincinnati harbor caught fire; she had a wooden hull. The second *Island Queen* was completed in 1925; she had a steel hull.

after five years of inconsistent and unprofitable results, the owners made it known that the *Cincinnati* was for sale.

Ready to satisfy the Commodore's unfulfilled vision for transformation of the Streckfus Steamboat Line into a fleet of steel-hulled craft, Joe Streckfus and his three younger brothers made an ambitious and bold wager: the *Cincinnati* would be moved to St. Louis in 1931. There, reconstruction on it would begin for a new life as a purposed excursion palace.

Wooden-hulled packets and excursion vessels were not directly in the sights of federal and state safety inspectors in the mid-1920s—but the Streckfus gentlemen were not oblivious to the incompatibility of wood and fuel. Streckfus Steamers Inc.—the name adopted in March of 1926 when the company was reorganized following the Commodore's passing—had a profound interest—some would say a fixation—on safety and best practices on the river.

It was clear that wooden-hull and infrastructure vessels burning coal or wood to stoke their boilers were doomed; the frenetic pace of change derived from the industrial revolution that made steel affordable—and oil readily available—demanded their eventual extinction.

> Smaller steamboats of the time burned 12 to 24 cords of wood every 24 hours, the larger ones 50 to 75 cords–enough to build 15 small houses.
>
> Such staggering demand for wood resulted in widespread deforestation and destabilizing of the river banks. Between 1821 and 1888, the Mississippi became increasingly wider and shallower, with the lower channel depth disrupting navigation and posing perils for all vessels. On average, a steamboat lasted 18 months.[197]

The 1931 acquisition of the *Cincinnati* from John W. Hubbard of Pittsburgh was done by Streckfus Steamers at a bargain price in the early

---

197 "Steamboat Graveyards Yield 'Time Capsules' to Salvagers," Jim Shur, Associated Press, July 7, 2002, *Los Angeles Times*.

New Blood—The Cincinnati: Steel & Oil

years of the global Great Depression. Over the course of the next two years, her multi-million-dollar transformation took place on the banks of the Mississippi north of the Eads Bridge at St. Louis.

Every last piece of the *Cincinnati*'s upper works of wood and glass was stripped to expose the fireproof steel of her massive deck. Here, with 26 individual watertight compartments, was the foundation of the Streckfus vision: the excursion steamer the *President*.

The *Cincinnati* (1924)
Courtesy of the Dave Thomson Collection at Steamboats.com

The *President*
Courtesy of the Dave Thomson Collection at Steamboats.com

AN ART DECO STEAMSHIP:
MAZIE KREBS PERFORMS DESIGN MAGIC

A bright, talented young lady left a lasting imprint on the design of the *President*—largely based on her novel interior plans for the ballroom and facilities. What an opportunity the *President* offered to Mazie G. Krebs: never before had there been a canvas of this scope and size.

The *President* became a model for a new generation of super-sized excursion vessels on the Mississippi. Krebs became a favorite of the Streckfus brothers; her creative art deco designs became the hallmark of the Streckfus Steamers organization. The sleek steel-hulled excursion behemoth, the *Admiral*, sister of the *President*, was to emerge on the scene in 1940.

Arthur L. Smith Personal Collection

The steel-hulled *President* needed a modern new look. Her interior was designed by a St. Louis upstart. Born in 1900, Mary Georgiana "Mazie" Krebs (nee Schoon) grew up in the St. Louis home of her maternal grandparents, who, like the late Commodore's parents, were German immigrants who made a home on the Mississippi.

Her father, John, a cattle dealer, and her mother, Mary, had divorced. Moving to her grandparents' home before she was 10 years old, nothing was going to be stale or boring for Krebs. She was destined for adventure, spending her early childhood traveling with the family vaudeville group, the DeMonieos, comprising her mother, aunt, and uncle.[198]

Krebs pursued and earned a diploma in industrial design from the Washington University School of Fine Arts, teaching dance along the way and working as a cartoonist, penning the comic strip "Cindy of Hotel Royale" that ran in a Chicago-based syndicated-newspaper service.

Leading to her important work in grassroots creative design for Streckfus Steamers, Krebs had applied her talent to fashion illustrations for St. Louis-based Famous-Barr department stores, later moving to Los Angeles as art director for another department store. Her hometown beckoned and she returned to St. Louis. There she joined the staff of Taylor-Rebholz, a leading graphic design shop specializing in outdoor posters, billboards, and giant displays.

Arthur L. Smith Personal Collection

Mazie G. Krebs
Find-A-Grave.com

The connection to big projects was deepened when Krebs joined Rebholz in Chicago to observe the planning underway for the Chicago World's Fair of 1933. In 1940, Krebs recounted her original connection with Streckfus Steamers. She told the *St. Louis Post-Dispatch*: "I got a lot of experience there in modernistic effects and stylized designing. Besides

---

198 "Ink-Slinger Profiles by Alex Jay: Mazie Krebs," Blog, February 26, 2020.

An Art Deco Steamship: Mazie Krebs Performs Design Magic

working on fair exhibits, I did some nightclub interiors, cocktail bars and murals."[199]

This fresh worldly experience was just what Joe Streckfus was looking for. Streckfus Steamers was already a Taylor-Rebholz advertising-design client. In 1933, while working on the Streckfus Steamers advertising account, Krebs became aware that the Streckfus brothers were planning a giant new excursion vessel, the *President*, that was going to eschew the traditional gingerbread scroll and filigree so common on steamers for so long.

A stated policy of Streckfus Steamers was to "not only to keep up-to-date, but to remain a day ahead of everyone else in the steamboat business."[200]

The radically oversized *President* would have a basic design exterior. Krebs had a herculean design assignment: to imaginatively create a jaw-dropping opulence for the new vessel now under construction on the banks of the Mississippi.

Arthur L. Smith Personal Collection

In a beauty pageant of sorts, the Streckfus Line brought in some 20 firms with established design credentials to offer proposals for the huge excursion side-wheeler. Taylor-Rebholz was originally put off by the challenge of a monstrous floating palace that demanded such unique custom work. But gutsy Krebs was undaunted and commented such to her colleagues. She said to the *St. Louis Post-Dispatch* in 1940, "That didn't scare me, so I asked Capt. Joe if I could submit some sketches."[201]

Based in Chicago at the time, Krebs recollects that she spent about a month, mostly on weekends, preparing sketches for the interior of the

---

199 Mazie Krebs article, *St. Louis Post-Dispatch*, Aug. 25, 1940.
200 Meyer, "Excursion Steamboating," pg. 167.
201 Resources: mainly "Ink-Slinger Profiles by Alex Jay: Mazie Krebs," February 26, 2020, Meyer ("Excursion Steamboating"), and Findagrave.com, Mazie G. Krebs.

steamer. "I just did what I thought should go into that boat, and I knew that I could do it."[202]

With her completed sketches in hand, she made an appointment to present them to Capt. Joe. "I put the sketches up on the steam radiators in his office and tried to explain what I had done."[203] Capt. Joe kept staring at her designs for a ballroom, powder rooms and a bar, as they were draped across the radiators.

"Capt. Joe just looked at them and didn't say a word. I remember I talked myself hoarse, giving him a build-up of what I had done and could do."[204]

Joe Streckfus, a curmudgeon of a riverboat master, kept staring harder and harder at Krebs' artistic design drafts. With Capt. Joe's silence Krebs grew nearly apoplectic. The reality was that Krebs' fresh, worldly experience was just what the Streckfus line was looking for in creating the *President*. He hired her.

The *President*
Murphy Library Special Collections/ ARC, University of Wisconsin–La Crosse.

Krebs said in 1940, "I found out later he said 'yes' because he didn't know how to say 'no' to me."[205]

To the shock of his brothers, Joe ended the competition. He was an enthusiastic supporter of this young woman and her standout design work. Krebs said in 1940:

Afterward, I found my sales talk had been unnecessary. [Capt. Joe] hadn't said anything because he had no criticisms to make. They were what he wanted and he quickly saw they were practical, for Captain Joe

---

202 Mazie Krebs article, *St. Louis Post-Dispatch*, Aug. 25, 1940.
203 Resources: mainly the Ink Slinger profile by Alex Jay; Meyer ("Excursion Steamboating"); and Findagrave.com, Mazie G. Krebs.
204 Mazie Krebs article, *St. Louis Post-Dispatch*, Aug. 25, 1940.
205 Sources: mainly the Ink Slinger profile by Alex Jay; Meyer, and Findagrave.com, Mazie G. Krebs.

An Art Deco Steamship: Mazie Krebs Performs Design Magic

knows every nut and bolt that goes into the building of a steamboat.... Captain Joe put me under contract....[206]

The *President* became a model for a new generation of supersized excursion vessels on the Mississippi. Krebs became a favorite of the Streckfus brothers; her creative art-deco designs became the hallmark of the Streckfus Steamers organization.

The sleek steel-hulled excursion behemoth, the *Admiral*, was to emerge on the scene in 1940. Krebs was cited in some publications as her "architect"; however, that was incorrect. Joe Streckfus picked Krebs to design the interior of the *President*, and with the *President's* exceptional reception, she was given carte blanche to create the *Admiral's* spectacular bandstand, dancefloor, and much-admired ladies' facilities.[207]

The *President*
Hogan Jazz Archive, Special Collections, Howard-Tilton Memorial Library. Tulane University

The *Albatross*
Courtesy of the Dave Thomson Collection at Steamboats.com

---

206 Mazie Krebs article, *St. Louis Dispatch*, Aug. 25, 1940.
207 Krebs retired in the 1970s and passed away in California in 1993; she was 93. Findagrave.com, Mazie G. Krebs.

The *Admiral* was originally the *Albatross*, built in 1907 for the Louisiana & Mississippi Valley Transfer Co. by the Dubuque Boat & Boiler Works, which had been the Iowa Iron Works until 1903 when Capt. John F. Killeen bought it, reorganized it, and renamed it Dubuque Boat & Boiler Works.

The *St. Louis Star and Times* reported on June 13, 1940:[208]

> Old-time rivermen must have turned over in their graves last night, for riding the river was a ship they never dreamed of—all steel, streamlined and air conditioned. And to make it all the worse on the old-timers, the ship was designed by a mere slip of a girl, Miss Mazie Krebs of 5059 Rosa Avenue.
>
> The ship is the S.S. *Admiral*, which made its initial voyage last night with a capacity crowd of excursionists, who spent most of their time wandering from vast room to vast room, exclaiming at sleek light tubing, sweeping staircases and functional furniture. But even more amazing than the S.S. *Admiral* is the designer Miss Krebs.

---

208 Findagrave.com, Mazie G. Krebs.

KIDS' STUFF AND POWDER ROOMS: THE ADMIRAL APPEALS TO ALL

With few exceptions, novel features incorporated in the SS *President* were expanded and further enhanced in the transformation of the rail transfer *Albatross* into the sleek, fireproof SS *Admiral*. For example, Krebs introduced her concept of four palatial Ladies Lounges anchoring the compass around the *President*'s expansive dance floor. These powder rooms were extremely well appointed and sported memorable color motifs: copper and jade, plaid, golden petal, and black and white.

These facilities on the *President* were an outstanding hit among female patrons and could only be improved upon for the *Admiral*—another four even larger, more opulent, and detailed versions were created.[209]

The Admiral
Arthur L. Smith's Personal Collection

Krebs decided that the *Admiral*'s powder rooms should go "Hollywood." The four facilities were named after movie stars Deanna (Durbin), Greta (Garbo), and Sonja (Henie), with the fourth simply, Glamour.

---

209 Blum, *The Steamer Admiral*, pg. 35.

The three movie stars were each at the top of their game in the 1930s.

Deanna Durbin was a Canadian-born actress and renowned vocalist who made her first film appearance opposite Judy Garland at age 14. Durbin appeared in numerous films and was credited with "saving Universal Studios." The wholesome Durbin was one of Hollywood's most compensated actors, with one of the world's largest fan clubs. A Streckfus Line magazine described the Deanna powder room: ". . . peach is the dominating color offset by white corrugated walls on which are painted Durbin's popular song lyrics."[210]

The Deanna Powder Room
The Verne Streckfus Collection

Swedish-born Garbo was one of the classic Hollywood stars. Garbo, whose career began in 1924 in silent film, became one of the world's leading actresses, known for her subtle, understated performances. Deeply private, Garbo avoided publicity and eventually retired to France. Garbo's look was aptly described by a Hollywood film critic as "trench coat, simple shoes, shirts, cigarette pants, slouchy hat and big sunglasses."[211]

The Greta Powder Room
The Verne Streckfus Collection

Streckfus Line magazine described the Greta powder room: "quaint charm of the old-world peasantry is placidly reflected in the Swedish-motif

---

210 J. Thomas Dunn, *The Admiral, A History* (J.R. Simpson & Associates, Inc., Little River Books Division, 2014), pg. 24.

211 *The Telegraph*, September 21, 2010, "To die for: Greta Garbo: Hilary Alexander celebrates the style and mystique of screen legend Greta Garbo." By Hilary Alexander.

segmented mirrors on the paneled outside walls and the round, glazed portholes. . . ."[212]

Sonja Henie, the Norwegian figure skater, dominated the ice, earning an unparalleled collection of Olympic and World figure skating titles won in the 1920s and 1930s. Henie gave up amateur status and moved to Hollywood. She seamlessly attracted global box office interest when she was introduced by Darryl Zanuck to musical comedies.

The Sonja Powder Room
The Verne Streckfus Collection

She was one of the most beloved and successful female actresses of the early 1940s. Streckfus Line describes the Sonja room as "a cool retreat of crystal beauty . . . a beautiful dream of glittering enchantment. Air-conditioned, the Sonja room seems degrees cooler (with) frosted windows, crystal fixtures, and pendants, giant white snowflakes and snow-covered shrubs on blue walls."[213]

The unique Glamour room was designed to be a young woman's make-up dreamland. It was described as having "tall, full-length mirrors, hung with swags of tasseled white cords and lighted by crystal-plumed sconces. . . . Fringe-skirted stools, before mirrors and crystal dressing tables, complete the illusion of a star's boudoir."[214]

The Glamour Powder Room
The Verne Streckfus Collection

---

212 Streckfus Steamers Magazine
213 *Ibid.*
214 Streckfus Steamers Magazine

The additional space afforded by the *Admiral*'s 360- by 100-foot first deck allowed the creation of a fabulous playground and arcade for children. An advertising bulletin stated, "Aboard the *Admiral* is the Main Deck Amusement Midway, making the steamer the largest floating funland in the world."

Flanking the midway, two Pitman-arm giant pistons roared with each turn of the sidewheels. In a lighthearted moment, the Streckfus brothers had painted the massive connecting rods with white and red stripes and named them after popular cartoon characters, Popeye and Wimpy.

The *Admiral*
Courtesy of the Dave Thomson Collection at Steamboats.com

The mid-section and stern of the first deck was a veritable floating carnival setting with a shooting gallery, penny arcade, photo booths, and amusement machines, including a mechanical model steamboat race. Rides and interactive machines for children were everywhere. Among this expansive amusement park on the water were refreshment stands, souvenir stores, and a three-ring Circus Cocktail Lounge for the adults.

Arthur L. Smith's Personal Collection

At the time of the *Admiral*'s introduction to the city of St. Louis on June 12, 1940, the ultimate investment funded by Streckfus Steamers was roughly $707,000. (In today's dollars, $13.9 million.)

CALLIOPES, ARCADES, POPCORN, AND SOUVENIRS

The goal of Streckfus Line was always to give the public a "good show" on every excursion. Like the calliope that heralded the arrival

Kids' Stuff and Powder Rooms: The Admiral Appeals to All

of Ringling Bros. and Barnum & Bailey Circus, Streckfus Steamers musicians pounded out upbeat steam piano tunes prior to riverboat boardings. Always eager to provide wholesome family entertainment, in St. Louis the Streckfus brothers introduced a massive amusement arcade on the first deck of the *Admiral*. Unfortunately, the presence of dangerous active machinery on the base deck of the *President* precluded the creation of a comparable arcade.

The Verne Streckfus Collection

The Verne Streckfus Collection

The Verne Streckfus Collection

The *Admiral*'s arcade was legendary among St. Louis youths. It featured nearly 150 activities, predominately mechanical games, but also booths, both photo and audio (create your own record), and Grandma, the legendary fortune teller. Pinball machines were active alongside hunting challenge games where customers took down bears and deer with electronic rifles and accurate light bursts. One of the most popular challenges pitted two contestants in a race of miniature riverboats, the *Natchez* and *Robert E. Lee*. Designed by Captain Wolter Schaab, the steamboat race was relatively expensive but prone to mechanical failure.

A legendary anecdote is told about the time Streckfus Steamers was forced to modify its photo booths. A malfunction jammed the machines and prevented several excursionists from receiving their strip of four photos. Streckfus personnel were confronted with racy photos displaying passengers with excessive exposure—pun intended! The fix was easy: much smaller curtains for the photo booths.

The Verne Streckfus Collection

The Verne Streckfus Collection

The Verne Streckfus Collection

Most arcade enthusiasts fed quarters into the wide array of wooden and metal ponies and cars. The rides for the youngest children were centered around a circular journey on the always sought-after carousel. Shops conveniently located in the high-traffic entrance to the arcade offered the smell of freshly popped popcorn to entice the crowd. If popcorn didn't seduce them first, most families were then tormented by the wonderful Streckfus Steamers giant ice cream bar.

A ride on the *Admiral* or *President* was not complete without some memento to bring home. Streckfus

The Verne Streckfus Collection

Kids' Stuff and Powder Rooms: The Admiral Appeals to All

Steamers souvenir stands were popular on all the company's vessels. The logoed ashtrays, beanies, buckets, post cards, pennants, and plush toys were reminders of that day's excursion. The stands also featured popcorn, peanuts, and candy for the ride home. Check out the surprising variety of Streckfus Steamers souvenir items that can be found in antique shops along the Mississippi and Ohio rivers. Here's a challenge to readers: search Streckfus Streamers on that massive database of internet exchange, eBay, the great dustbin of Americana.

Courtesy of the Dave Thomson Collection at Steamboats.com

THE BROTHERS COLLIDE

There are many accounts of "The Streckfus Line" and the family's influence on the riverboat-excursion trade and on the migration of jazz. Captains Alan Bates and Clarke Hawley devote an entire chapter of their historical account, *The Excursion Boat Story: Moonlite at 8:30*, to the Streckfus line.[215]

Doc Hawley on the Natchez Callyope [sic]
Courtesy of the Dave Thomson Collection at Steamboats.com

The accounts and views presented by Bates and Hawley in *The Excursion Boat Story* (1994) describe the Commodore, the Streckfus brothers, and their riverboats, children, and family. The author met with the late "Doc" Hawley who, at 86, was charming and an articulate riverboat master. Doc Hawley spent a good chunk of his career on the Streckfus line and was an accomplished master of the calliope.

According to Bates and Hawley's book, "the Streckfus Family did not live in perfect harmony."[216] In interviews with the Commodore's descendants, none disputed that there were ongoing areas of friction, of

---

215 Bates and Hawley, *Moonlite at 8:30*, pgs. 155–160.
216 Bates and Hawley, *Moonlite at 8:30*, pg. 158.

course.[217] How else could an enterprise have adapted, innovated, thrived, and survived for 100 years?

In New Orleans in 1940, the piers and docks[218] were at operating capacity, teeming with traditional commercial trade—loading and unloading produce, other goods, and industrial machinery.

With the prospect of military action on the horizon, there was an unusual battleship-gray concentration of U.S. Navy and U.S. Coast Guard vessels moored at the port. The pace of traffic in New Orleans was alarming as ocean-faring freighters, river barges, tugboats, and ferries were constantly competing for lanes of travel.

Ferry crossings, north to south, were at Audubon Park (Walnut Street Ferry), Napoleon, Louisiana, and Jackson Avenues, Canal Street and Esplanade Avenue. At the Napoleon crossing, the river was 2,800 feet wide and 200 feet deep, according to a Shell Oil Co.-sponsored motorists' map.[219]

Despite the growth in auto transportation, there was only one bridge for motorists—the Huey P. Long Bridge upriver of the Garden District. Meanwhile, for those traveling by air, by air, the city now hosted two civilian airports. The U.S. Navy had an aircraft base on the southern bank of Lake Pontchartrain near the Southern Yacht Club and municipal harbor.[220]

So Capt. Roy Michael Streckfus, 52, placed a phone call to Streckfus headquarters in St. Louis. The senior Streckfus brother, Joseph Leo, 53, was in a particularly good mood that day: The Streckfus Line was profitable, shareholders having been rewarded with dividends of $1 per share in both 1938 and 1939—despite the ongoing Great Depression. The financial strength of Streckfus Steamers was solid; the company was a

---

217 Interviews conducted by the author.
218 New Orleans on the east; Algiers (a NOLA neighborhood), west. However, as the winding river travels west-east here, downtown New Orleans sits on the northern bank; Algiers and Gretna, Louisiana, sit on the southern bank.
219 NOLA subreddit post, user Petrarch1603, accessed March 11, 2019.
220 New Orleans' "Dueling Oaks" were at the southern end of City Park across from the Fair Grounds horse-racing track. The city's "Suicide Oak" was nearby. NOLA subreddit post, user Petrarch1603, accessed March 11, 2019.

The Brothers Collide

major philanthropist to churches, universities, and charities of St. Louis and New Orleans.

And remarkably, financed by operating cash flow, the all-steel, fire-resistant, air-conditioned, streamlined, and non-sinkable *Admiral* was approaching completion, having been built on the hull of the *Albatross* for roughly $500,000. ($10.8 million in 2023 dollars.)

In January 1939, Joe, general manager of Streckfus Steamers, had been awarded by the shareholders an annual salary of $15,000 ($325,000 in 2023) plus participation in profit-sharing.

The general economy was vibrant, and Streckfus Steamers was expecting more good times ahead. For brothers Joe and John, who managed the Gateway City operations and Mississippi and Ohio waters north, Streckfus Steamers was at the top of its game. Sure, there was talk of a reluctant U.S. entry into World War II. But here, near the Eads Bridge, the *Admiral* was in her last days of preparation for a grand re-launch in the spring.

But wait. Not all was well in New Orleans. Roy and younger brother Verne were concerned that the Streckfus Steamers operations in the Crescent City were in great jeopardy. It was time for a passionate showdown. A formal telephone appointment was scheduled from the Streckfus wharf boat offices in each city. At the foot of Canal Street, Roy and Verne huddled beside the phones connected to Joe and John at the foot of Washington Avenue.

Roy, as told to his grandson, the author, minced no words on his call to Joe: "The business model and operations of Streckfus Steamers must change immediately. Joe, the *Capitol* is too old, waterlogged, and fragile to continue excursion operations here in New Orleans. Industrial activity in the harbor is at a frantic pace and I fear a disaster should the *Capitol* collide with another vessel."

The wooden hull of the *Capitol* would be reduced to splinters in a moment if it were to collide with a Navy vessel or industrial barge. "The loss of life of our passengers and crew would be staggering," Roy said. "For safety's sake, Verne and I are throwing down the gauntlet. We will no longer operate the *Capitol* here in the Crescent City. She must be retired from excursion service at once."[221]

Joe was flabbergasted. "Roy," he said, "business is going great here in St. Louis and for all of our active vessels on the Ohio and northern Mississippi environs. Business and profits have never been better! And, as you know, we are on the cusp of adding [our art deco ocean-liner] the *Admiral* into service."

The *Capitol*
Courtesy of the Dave Thomson Collection at Steamboats.com

Roy responded, "Yes, we're very proud of our company and our accomplishments." But the nearly spotless safety record of Streckfus Steamers "is a hallmark and that record is not worth putting at risk for another dollar. A serious accident with the *Capitol* would be devastating and could cripple all of our excursion businesses. For Streckfus Steamers, it could be worse than another *Eastland*."

At this point in the exchange, Joe was said to have been brought to tears.

Capt. Verne W. Streckfus aboard the *Capitol*
The Verne Streckfus Collection

Roy persisted: "Because times are good and we are on financial bedrock, the *Capitol* must be retired and sent to salvage. In short order, the older wooden-hulled boats in our fleet should also be scuttled."

Joe was not convinced. He shouted to his younger brother, "Roy, if that's your final position, you are fired!"

---

221 As told to the author, the source's grandson.

The Brothers Collide

Infuriated, Joe paused for 30 minutes. He then madly dialed the *Capitol*'s office and asked to speak to Verne Walter. Joe pleaded with Verne to accept responsibility for the *Capitol* and to continue operations at New Orleans.

Without hesitation, Verne replied, "Roy knows the boat better than I do and she's his regular boat. I don't want to run her either."

The warm-hearted and emotional Capt. Joe could not hold back his seething anger. Why upset today's smoothly functioning Streckfus Steamers operations? Boiling with rage, he shouted, "Verne, you too are fired!"

On a typical day, the devoutly Catholic Streckfuses were at peace with each other; communication was friendly and constant. The four brothers' families interacted regularly as their seasonal travel from New Orleans to St. Louis to Davenport, Iowa, and St. Paul (and Cincinnati and Pittsburgh) moved like the annual waxing and waning of the rivers' crests.

St. Louis had been the undisputed Streckfus headquarters since 1911, when the company bought the Diamond Jo Line and attendant riverfront real estate. Acquisition of the line had demanded intense managerial effort from Day One. The family relocated to St. Louis immediately; Diamond Jo's two sternwheelers and two sidewheelers were stationed in the Gateway City at the time.

In the nearly 30 years of tramping among hundreds of riverfronts since—and the additional prior 27 years as Acme Packet Co., commencing before the oldest son, Joe, was born—the Streckfuses had vastly expanded their geographic presence and steel-clad their reputation for quality river-excursion service.

The year 1940 was ideal timing for major, strategic business action: The *Admiral*, the new flagship of the Streckfus fleet, was nearly ready. Meanwhile, the equally massive steam cruiser, the *President*, was operating out of St. Louis and points north.

It was time for the *President* to move to the Crescent City. And move it would: The *President* would command the lead position of excursion trade in New Orleans for the next 40 years.

The imminent displacement of the *President* at St. Louis by the *Admiral* and Roy and Verne's significant ownership in Streckfus Steamers—their birthright, but further earned by hard work beginning when each was old enough to walk—presented a viable negotiation tack.

After consulting local legal counsel and financial advisors, Roy and Verne knew they had leverage—they could start their own excursion-steamship business in New Orleans, competing against their brothers, if necessary.

President—**Novelty Dye Cut Cartoon Postcard**
Courtesy of the Dave Thomson Collection at Steamboats.com

Using logic (check) and leverage (checkmate), Verne and Roy demanded Joe and John surrender clean and clear ownership of the *President* as a partial swap for their Streckfus Steamers shares.

WWII & THE EXCESS PROFITS TAX

Soon, the U.S. entered World War II. As had been the case during World War I, the four Streckfus brothers (now in their 50s) received Class Five determinations from the draft board. The Class Five ruling governed licensed pilots on inland rivers—they received deferred classifications.

The launch of the stainless, fireproof mega-steamers, the *President* in 1933 and the *Admiral* in 1940, heralded a new peak in activity for Streckfus Steamers. Meanwhile, the remaining two wooden hulls, those of the *Capitol* and the *Senator*, were being made ready for their final days on the water.

The Streckfus line had undergone a transformational period through the Roaring '20s, Prohibition, and the Great Depression. Following the dream of the Commodore, the company judiciously reinvested profits and capital through the 1920s and 1930s to build its future: Steel-hulled, palatial excursion vessels.

But maybe times were too good for Uncle Sam. The *Admiral* emerged on the scene in mid-1940 and was immediately embraced by the entire city of St. Louis. With World War II's epic arrival on December 7, 1941, Streckfus Steamers braced for tough seas: shortages of materials, fuel, food, commodities and—most dear—experienced crew.

The *Admiral*
Arthur L. Smith's Personal Collection

That said, the *President* and *Admiral* were both doing a brisk excursion and moonlight cruise business. Enlisted men on shore leave joined with local folks for clean entertainment and hot jazz. The Streckfus boats were never short of passengers and respectable profits.

The crisis of a national war and demands for military personnel and capital pressured Congress to enact several statutes aimed at "clawing back" excess or "windfall" profits. The challenge to lawmakers was to identify what were these excess wartime profits (i.e., gouging) in contrast to normal, "peacetime profits."

The IRS determined that Streckfus Steamers was too profitable in 1942 and 1943, probably reflecting the fact that the *Admiral* was a late entrant to the company's recent commerce. The company was subject to the new Excess Profits Tax, which was substantial and unprecedented.

Facing what would be a more than $1.5-million tax bill ($26 million in current dollars) and further tax and/or fines, Captains Joe, Roy, John, and Verne were at an impasse. At the time there were other issues: trained crew were leaving for active military service and fuel and provisions were increasingly difficult to procure.

Streckfus Steamers was forced to cancel the *Admiral's* entire 1945 season. By spring of 1946, she resumed cruises. The tax dispute continued to daunt the firm for many years. Eventually, a compromise with the IRS was reached.

THE JEFFERSON ARCH CHALLENGE

The Streckfuses met with more government interference. Since the Streckfus Line had operated on the western bank of the Mississippi in St. Louis since the 1911 Diamond Jo acquisition, the company had—by commercial strength alone—homesteaded the prime waterfront at the foot of St. Louis's Main Street, a.k.a. Washington Avenue.

Streckfus enjoyed this location for half a century before work began on "The Arch."

The Jefferson monument—the pride of St. Louis—was designated "The Gateway to the West" and stands an impressive 630 feet, the tallest man-made monument in the Western Hemisphere. The concept for the memorial came from Luther Ely Smith and St. Louis Mayor Bernard Dickmann between 1928 and 1933. The Jefferson National Expansion Memorial Association (JNEMA) stated as its goal:

> A suitable and permanent public memorial to the men who made possible the western territorial expansion . . . particularly President Jefferson, his aides Livingston and Monroe, the great explorers, Lewis and Clark, the hardy hunters, trappers, frontiersmen and pioneers who contributed to the territorial expansion and development of the United States.[222]

As part of the grand vision for the memorial, the St. Louis fathers recognized that a major revitalization should be undertaken for the St. Louis waterfront. For Streckfus Steamers and the *Admiral*, this began a lengthy feud over access to the river—and the company's wharf rights. Railroad tracks that paralleled the river obstructed views and led to a series of tunnels anchoring what was to become the Riverfront National Park.

Captains Joe and Roy Streckfus recognized the folly of an early plan, which would have eliminated nine of the 12 east/west streets whose terminus

---

222 Wikipedia article on the Great Arch.

The Brothers Collide

was at the river. The company engaged in a furious campaign of letters and political lobbying to address riverfront access for all riverfront commerce.

In the end, the area between Eads Bridge (Washington Street) and Poplar Street Bridge (Chouteau Street) was closed to create an unobstructed vision of the eventual monument. For the Streckfus Line, all its efforts produced only a Pyrrhic victory: Washington Street was saved and remained the main thoroughfare to the company's operations. However, easy access was forever restricted by the memorial and park.

In an interview, Capt. Roy, then president of Streckfus Steamers, was said to have remarked, "I was told that thousands would visit the Arch and enjoy a pleasure cruise on the *Admiral*. Well, I'm still waiting."[223, 224]

The *Admiral*
Arthur L. Smith's Personal Collection

The development of the Jefferson Expansion Memorial got underway in earnest in 1935 when President Roosevelt allocated an 82-acre historical site. Design competition, under the auspices of the National Park Service director and JNEMA founder Luther Smith, was kindled in 1945 by grants totaling nearly $250,000. Finnish American architect Eero Saarinen presented the winning design and President Eisenhower signed a bill authorizing $5 million for construction in 1953.

Streckfus Steamers was regularly interrupted by work on the arch and park during the construction (1962–1965). On October 28, 1965, Vice President Hubert Humphrey observed the fitting out of the 10-ton, eight-foot-long keystone by helicopter. Nearly 800,000 student signatures and assorted memorabilia were included in a time capsule.

---

223 "Top Man on the River," *St. Louis Globe-Democrat*, June 9, 1966.
224 Actual quote: ". . . people told me a couple of years ago, 2,000,000 people a year would be coming here to see the Gateway Memorial Arch and it would swell our business. I'm waiting for them."

LOOSE LIPS SINK SHIPS

In their book *Moonlite at 8:30*, Hawley and Bates level the charge that the Streckfus line "had a penchant for secrecy that almost amounted to paranoia. . . . Crews were discouraged or even forbidden to talk to the press about the boats or the company and the family members were as close-mouthed as they demanded others to be."[225]

Long before the War Advertising Council's campaign, "Loose Lips Might Sink Ships" during World War II,[226] the Streckfus family was practicing limited information-sharing about its own business. The Streckfus way centered on a strict policy to button-hole information; it was just "good business." Similarly, great effort was made to eschew careless talk and to avoid spreading critical data or financial information about its broad-based excursion steamer operations.

On his first assignment, William Carroll was introduced to the intentional secrecy that was the Streckfus way. Carroll, the new son-in-law of Capt. Joe, had been assigned to the gangway as passengers were boarding the *Saint Paul*. Using a hand-held device similar to those employed by rail conductors, Carroll pressed down on the counter as each passenger embarked.

A piece of tape had been carefully pasted over the counter window. He had yet to please his father- and uncles-in-law. He was not yet allowed to know ticket sales until he was indoctrinated as a master in the Streckfus fleet. Captain William Carroll later worked tirelessly to "earn his chevron" as a Mississippi River licensed master pilot. He would grow to be an important senior officer of Streckfus Steamers.

Capt. D. Walter "D.W." Wisherd reminded Capt. Edgar Mabrey of the company's policy of keeping its business to itself in 1934:[227]

To: Captain William Mabrey, Steamer *Washington*, Steubenville, OH

---

225 Bates and Hawley, *Moonlite at 8:30*, pg. 155.
226 Security of War Information—Loose Lips Sink Ships (1942–1945), Ad Council.
227 Bates and Hawley, *Moonlite at 8:30*, pgs. 155–156.

My dear Captain:

From the articles that have been appearing in *The Waterways Journal*, you or someone of the crew have been talking too much about the Company's business.

In the June 23rd issue of *The Waterways Journal*, under the Clarington news, Gable had an article about the Steamer *Washington* going down to Cincinnati for a Negro excursion, etc. This was before the date of the colored excursion out of Cincinnati and there was no one except you and Elder that knew we were going down there, so that one of you gave him information or else you have been telling other members of the crew. In the issue of July 14th, you are quoted in regard to the four boilers not burning any more coal than the three that were on her and if Donald Wright had not said anything more, there would have been no harm in this, but he goes on mentioning where the boilers came from, which is not good publicity.

In another item, Donald Wright, in speaking of the *Washington* having capacity July 4th, mentions that this was the fourth time this season that she had reached capacity. While we are pleased that this is true, it is the Company's business and not for publication.

In future I do not want you or any of your crew, when talking to Donald Wright or any reporters for *The Waterways Journal* or any other paper, to give them details as to the amount of coal we consume, the speed we make with the boat, or the number of passengers carried, etc. as this is private.

If you have to talk to these fellows, talk about the nice wife and family you have.

Please take up this matter with Mr. Elder and see that we do not get any more publicity in regard to our business.

Yours truly,
D.W. Wisherd, Traffic Manager

THE STRECKFUS RIVERBOAT DYNASTY

Streckfus Steamers
Pittsburgh PA

No Streckfus descendant wishes to contest that the clan was very close and inwardly focused. The Streckfus steamboat legacy has been criticized for what some have seen as excessive secrecy and a refusal to share information—and tightfistedness with money and wages.

However, the longevity of the Streckfus excursion empire on the Mississippi was not rooted in Dickensian Scrooge-ness. To the contrary, at its core, Streckfus ethics were a testament to honesty, the fair treatment of employees, and a conservative nature about information sharing.

CAPT. D. WALTER WISHERD

D. Walter Wisherd shares a colorful past as a legendary steamboat owner, pilot, and captain on the Ohio, Missouri, and Mississippi rivers. For the Streckfus clan, the mention of the Wisherd name evokes great emotion as, over the years, Walter Wished was a charming, unpredictable scoundrel.

Working with the Commodore in the early years, Wisherd ranged from being a special partner and, after a gap, a trusted Streckfus employee who managed the Streckfus Line's Ohio River operations. Always an opportunist, Wisherd later soured on his Streckfus affiliation and metamorphosed into a head-to-head cutthroat competitor.

In the early years of Streckfus Steamers activity, Wisherd must have been a close friend of John Streckfus. In 1896, admittedly well before the riverboat mantle of "Commodore" was established, John Streckfus and Acme Packet Company acquired a small packet, the *City of Winona*. The *City of Winona* was immediately repurposed to excursion duty in a working combination with the barge *Acme*. In 1901, Streckfus already had the *J.S.* operating profitably with Wisherd at the helm. After her conversion in 1905 the *City of Winona* was renamed the *W.W.*

The Brothers Collide

Like the Commodore, Wisherd's early steamboat activity on the Upper Mississippi (1894–1899) ranged between Quincy and Burlington when he owned and operated a small packet, the S.R. *Van Metre*.[228] Thus began Wisherd's remarkable string of more than 50 years of buying and selling steamboats and boldly attempting to develop new excursion markets.

S.R. *Van Metre* (Packet, 1888–1899)
Murphy Library Special Collections/ ARC, University of Wisconsin–La Crosse.

Along the way he briefly owned the *Prince* and its barge the *Princess* (1896), the excursion barge *Daisy W.* (1918) named for Mrs. Wisherd, and the *Keystone State* (1914) which was converted into the first of two ill-fated *Majestic* steamers.

The *Rees Lee* became the *Majestic II* in 1916 and, in 1921, Wisherd ventured to open an excursion market in Kansas City. (That failed because of exceptionally low water levels.)

Captain "Buck" Leyhe, of Eagle Packet fame, was critical of Wisherd's use of the name *Majestic*, citing a host of bad omens. Certainly, the fate of the first *Majestic* seemed pre-ordained as she had barely left the shipyard when she sank irreparably; her hull was pierced by an unmarked water intake near Chain of Rocks, a 17-mile series of rock ledges above St. Louis.

Leyhe noted that the *Majestic II* had colors that foretold bad luck: red carpet in the captain's quarters and blue paint elsewhere. According to sailors' superstition, painting a vessel the color of the sea (green or blue) was thought to bring bad luck and red-haired people were considered unlucky. "M" was also an unfortunate choice, as it is the thirteenth letter of the alphabet.

---

228 Bates and Hawley, *Moonlite at 8:30,* pg. 85.

The *Majestic II* was consumed by fire in May 1922 while docked at Havana, Illinois. Salvage was not an option.

Wisherd had two important stints of employ by Streckfus Steamers: from 1905 to 1912 when he served as passenger agent, and from 1925 to 1942 when Joe Streckfus and his brothers appointed Wisherd manager of Ohio operations, including the *Saint Paul, J.S. Deluxe, Washington,* and *Senator*. Wisherd operated out of Cincinnati and Pittsburgh and might have remained with Streckfus for many years more if World War II had not intervened, diverting its excursion crews to essential river barge work.

After the loss of *Majestic II*, Wisherd donned his dealmaker hat and, on the advice of noted financier John W. Hubbard, tossed in a bid for the uncompleted hull of the *Louisville*, under construction at Midland, Pennsylvania. The *Louisville* hull was towed to Cincinnati where the craft was elegantly completed as the mega-steamer *Island Queen*.

Wisherd had great contacts in Cincinnati with the Coney Island Co., operators of the popular amusement park; in a deft sleight of hand, he purchased the *G.W. Hill* and modified it to be the sister ferry, the *Island Maid*.

Not content to be idle, Wisherd seized the opportunity to acquire the *Dorothy McBride* in a U.S. Marshals' sale; the vessel was confiscated from Capt. Birch McBride in 1933. Wisherd was not yet done: Immediately he ordered four-foot-tall letters proclaiming the vessel the *W.W.*

WISHERD AND THE *ISLAND QUEEN*

Long active on the Ohio, the *Cincinnati* and the *Island Queen 2* were sister packets that emphasized passenger traffic. The *Cincinnati* boasted 350 well-appointed staterooms for its overnight passengers between Louisville and Cincinnati.

The original *Island Queen* was built 1896 and may have well been the first "excursion boat" for daily passenger traffic—on the Ohio. Commodore Streckfus launched his *J.S.* in 1901—on the Mississippi. The principal route served by the first *Island Queen* was from the city of Cincinnati to a grand amusement park built on Parker's Grove, near Cincinnati, Ohio, and renamed by a new owner, Captain J.D. Hegler, "Ohio Grove, The Coney Island of the West."

Island Queen (Excursion boat, 1896–1922)
Murphy Library Special Collections/ ARC, University of Wisconsin–La Crosse.

For many years, the *Island Queen* enjoyed tremendous success ferrying crowds to and from the amusement facility and tramping the Ohio River. In 1922, a dark cloud of bad luck hung over her when a roof deck collapsed; later that same year, she and three packets were engulfed by flames while docked at her home harbor. Nothing was salvageable.

The new *Island Queen*: This big steel sidewheeler was built in 1925 by Streckfus friend and former employee Capt. Wisherd. As had the first *Island Queen*, she served the local Cincinnati market for excursion trips to what had been renamed simply Coney Island. With a rated capacity of 4,100 passengers,[229] she tramped the Ohio during the next 22 years, including in brutal competition with Streckfus's *President*.

Island Queen (Packet excursion 1923–1947)
Murphy Library Special Collections/ ARC, University of Wisconsin–La Crosse.

---

229 Bates and Hawley, *Moonlite at 8:30*, pg. 144.

PART V

The Sons Rise

AS TOLD BY JOSEPH LEO STRECKFUS

Joseph Leo Streckfus passed away on January 15, 1950. He, with his father, had ordered riverboat jazz into life; he promoted it for forty-two years. Here is his story, as imagined by the author.

I am Joseph Leo Streckfus, the eldest son and one of eight children born to John and Theresa Streckfus. I have three older sisters and three younger brothers. One sister, Theresa Agnes, died in her first year; another sister, Nina Agnes, died at the age of 10.

My father, John, was a great visionary and entrepreneur. He was also a calculated risk-taker. Yet, at the same time, he was frugal and an incredible manager of people and riverboats. While "the Commodore" may have been criticized for naming his first excursion steamboat the *"J.S.,"* John Streckfus was never boastful or pretentious.

I love my elder sisters, Lily, Anna, and May most dearly. With my younger brothers, Roy, John, and Verne, we remain close-knit and family-centric. We are of second-generation German American heritage and, as such, we will not suffer conjecture, unfounded assertions, and bad-mouthed gossip.

My grandfather Balthazar and grandmother Marie emigrated to the United States in the middle of the 19th century with my two aunts, Barbara and Catherine, and Uncle Michael. They hailed from the Bavarian town of Laudenbach, northwest of Munich.

THE STRECKFUS RIVERBOAT DYNASTY

Formal portrait taken January 5, 1920, of Commodore John Streckfus with his four sons. Left to right: Roy M., Joseph L., Commodore John Streckfus, Verne W., John N.
Author's Family Collection

Grandfather Balthazar and grandmother Marie settled in 1851 in Edgington, Illinois, southeast of Rock Island. My father was born in Edgington as were all of his younger siblings. Famously, my Uncle Michael, who was born during the family's crossing of the Atlantic, did not go into the family steamboat business.

My entire life has centered on riverboats, safety, and the entertainment of our millions of passengers who embarked on our fleet over the many years my family has conducted commerce on the mighty Mississippi and its tributaries. Our father was never officially titled "Commodore," but this was the role he played in our lives as he created a magnificent fleet of excursion steamers that came to be widely popular and loved—our mighty Streckfus Steamers line.

As Told by Joseph Leo Streckfus

Oh, the music.

It has been said that the Streckfus excursion steamers floated on the backs of the exceptional musicians who entertained our clients from 1901 onwards. It is also true that my brothers and I all were accomplished musicians—Roy and Verne, violin; John and I, piano. Riverboat music and the birth and nurturing of jazz are found in Streckfus DNA.

Music, the best numbers performed by the most creative and talented musicians we could find, made our fleet unique up and down the Mississippi. Over the years, many competitors challenged us in all of our markets, from "tramping" to head-to-head business warfare in our principal cities of operation: St. Louis and New Orleans.

Offering a wholesome, family atmosphere drenched in outstanding music of our time was the hallmark of our Streckfus Steamers franchise.

Of the Commodore and Theresa's four sons, I was the tallest and sturdiest of the lot. Some accounts have described me as "fleshy," but I prefer the observation that I was a big man, filling big shoes with a muscular, solid frame.

Fate Marable's Society Syncopators: Warren "Baby" Dodds, William "Bebé" Ridgley, Joe Howard, Louis Armstrong, Fate Marable, Dave Jones, Johnny Dodds, Johnny St. Cyr, George "Pops" Foster.
Hogan Jazz Archive, Special Collections, Howard-Tilton Memorial Library. Tulane University

In a 1919 photograph taken onboard the SS *Sidney* of Fate Marable's Society Syncopators, you will observe an imposing figure wearing a fedora (me). Marable is centered behind his piano and his illustrious nine-piece combo. Louis Armstrong is on cornet. I am standing behind David Jones (mellophone), Johnny Dodds (clarinet), and Johnny St. Cyr (banjo). My younger brother John is a distant figure in the panorama created by an unidentified photographer.

1896—My career on the river began in 1896 when I was 10 and performed odd jobs on the *City of Winona*. After Rock Island High School, I enrolled at Notre Dame University, studying business. South Bend, Indiana, was great, but I only completed one year as our steamship company needed me to assist in 1905 in the upgrading of the *City of Winona* into the excursion *W.W.*

A memorable recollection was when my dad sent me off to college and ordered, "I don't care what you study, but don't come home until you can play twelve pieces on the calliope." It was a challenge, but I mastered "My Alamo Love" and other compositions as required.

The next step to please Dad was to train as a licensed riverboat pilot. At 21, I first took the helm of the *W.W.* as Captain (1908). I worked and studied hard and gained the river "rank" of "double ender" with the award of two certificates as licensed steam engineer and licensed master-pilot.

1910—Streckfus Steamboat Line Co. was organized at Rock Island on August 18, 1910, by Capt. John Sr., myself, and Roy. At that time, our stated capitalization was $250,000. We moved quickly after the loss on June 25 of our beloved *J.S.* excursion steamer. Dad was 55 and Roy and I were 21 and 23, respectively.

The Company started with a total of 14 stockholders and paid-up capital stock of $138,473. Our assets consisted of the steamer *W.W.*, its barge *Acme*, and partial ownership of a Rock Island warehouse. The bulk of our capitalization was $106,250 of cash, primarily insurance proceeds from the *J.S.* disaster.

1911—In January 1911, the company purchased from Jay Morton of Chicago the Diamond Jo Line Steamers and property for $150,000, paying $75,000 cash and giving notes at 6% for the balance of $75,000 over a period of four years.

This Diamond Jo Line property consisted of the passenger and freight steamers *Saint Paul*, *Quincy*, *Dubuque*, and *Sidney*, a St. Louis wharf boat, two wooden and one steel barge, 15 wooden warehouses, two steel warehouses, and two lots of real estate.

Returning to our excursion steamer roots, conversion work began immediately on the steamer *Sidney*. The Commodore knew what changes—elimination of staterooms, creation of a large dancefloor with a bandstand—were essential from prior experience with the *City of Winona/W.W.*

The Sidney was transformed from a passenger-freight steamer to excursion-focused trade at a cost of approximately $41,000. We moved quickly and our other three packet steamers, the *Saint Paul*, *Quincy*, and *Dubuque* were overhauled and scrutinized for safety. This packet fleet was made ready for traditional passenger-freight business between St Louis/St. Paul and St. Louis/Burlington, Iowa, and were operated in that territory that summer season.

The steamers *Sidney* and *W.W.* were advertised and scheduled to operate between Alton, Illinois and St. Paul, Minnesota, in the excursion trade. Unfortunately, that year we had one of the lowest stages of water in history with a mere 3.5 to 4 feet in the main channels of the Upper Mississippi River. We had few alternatives that first year but to shave our schedules 50%, and the low volume of freight trade ballooned our fixed cost of operations.

Our first year generated a troublesome loss of $7,000.

1912—The Commodore was fearful of continuing drought and sluggish commercial activity and, during the winter, approached original investors and raised $21,000 of fresh capital stock.

While the years 1912–1915 were again challenged by excessively low water, we were able to keep all five of our steamers productive. We generated profits of $15,000 to $28,000 for our next two years and moderate losses of $9,500 and $2,700 in 1914–1915. Although we had been able to remain current on interest on our outstanding 6% notes, a showdown was at hand: Jay Morton wanted the balance of his $75,000 of owner financing.

The sinking of the *Titanic* in 1912 reinforced our commitment to preparation, safety, and defensive navigation. Just a few years later, in 1915, the *Eastland* disaster in Chicago focused us on seaworthiness and proper ballast. We also instituted the whaleback test on all our vessels.

From the beginning of our operations in 1911 through the year 1916, the Mississippi River remained at the lowest continued state in its history. Steamers were unable to make their scheduled time, unable to carry freight cargo, and schedules were delayed eight to 10 days stemming from challenges to navigation—all resulting in added expense and limiting net revenue.

All through this period the company had the expense of maintaining its steamers and warehouse properties in good condition and, at the same time, we, the Streckfus family, were guarantors and obligated to retire the original purchase notes in four tranches—this year having the last note of $20,000 due.

1916—Through the Business Men's League (now the St. Louis Chamber of Commerce), I worked closely with my dad and brothers to contact each of our close ties with prominent St. Louis businessmen. At our behest, Mr. Murray Carleton, George Simone, and Alfred Shapleigh called a dinner meeting of the organization. At that event, the Commodore gave his vision of building a world-class steamer fleet which would provide entertainment and commerce along the entire Mississippi and Ohio. The reception among the St. Louis business community was encouraging; subscriptions were taken for First Mortgage 7% bonds and, with the continued help of this committee, proceeds of $20,500 were obtained.

With the proceeds of these bonds, we were able to pay off the last purchase notes to Jay Morton. The monies we raised brought the total outstanding capital stock of Streckfus Steamboat Line Co. to $179,973.

Author's note: No additional common stock was raised by the company until 50 years later (1965) when Streckfus Steamers suffered a liquidity crunch.

1916—Woodrow Wilson, running on a platform seeking to avoid military conflict, was elected president in 1916. Thomas Riley Marshall, Wilson's somewhat estranged vice president, famously remarked, "What this country needs is a really good five-cent cigar." I bring up cigar levity as we were extremely sensitive to safety and fire prevention on all of our vessels and banned smoking of any tobacco other than extra-long "Streckfus Stogies." Our cigar brand was manufactured to automatically extinguish when left unattended.

While tensions abroad in Europe simmered in 1916, our four vessels remained active and we inched out a profit of $15,000. The continuing success of the *Sidney* in the excursion trade supported our initiative to convert our largest packet. At a cost of $41,000, the freight-passenger steamer *Saint Paul* was retooled to focus on the tramping market between St. Louis and St. Paul.

1917—Shortly after Wilson gained office in April 1917, the United States was forced to enter World War I. German submarines were targeting American merchant vessels and Great Britain, France, and Italy were desperate for economic and military support.

Given our positions in transport and river commerce, my brothers and I were not drafted. The "Great War" was tough on American industry and our business felt the pain, posting a loss of $5,000. Savings in banks were frozen over the summer months. Railroads were taken over by the government and our combination railroad-excursion business was canceled. We were forced to lay up all but two of our boats.

1918—The Mississippi and Ohio steamer business was under great duress from an extremely cold winter. In March of 1918, an unforeseen harbor freeze destroyed all the Eagle Packet Co. excursion boats formerly operating out of St. Louis.

Fortune had smiled on us, as we had chosen to winter our fleet of northern vessels in Dubuque, where milder conditions prevailed. Now, with the Eagle fleet virtually eliminated, we began plans for conversion of the *Quincy* and *Dubuque* to the excursion trade.

We opened the season at St. Louis with the majestic *Saint Paul*, sailing out on Decoration Day. We ran an advertisement in the Gateway

City newspapers: "One block long, 75 feet wide, 5,000 passengers, three roomy decks open on all sides, 500 rockers, 2,500 comfortable seats, 5,000 electric lights, 1,000 electric fans. Best dance music in the United States, 1,500 couples can dance on the dance floor at one time."—*St. Louis Argus*

The *Saint Paul* enjoyed a successful season, enabling the company to recoup its entire cost of remodeling and showing a modest profit at the end of her first season. The Commodore and my brothers saw an opportunity to differentiate the excursion market and operate two steamers in St. Louis.

Thankfully, the Central Powers disbanded in 1918 and the war officially ended with the Armistice of 11 November 1918. With a strong peacetime economy at hand, our prospects were excellent.

1919–1925—In 1919 we remodeled the side-wheel steamer *Quincy* into the new excursion steamer *J.S. Deluxe* at a cost of $80,000, advertising and operating as a new experience with the equivalent of ocean-liner service on the Mississippi. Granted, we tested the market with $1 and $1.50 fares with encouraging results. The steamer *J.S.*, as well as the *Saint Paul*, enjoyed a nice season, enabling the company to pay off the cost of the *J.S. Deluxe* conversion while still leaving a net profit for the year of $14,000.

In the spring of 1920, our sternwheel *Dubuque* was moved to the shipyard in Keokuk, Iowa, and transformed for the princely sum of $131,000. She had been lying idle for the previous two years. The *Capitol* emerged with gorgeous lines and ornate gingerbread and became our family's most loved and admired wooden hull.

With the profits of that year, we were able fund the upgrade and still generate $11,700 of black ink. By this time, all of our equipment was completely devoted to the excursion trade. We no longer were in the freight-hauling business and various wharf, floating equipment, and idle warehouses were no longer needed and were divested.

During 1921, we were able, for the first time, to give our steamers' hulls a general repair and overhauling—and, after taking care of that expense, we ended the year with a net profit of $48,000. It had been a decade since

As Told by Joseph Leo Streckfus

the Diamond Jo transaction, and the Streckfus line was a pure excursion company now.

We had parted with the *W.W.* and we now were looking ahead—not just to expanding our geographic reach but to our future in steel.

The Roaring '20s were great years for St. Louis and for our riverboat operations. Looking back to post-war days, President Warren Harding inherited a strong and bottled-up economy which, upon his death in 1923, was passed to Calvin Coolidge. Our Streckfus line benefited from "the Coolidge years" of robust economic expansion. Interest in our fleet of excursion vessels, like the strong demand for autos and housing, accompanied this period of unprecedented prosperity. I liked Coolidge and his dry sense of humor and brevity of speech. One biographer said it well: "He embodied the spirit and hopes of the middle class, could interpret their longings and express their opinions. That he did represent the genius of the average is the most convincing proof of his strength."[230]

Annual corporate profit was strong and consistent, ranging from $91,000 in 1922 to $188,500 in 1925. Working purely within operating cash flow, our enterprise was able to retire the $21,000 of the 7% bonds issued a decade earlier.

It was time for our workhorse steamer *Sidney* to be recognized and benefit from a much-deserved facelift. Emerging from the shipyard in Moundsville, Indiana, the *Washington* embodied the quality design and gingerbread lines of her sisters.

With the *Saint Paul* and *J.S. Deluxe* enjoying a great reception in St. Louis, the *Capitol* was reassigned to New Orleans to fill the *Sidney*'s absence. Now it was time to venture forth north and east to ports on the Ohio, and the *Washington* was ready.

Our old friend and new competitor, D.W. Wisherd, now had his own excursion vessel, the *Majestic*. Somewhat under-sized at 225 feet, she was tramping the upper Mississippi and Ohio as far as Pittsburgh. Wisherd

---

230 https://en.wikipedia.org/wiki/Calvin_Coolidge. Quoting Claude Moore Fuess, (1940). *Calvin Coolidge: The Man from Vermont.* (New York: Little, Brown and Company, 1940).

was a master entertainer and had added a miniature railroad and merry-go-round to the *Majestic*'s top deck. Again, fortune smiled on our Streckfus clan when, just as the *Washington* was ready to leave the shipyard, the *Majestic* was consumed by a fire in early 1922. While we regretted our former employee's loss, a competitor was now eliminated.

Evidence of a lasting friendship with Wisherd was our decision to hire him as general manager of our Ohio river operations in 1925. He and the *Washington* performed admirably, managed from offices in Cincinnati and later (1931) in Pittsburgh.

Capt. John Streckfus, the Commodore, our president and general manager, died on October 12, 1925, at the age of 69. His cause of death stemmed from a loss of blood after an accident. My brothers and sisters mourned the loss of our father, the Commodore—a great and bold riverman and entrepreneur.

I succeeded my father as president and general manager.

1926-ONWARD, AS TOLD BY JOE STRECKFUS

My brothers, Verne and Roy, were based in New Orleans and, in the fall of 1925, extensive repairs were made on our *Capitol* at nearby Slidell, Louisiana. All of our northern steamers had solid seasons and the company ended the year with a profit of $188,500—a return of about 26% on the capital stock and earned surplus of the company.

1926—On March 2, 1926, Streckfus Steamers Inc. was incorporated under the laws of the state of Delaware with 50,000 shares, no par value, Class A, and 100,000 shares, no par value, Class B. Streckfus Steamers acquired all the assets and assumed all rights of Streckfus Steamboat Line Co., an Illinois corporation that was later dissolved. Class B stock was distributed at the basis of 27.8 shares for each share of the Streckfus Steamboat Line stock held.

Later that year, we created a subsidiary, the Steamer Service Co., which was incorporated in the state of Missouri. The year 1926 generated income of $142,000. However, stock market turbulence required a deduction of $25,000 for shrinkage in the value of securities held.

While the Roaring '20s continued to percolate in 1928, there were visible economic storm clouds on the horizon. The Coolidge years of great growth and productivity were waning, and Coolidge wisely declined the opportunity to seek another term in 1928. Speculation around frothy markets greeted Herbert Hoover when he assumed the presidency in 1929.

Notwithstanding combined losses on stock securities of $50,000, the company was solidly profitable in 1927–1928 and generated roughly $200,000 of adjusted net income. Wall Street took notice of our operating and financial success and came calling just as we were looking ahead to replace our aging fleet of wooden hulls.

St. Louis-based investment firm Knight, Dysart & Gamble agreed to underwrite the issuance of $500,000 of Streckfus Steamers Inc. Class A stock. Our proposed "use of proceeds" was to build a new steel non-sinkable excursion steamer. However, the underwriting was never consummated as a sharp downdraft in the stock market took place. Knight, Dysart & Gamble went out of business.

Talk about bad timing! Our dominant position on the waterfront in New Orleans had been built up since the turn of the century by the *J.S.* and *Sidney*. The year 1929 and the early 1930s would not be kind to launching new businesses. Nevertheless, local New Orleans merchants saw an opportunity, invested in a total remodeling of the steamer *Greater New Orleans*, and entered into competition. During the tramping off-season, I managed the *Capitol* in New Orleans, offering afternoon sight-seeing and nightly dance trips.

Desperate in competition, the local interest owners of the *Greater New Orleans* brought great pressure on port officials to exclude the *Capitol* from our regular landing place at the foot of Canal Street. At the same time, their extensive advertising and discounting campaign slashed our profits to a minimum.

As time went on, the *Greater New Orleans's* harbor activities were curtailed and the vessel began to visibly deteriorate. It was clear that her owners were losing money and Streckfus Steamers feared that the vessel could experience a collision or fire tragedy. It came as no surprise when the investment group made overtures of selling their boat to us.

After tough negotiations, a deal was finally consummated: We owned the *Greater New Orleans* at a rock-bottom $27,500. Recognizing her poor state of repair, we immediately withdrew the *Greater New Orleans* from service. We began to "part out" the valuable, useful assets, including her boilers, which were transferred to the *Senator/Washington*. After laying her up and stripping her down, the short-lived vessel was junked.

Oct. 24, 1929—Our Company was in for a very painful jolt when the "Black Thursday" stock market crash hit on Oct. 24, 1929. We had enjoyed prosperity and now we were forced to tighten our commercial belts and move to survival mode. Our loss in 1929 reflected bank charges and a markdown of securities and bonds in the amount of $86,000. The Great Depression, like the "Great War" experienced in the prior decade, was anything but "Great!"

Chaotic market conditions persisted in 1930; losses on securities liquidated and shrinkage in the portfolio amounted to an ugly $125,000 contraction in our balance sheet. At its low, the stock market's value had shrunk by 90%. We were fortunate that we had liquidity and no debt, but the downturn was, nonetheless, severe in all respects.

On Dec. 12, 1930, I stated to the Streckfus Steamers Inc. board of directors, "This year, 1930, we have not maintained the rate of progress of the preceding nine years. In a measure, our challenges were severe and many."[231]

Among them: the lowest water in 64 years; adverse and inaccurate newspaper reports of readings resulting in the stranding of boats, rescuing of passengers, etc.; a summer of drought and crop failures; and economic depression.

---

231 Source: Streckfus Steamers family records.

I then reported on salaries and bonuses: "Whereas the Season of 1930 has not been a profitable season, but a year of business depression, drought, with no immediate signs of any marked improvement, it is imperative that our management curtail operating expenses."[232]

I reduced my salary about 40% alongside the officers of our company. Roy, John, Verne, and Hilmar Lax accepted salaries and bonus reductions of approximately 20%. While the Company elected to issue a dividend of 50 cents per share ($25,000) for the year, management cautioned that further dividends would be curtailed and that the net loss for the year's operations was $13,900.

The company braced for further belt-tightening. I remarked to shareholders in the annual business review:

> On account of business depression throughout the United States in 1930, our business, like others, suffered and, in order to meet the issue, all salaries have been sharply curtailed. The Season of 1931 is at hand and before us. It is doubtful that business will return to normal by summer and it is not practical to contract for highly paid executives, boat managers and passenger agents. However, the business of Streckfus Steamers is a specialty business; it requires experienced and well-trained men to manage it safely and efficiently.

At this time, the Company adopted a plan for executive remuneration which held salaries flat when profits were low and implemented a program to distribute a percent of profits in better economic times. The formula that was adopted was geared to the organization attaining net profits of $25,000. Below that level, there would be no profit-sharing. As corporate earnings climbed above this bogey, a graduated incentive plan would take effect, whereby officer bonuses would rise from 0.5% to 1% of base salary.

---

232 Source: Streckfus Steamers family records.

Moved by John Streckfus and seconded by Joseph Schaab, the Streckfus Steamers profit-sharing arrangement was put to a vote. It passed unanimously.

The years 1929–1932 are often cited as encompassing the worst times of the economic collapse in the United States. Industrial production and consumer prices fell by a third and unemployment surged sixfold. My brothers all agreed to voluntary salary reductions of 20% or greater and there were no profits and, therefore, no awards under our compensation plan. As general manager, I saw my salary from the company reduced from $25,000 in 1929 to $18,000 in 1930 and further to $15,000 in 1931.

I do not think that our response to the Great Depression was defensive or that our activities were curtailed. We saw opportunities and acted on them.

1931—Competition from the steamer *Greater Pittsburgh* evaporated in 1931 when she was destroyed by fire. The misfortune was our opportunity. We acted to rearrange the schedule of our steamer *Washington*. Familiar to the Ohio River from prior voyages out of Cincinnati, she entered the Port of Pittsburgh for the first time.

The federal government lock at Hastings, Minnesota, was finally completed in 1931 and removed another roadblock to our Upper Mississippi excursions. The expectancy was that the pool at St. Paul above the lock would be flooded no later than June 1. As a result, we scheduled our steamer *Capitol* into St. Paul for excursion on three different occasions that season.

On Sept. 4, 1931, the steel sidewheel *Cincinnati* was purchased for $100,000 from John W. Hubbard with $50,000 in cash and the balance in three notes extending over three years. Approximately five years old at the time, the solid steel hull *Cincinnati* had operated from that eponymous city in the passenger trade to Louisville.

She was relocated to St. Louis for renovation, and we planned to operate her there upon completion. We immediately began removing all wooden superstructure down to the steel second deck, and then erecting a steel superstructure that would be as fireproof as possible, converting it into a high-class excursion steamer.

Our consolidated income and expense statement show a net loss for the year of $216,000, largely reflecting "reserve in shrinkage" in the market value of securities of $225,000. Loss on securities sold was $110,000.

1932—At the annual directors meeting of Jan. 11, 1932, we reported to shareholders that great progress had been made in our complete retrofit of the *Cincinnati*, to be renamed the *President*. We gave recognition to the flip side of the recession: valuable, industrious, and thankful labor on the Mississippi. John Streckfus had assumed leadership in design and construction and stated that he expected completion of the boat so as to enter service in the spring of 1933.

While our company was quite active throughout the Depression, times remained tough. With the scarcity of money and our demands for expenditures on the *Cincinnati*, it was deemed advisable to pass on the dividend to the stockholders until a more favorable time.

1933—[As] Our general manager and president, I offered the following at the shareholders' meeting in 1933. I was not sanguine.

> A year ago today at the time of our Annual Meeting we all felt that the business depression had hit bottom and that business conditions couldn't get any worse. Contrary to our expectations, business conditions continued on the decline. Depressed conditions were reflected in demand for our excursion fleet. Like many merchants, we were obliged to cut our ticket and concession prices. Moreover, the volume of our clients dwindled and the people we did handle didn't have the money to spend; through November our gross revenue plunged $182,000.
>
> In the operation of our Steamers, U.S. Maritime Laws and Regulations require a minimum number of crew to be retained

on each excursion voyage. At the same time, our expenses such as fuel, maintenance, insurance, advertising, etc. remain the same. A threshold of clients must be attained before any profit can be expected—over which point, our income climbs sharply once we clear the straight operating expense burden. But there is evidence that the worst days of the economic bust are in the rear view mirror; the magnitude of our annual loss on securities was trimmed to $26,000 the year and we eked out an equivalent profit.[233]

I elaborated further:

The year 1933 will go down in history as one of severe business depression. On March 4th all banks were closed for two weeks. Many are still closed. The army of unemployed has been fed by the Government, State, City and private funds. Numerous business concerns failed. In all, the year was a hectic one for business in general. Our company did manage to finance the building of our Steamer *President*—a major accomplishment and one fortunately completed when wages and construction materials prices were at their lowest. By this means we were able to keep our crews employed and enabled them to provide for their families.[234]

While adverse conditions and cash stringency delayed finishing the *President*, we questioned whether we would be able to start our season on June 1 as originally planned. However, we did complete the *President*, delaying her maiden trip to July 1, 1933. Our sidewheeler was the first five-deck, all-steel, most fire-resistant steamer built on western rivers, with 24 water-tight compartments in her hull, making her non-sinkable, being

---

233 Source: Streckfus Steamers family records.
234 *Ibid.*

certificated and equipped with life-saving equipment to carry 3,300 passengers, passing a U.S. government stability test.

The year 1933 remained mired in economy like quicksand. Nonetheless, the *President* proved a phenomenal hit with the public and we closed a very successful season in the middle of September. The *President* entering the St. Louis excursion trade enabled the company to place the deluxe sidewheel *J.S. Deluxe* on the Upper Mississippi and Ohio rivers, introducing that high-class steamer to the excursion trade.

That venture proved profitable and our company experienced a welcomed net profit: $68,000.

1934—Although business conditions for Streckfus Steamers were on the rebound, executive salaries were held at their lower base. But now the company could clear its profit-sharing hurdle with a net of $90,000 and bonuses of roughly 1% of base salary awarded. Another positive was the reinstatement of a dividend of 50 cents per share of $25,000.

I remarked:

The past year of 1934 found business still in the depressed state, one-fifth of workers unemployed. However, the general trend is upward. Few businesses made a profit, but the majority of companies did substantially cut down their losses from that of former years. Our company was fortunate in finishing the year with a profit under the existing conditions, with no serious accidents. During the year we paid off all bank loans and completed the purchase of the Steamer *Cincinnati* by paying the last note due during the year. In addition, we set aside $25,000 for a dividend.

Of negative note, the Steamer *Morro Castle* suffered a disturbing marine accident that cost the lives of a number of passengers and crew on the high seas. We must brace for further stricter regulation in the operations of our Steamers in the future. Moreover, such repercussions may bring forth some drastic laws, making our wooden Steamers almost impossible to operate at a profit.

With the completion of the locks and dams system on the Upper Mississippi, we can look forward to better operating conditions in that section of the river. While not completed for the year 1935, we will be able to use three or four pools recently completed, which will substantially help our upper river trade.[235]

1935—In October, the executive committee reported that they were considering the advisability of buying or building a new steel vessel. All four brothers were intrigued to learn of the availability of the massive railroad transfer *Albatross* located at Vicksburg, Mississippi. Could the *Albatross* be purchased for a reasonable figure?

Annie Amantea Blum says in her book, *The Steamer Admiral and Streckfus Steamers, A Personal View*, "The *Admiral's* story begins with the *Albatross*. *Albatross* was the given name of a railroad transfer boat, or as some say, a ferry for railroad cars. The name *Albatross* had been used for other boats and ships; for instance, the wooden hull gunboat used during the Civil War. It is amazing to consider that river boats like the *Albatross* could carry the weight of railroad train cars on deck, thereby taking the place of a bridge."[236]

Oct. 21, 1935. Streckfus Steamers Incorporated—Minutes of Directors Meeting reads as follows: "The Executive Committee reported that they were looking into the advisability of buying or building a new steel vessel, and it was arranged if the *Albatross* could be purchased for a reasonable figure, to make the deal."

Nov. 18, 1935. Streckfus Steamers Incorporated—Minutes of Directors Meeting reads as follows: "We have purchased the steel Steamer *Albatross*

---

235 Source: Streckfus Steamers family records.
236 Blum, *Admiral*, pg. 19.

from the Illinois Central System. This Steamer's hull is in splendid shape and should make us a real Steamer. It is my recommendation that this Steamer be rebuilt at once into a first-class excursion boat. We now have two steel and four wooden boats. I am quite sure it will only be a matter of a few years when all wooden boats will be obsolete. We should keep this in mind and replace our wooden Steamers with steel Steamers as soon as possible. Upon motion made and properly seconded, the President was authorized to proceed on the plan for rebuilding the Steamer *Albatross*, this work being done by the Steamer Service Company, a subsidiary of Streckfus Steamers Incorporated, and the necessary funds being transferred to the Steamer Service Company to finance this work."

January 13, 1936. Steamer Service Company—Minutes of the Annual Stockholders Meeting read as follows: "The Chairman reported the purchase of the Steamer *Albatross* on behalf of the Steamer Service Company from the Yazoo & Mississippi Valley Railroad Company, for the sum of $25,000 and stated as soon as the bill of sale and final papers are received, the Steamer Albatross will be brought to St. Louis."

July 1, 1936. Streckfus Steamers Incorporated—Minutes of the Directors Meeting reads as follows: "Next in order, Mr. Jos. Streckfus submitted to the Directors present, the proposition submitted by Miss Mazie Krebs under date of June 29, 1936, covering the design and ideas for the new boat. However, because of the possibility of being unable to finish up the interior in time for the 1937 season, it was decided by the Directors present to withhold making arrangements for the designing of the interior until a later date. Joseph Streckfus was authorized to write Miss Mazie Krebs to this effect."[237]

Meanwhile, Mazie Krebs had prepared draft interior design plans for the conversion. Such plans were deferred as work could not be finished in time for the 1937 season.

---

237 Blum, *Admiral*, pg. 86.

Shareholders were informed:

It is currently estimated that expenditures on the new boat to date will run approximately $47,000 and that it will take at least an additional $300,000 to finish the Steamer. Authority for such expenditure to complete the conversion was approved. The *President* remained a great draw and a profit of $100,700 was booked along with distribution of the regular dividend.

Progress is being made on the building of our new steel Steamer, which, when completed, will be one of the largest and most up to date Steamers plying inland waters, and will be our second steamer built of Steel.

As we anticipated, the late Steamer *Morro Castle* and *Mohawk* disasters prompted the Bureau of Steamboat Inspection, as well as Congress, to enact more rigid laws and regulations governing all Steamers carrying passengers; read: additional expense in our operations to comply.

The Director of the Bureau had gone on record (at a committee meeting of Congress) with the statement that there are over 200 boats in the United States that are built of wood, more than 20 years old, and are obsolete and should be junked. Proportionately, we have four wooden Steamers in our line that are of wood and well over twenty years of age. To replace the wooden hulls with steel fire-proof modern hulls, Streckfus Steamers will eventually be obliged to write off these wooden Steamers at a loss. With some good fortune, extra profitable business from new modern Steamers should more than offset that loss. The executives and board contemplated options to provide funds for a third steel boat.

1937—With investment in the *Albatross* conversion measured at $51,500, excursion schedules and plans for the five vessels in operation were established. Extreme floods on the Ohio postponed the opening of the *Washington* excursion schedule until July 1. With the *President* and *J.S. Deluxe* stationed in St. Louis, the steamer *Saint Paul* would visit all cities enroute to Pittsburgh. Stationed in Pittsburgh during the summer of 1937, the *Saint Paul* was under the auspices of Capt. D.W. Wisherd, who handled sales and management of her operations.

A continuing impact of the Depression on the availability of important materials slowed progress on what would be named the *Admiral*. Company plans for operating the *President* upriver to St. Paul were also confounded by delays in the completion of the Upper Mississippi lock system, especially the lock at LeClaire, Iowa. A dividend of $1 per share was paid to stockholders of record December 6, 1937, totaling $50,000.

With expenditures on the new steamer at $134,000 by December, the final consolidated income and expenses statement showed a net profit for the year 1937 of $89,000 despite $55,000 in further markdown of securities.

Cash flow from operations was sufficient for an increase in the dividend to $1 per share. The general manager's report stated: "Work on our second large steel steamer is progressing nicely. Our aspirations are that the *Admiral* will be last word in an up-to-date excursion vessel, built in accordance with the latest ideas for construction of a fire-proof non-sinkable vessel."

1938—Under Capt. Wisherd, the results of tramping operations of the *Saint Paul* on the Ohio River and all cities enroute to Pittsburgh were quite encouraging as were summer operations out of that city. It was decided not to operate the *Washington* this season, but to lay her up in winter quarters at Paducah until autumn.

Bids for the air conditioning installation aboard the *Admiral* were submitted by Tate & Tate, York Ice Machinery Corp., and Carriers Corp. After full consideration and examining existing installations by the companies, it was decided to place the contract with Carriers at a cost of $49,000 less a 2% discount.

In the annual report to stockholders, I noted:

In view of the rigid rules of the Bureau of Marine Inspection & Navigation Service at Washington against all wooden vessels, which have been classed by them as fire traps and unsafe, it was decided to close the season of the Steamer "*J.S.*" at St. Louis, and dismantle and abandon that Steamer.

It was decided to widen the Steamer *President* with the addition of sponsons. Plans were drawn up and Todd-Johnson Dry Docks, Inc. in New Orleans was awarded the contract for $31,900 according to specifications and blue-prints submitted for the work. On the new boat front, expenditures to date had climbed to $274,000.00.

Income of $95,000 was attained, profit-sharing was funded, and a dividend of $1 per share was distributed.

Management gave the following accounting of the activities of the Streckfus fleet: *President* at New Orleans—Enroute New Orleans to St. Louis and berthed at St. Louis; Str. *Capitol* at New Orleans—Enroute to and from St. Paul, and at St. Paul; Str. *Saint Paul* enroute to and from Paducah and Pittsburgh, and at Pittsburgh; Str. *J.S.* enroute New Orleans, La. to Red Wing, Minn.; Str. *Washington*—retired; Str. *Albatross*—being reconstructed at St. Louis by the Steamer Service Company.

General economic conditions had begun to deteriorate again, forcing expense reductions concomitant with the 20% retreat in gross business income. At the same time, the *President* required an additional investment of $40,000 which reduced net cash from operations materially.

Over the course of 1937 and 1938, the company accepted the reality that wooden-hulled steamers were facing sunset. As a result, it retired the *Washington* and *J.S. Deluxe*; both were sold for scrap in December 1938.

Unexpectedly, the Port of New Orleans, on a 14-hour notice, raised the company's wharf charges 500%—from $300 per month to $1,500. In response, the two Streckfus steamers operating there were mothballed, pending a negotiated reasonable adjustment.

Positive news emerged that work on the *Admiral*—the new all-steel, fire-resistant, air-conditioned, stream-lined sidewheeler—was nearing completion at a total cost of approximately $500,000. The Streckfus family and shareholders were confident that the giant art-deco excursion boat would be a moneymaker.

1939—It was decided to arrange for the dry docking of the *Capitol* and *Saint Paul* at Paducah at the close of the summer season. Here, the company would authorize any necessary repairs and any additional improvements ordered by U.S. inspectors. Thorough examinations would be performed by these inspectors while the steamers were in dry dock.

Several new vessels were acquired in late 1939 including the diesel tug *Turnbull* and a steel barge belonging to the Southern Coal, Coke & Mining Co. and the tug *Susie Hazard*, which was bought in a foreclosure sale.

Consolidated income for the year was $84,000 and a $1 dividend was declared.

1940—Streckfus Line closed its 28th year in business.

Updates on the fleet were as follows: The *President* was at New Orleans, enroute and at St. Louis; *Capitol* was at New Orleans, enroute and at St. Paul; *Saint Paul*, enroute on Ohio River, and at Pittsburgh; *J.S.* and *Washington*, sold to a wrecking company, St. Louis; *Albatross*, under construction at St. Louis by Steamer Service Co.; *Susie Hazard*, steam tug, and *Turnbull*, diesel tug, both purchased in Autumn 1939; and a steel barge, also purchased in Autumn 1939.

Management remarked that the *President*, with new sponson sides, performed excellently and was solidly profitable and now being conditioned for the upcoming season. The *Saint Paul* was placed in dry dock at Paducah, given a new bottom and general overhauling and modernization. While the operations and financial contribution of the *Capitol*'s season were on par with 1938, the sternwheeler was also extensively repaired and retrofitted with attention to considerable replacement of its hull.

THE STRECKFUS RIVERBOAT DYNASTY

As general manager, I reflected in January 1940, as per meeting minutes:

War between Germany, England and France, and Russia with Finland, now some three months old, is already having a crimping effect on our business here. Some 16,000,000 men remain unemployed. A seemingly never-ending series of restrictions emerge every day: new taxes, Social Security regulations, union activities, Wagner Act. These burdens have made our business finance extremely challenging and have slowed the recovery of our overall maritime operations. Even through years of depression, Streckfus Steamers has continued to prosper. Our entire organization has been alert, careful, and at the same time energetic and progressive. Our future is bright and I am sure we can look forward to better days. In conclusion, I wish to express my appreciation to the stockholders and our staff for their co-operation, and also to the public for the many evidences of their confidence in, and goodwill toward, our company.

Respectfully submitted.
(signed) Jos. Streckfus, President

IN THE WORDS OF
CAPT. ROY MICHAEL STRECKFUS SR., 1888–1967

Roy Michael Streckfus is my name, riverboat captain and executive manager of the largest, longest-lived excursion steamboat fleet ever to ply the Ohio and Mississippi rivers—and connecting tributaries.

Born October 8, 1888, I am one of four sons of the Commodore and Theresa, nee Bartemeier. My father, John Streckfus, married in 1880 and, by 1881, Elizabeth Mary, a.k.a. Lily, was born. Subsequent years brought additional girls, Anna (1883) and Mary (1885), who preferred to be called May.

Captain Roy Streckfus in his office on the *Capitol*
Courtesy of the Dave Thomson Collection at Steamboats.com

After three daughters, my father and mother embarked on a spree of introducing male sons into this world—all with riverboat blood in their veins. The first was Joseph Leo (Feb. 1887), then me, then John Nicholas (1891) and Verne Walter (1895).

Another sister, Theresa Agnes, died in her first year when I was six years old. I remember the family standing beside her tiny bed as she took her last breaths. I lost my other younger sister, Nina Agnes, when I was 19 years old; she died when she was only 10 years old.

Among the four Streckfus brothers, I was bestowed with the only sons. My brother John and his wife were childless. Joe and Verne and their wives were each blessed with offspring—all daughters.

Like my father before me, I was touched by riverboat great fortune. Whether divined from Poseidon or Neptune, my late wife Isabel, who passed away in 1939, and I were blessed with three daughters and four sons. All the boys loved the Mississippi and, through the ranks, became celebrated riverboat captains themselves.

My boys were John Curran (1917), whom we called Curran; Roy Michael (R.M.) Jr. (1921); Robert Bernard (1926); and William Sauvage (1933).

Isabel and I also enjoyed the great fortune of three wonderful daughters: Junie (1908), whom we lost to the Spanish flu in 1919; Mary (1924) and Lily Ann (1928).

Following German tradition, it was my elder brother, Joe, who was given the latitude to attend college. In our Roman Catholic way, where else could Joe have gone but Notre Dame? I too wanted to attend university, but my father would have none of it; there was too much to do on our excursion vessels.

I was in my early 20s when the family embarked on the ambitious undertaking of buying four wooden packets of the Diamond Jo line. There was intense work to be done in revamping the four packets and the Commodore impressed upon me, "There are challenges out there on the Mississippi, which will teach you more than you could ever learn in a classroom."

Let the record show that, in the off season from Streckfus Steamers commerce, I did find time each year to master the basic courses in business school. However, as I have said on many occasions, "My college was out there, on the Mississippi." And indeed, it was: I captained our vessels from St. Paul to New Orleans and back on hundreds of trips, where I navigated the treacherous twists and turns of the mighty river.

In the Words of Capt. Roy Michael Streckfus Sr., 1888–1967

During my 79 years on the river, no radar or precise GPS electronic signals existed to illuminate the way. We worked from maps, red and green channel markers, horns, and light beacons. These visual aids were supplemented by constant ongoing communication with other captains. We used every tool available to Mississippi river transport, but it was primarily based on good and bad past experience: prior knowledge of where the sandbars and snags were located that allowed our passage.

My father, the Commodore, gained his success from hard work, cautious risk-taking and trial and error. As a family we all agreed with the acceptance of "fast failure" and lived by the apt observation, "Good judgment comes from experience BUT experience comes from bad judgment."

My daughter Lily said this about me:

Captain Roy Streckfus was forever on a quest for learning about the river and the mechanics of the Streckfus Steamer fleet. He understood navigation and operation of boats in his command under marine law. The captain must be a businessman yet responsible first for the safety of his passengers and crew. He had to maintain the vessel along with his understanding the nuts and bolts of engines such as the pair of 1,000 horsepower steam engines on the excursion vessel, *President*. The boat had a chief engineer and multiple assistants. But the responsibility of keeping the machinery going was his.

There were many times when I observed my dad draw a picture of an important but failing part. With this design in hand, he had a copy made at the machine shop onboard and put back in place, just in time for another trip on the river. Keeping a schedule was sacred to the success of the Streckfus Steamers fleet. Our customers, young and old, could count on the steamers leaving the dock precisely when scheduled.[238]

---

238 Lily Streckfus Smith journal, Sept 15, 1995.

By the year 1967, I was known as "Dean of the Mississippi." Granted, this was an accolade I earned after a full life of riverboat oversight and a ton of experience, making every mistake in the book. One colleague remarked, "He knows the excursion business and the twists and turns of the river from stem to stern."

For the unexpectedly short 25 years of our matrimony, I was intensely devoted to my wife Isabel Lourdes McPartland (1891–1939). I first met Isabel at Burlington, Iowa, while piloting one of our steamers. Let the record show that I had to go to great lengths to meet and court Isabel McPartland; I first saw her riding a beautiful white stallion along the banks of the river, upriver from the town of Burlington. I had been transfixed by her style and beauty and immediately began an investigation as to who she was—and, of course, how I could introduce myself.

Isabel McPartland Streckfus
Arthur L. Smith's Personal Collection

When the *Saint Paul* docked at the wharf in downtown Burlington, I set off on a mission: Find that beautiful young lady I saw riding along the bluffs of the western shore of the Mississippi. The year was 1912—the first full year Streckfus Steamers operated the Diamond Jo fleet and the *W.W.*

I was 24; Isabel was 21.

Also known as Isabella and Isabelle, she was the fourth daughter of Bernard McPartland (1853–1891) and Mary Curran (1855–1931), both of generation Irish American heritage, born in Rhode Island and Iowa, respectively.

Her father was a railroad man. The 1879 census data indicate that, at age 26, he was employed as a "locomotive engineer." After marrying Mary in 1876, they were blessed with Kathryn (1878), Mary (1881) and

In the Words of Capt. Roy Michael Streckfus Sr., 1888–1967

Gertrude (1886). Their son, Barney, perished in 1901 at the age of 16. Records indicate the death was of unknown causes.

My Isabel entered the world on May 22, 1891. A grim introduction awaited her: Within 24 hours, her father Barney was gone.

Apparently with no evidence of illness or incapacity, Barney McPartland had been rushed to the hospital after a coronary attack and immediately expired on May 23, 1891. A good man, Barney had been a good provider to Mary and their family. With perseverance and hard work, he had climbed to the rank of railroad conductor.

However, death and disability benefits were nonexistent or trivial (if any) at the time and Mary found herself in a quandary—no husband, limited (if any) pension and insurance benefits, and four youthful daughters, ranging in age from 13 to one day old.

Mary Curran McPartland's sister-in-law, Mary Agnew, had married a gentleman named John J. Curran (known as J.J.). To confuse matters for later historians, John H. McPartland (Barney's brother) had married Ella Curran (Mary Curran McPartland's sister).

Mary Agnew Curran was born in Ohio. At the time of Isabel's birth, she and J.J. were childless but enjoying a well-appointed life. One of Burlington's most successful citizens, J.J. was active in state and local politics while serving as postmaster general. J.J. was a gifted businessman, and he and Mary were enjoying the affluence afforded by his successful chain of tobacco shops.

Mary (Agnew) Curran reached out to her McPartland sister-in-law during this period of bereavement for Bernard and suggested that Isabel live with her and John. Historical records indicate that Isabel and her adopted parents were extremely wealthy; by 1910, Isabel's 19th year, the Currans employed eight "servants" who ranged in age from 18 (Mark, the storekeeper) to 70 (M.M., the bartender).

At this time in U.S. history, there were no social benefits for the poor and under-employed. Therefore, it was not uncommon for a well-to-do businessman like J.J. Curran to employ and indirectly offer a form of philanthropy to many "servants." Certainly, there must have been some family turmoil and jealousy among Isabel, her mother, and three sisters regarding daughter No. 4's immense good fortune under the Curran roof.

In two years, Isabel and I wed after the first mass at St. Paul's Church in Burlington, the heart of what were then identified as the Tri Cities. The local newspaper, The *Davenport Democrat and Leader*, commented in its society pages:

> One of the greatest matrimonial surprises of the season was celebrated—Miss Isabella McPartland and Mr. Roy Michael Streckfus—with the Rev. Father Thomas Galligan officiating. While the intentions of the bridal couple were not altogether unknown to the immediate family, the wedding came as a complete surprise to the relatives and host of good friends of the young couple.
>
> The bride is one of Burlington's handsomest brunettes, a graduate of St. Joseph's College, Dubuque, and great favorite in a large circle of friends. She wore a very becoming navy blue crepe de chine gown, with a corsage bouquet of sweet peas and a black French hat for the ceremony.
>
> (Isabel) . . . is the youngest daughter of Mrs. Mary McPartland and has been making her home for a number of years with her uncle and aunt, Mr. and Mrs. J. J. Curran of Burlington.
>
> Captain Streckfus is a well-known river man, looking after his father's interests in the big Mississippi, and has the congratulations of his host of friends in Burlington.
>
> Business interests of the bridegroom will not permit an extended wedding trip at present. Instead, the young couple will take a tardy matrimonial jaunt in the fall. Captain and Mrs. Streckfus will make their home in New Orleans.

Burlington's population was predominantly Irish, while Rock Island's was primarily German; our Irish/German ancestry was doubly appropriate, having in common our Catholic faith.

In the Words of Capt. Roy Michael Streckfus Sr., 1888–1967

When the summer season came to a close, Isabel and I did enjoy a fabulous honeymoon. Forsaking an ocean-liner cruise, we spent our honeymoon visiting the major eastern cities of New York, Boston, and Philadelphia.

Managing the *Capitol* and the *President* led me to build a home at 15 Versailles Boulevard in the heart of the New Orleans Garden District. The lot on which the house was erected was originally No. 13. But Isabel was somewhat superstitious; thus, the renumbering.

Not unusual for turn-of-the-century medicine, early deaths were both common and often lacking the telltale warnings of ill health.[239]

Isabel and Roy Streckfus
Arthur L. Smith's Collection

---

239 Isabel may have been a carrier of a rare form of heart disease: hypertrophic cardiomyopathy (HCM). While medical records were sparse then, the abrupt death of Bernard (Barney) at only 37 is consistent with this medical condition. HCM heart disease may have taken Isabel's father and, in 1939, it took her. At the time, HCM was not recognized. However, the symptoms she displayed in the years prior to her premature death are consistent with this diagnosis. HCM was later manifest in our sons, R.M. and John Curran, both of whom died prematurely. Additionally, Curran's daughter, Linda; R.M.'s daughter, Donna; and Lily Ann Streckfus Smith's grandson, Dustin Arthur Smith, all evidenced HCM symptoms.

THE STRECKFUS RIVERBOAT DYNASTY

After losing Isabel in 1939, I never remarried and turned my attention entirely to my children—and the boats. I had tough shoes to fill as Isabel left me with a son just five years of age and a daughter, 10. Their siblings were only slightly older at 12, 14, 16, and 20.

Isabel and I also enjoyed the great fortune of three wonderful daughters: Mary (1924–1959), Lily Ann (1928) and Junie, who succumbed to the Spanish flu in 1919 when 11 years old. Junie was one of my favorites.

Lily had two children: Arthur Lawrence Smith (1952), the author of this work, and Ellen Isabel Smith Brown (1958). Mary had just one son, Streckfus Dufour (1947). [Author's Note: He passed near the millennium.]

Joe's daughters and Verne's daughters achieved, on their own, many local friends and extensive reach in St. Louis and New Orleans. Joe's three daughters were well known on the social circuit in St. Louis, while Verne's daughters were equally ensconced in the always vibrant activities of New Orleans. William Carroll, a Bostonian, married Joe's daughter Maysie and was soon active in management of the Northern district, becoming a licensed pilot and ultimately, master of the *Admiral*.

Throughout my career, I was a vocal proponent of thoughtful development of the Mississippi regarding bridges, locks, and general navigation. In the early years of steamboat commerce on the rivers, the fast development of the railroads led to great animosity among the two camps. For obvious reasons, railroads sought low-level, low-cost river crossings. But steamers needed consistent clearance under the bridges and clearance was exacerbated during flood tides.

An example of the conflict was a bridge in Minneapolis that was constructed with an inferior height. The result: Steamers like those of the Streckfus line could not travel north when the river was elevated. To overcome the limited clearance of low auto and rail bridges, it was necessary that steamers hinge their smokestacks to permit acceptable passage.

In 1967, I had been appointed to a special Coast Guard panel as a representative of the Western Boat Operators. That committee was focused

In the Words of Capt. Roy Michael Streckfus Sr., 1888–1967

on navigational problems and regulations regarding marine transport on the rivers.

My family and I took keen interest in the development of the 29 lock-and-dam systems that were constructed between 1930 and 1940. In its whole, the lock system was an ambitious and costly engineering marvel. A series of locks were constructed to ameliorate thorny stretches of the river, such as the appropriately named Chain of Rocks just north of St. Louis. Our firm's presence in the super ports of St. Louis and New Orleans gave us a place at the table when important local and national regulations were gestated.

It was a lengthy and hard lobbying effort by my brothers and me to see that the NOLA crossings to the West Bank (the Huey P. Long Bridge and the Greater New Orleans Bridge, now known as the Crescent City Connection) were of adequate height. Similarly, in St. Louis, the Streckfus organization was consulted prior to construction of the Eads and Chain of Rocks bridges.

Capt. Roy M. Streckfus aboard the *Admiral*
Murphy Library Special Collections/ ARC, University of Wisconsin–La Crosse.

While my brother Joe was executive manager of the overall Streckfus enterprise, he deferred to me the responsibility of regular travel to Washington, D.C., and testimony before Congress on river development initiatives and regulations. While these activities took me away from time with family, I accepted the responsibility with great enthusiasm.

OBITUTARY FOR ROY MICHAEL STRECKFUS SR. (1888-1967)

Capt. Roy Michael Streckfus Sr., born at Rock Island, Illinois, on Oct. 8, 1888, passed away on Oct. 11, 1967, and was buried at Sacred Heart Cemetery in Burlington, Iowa. He was 79.

"One of four sons of the late John Streckfus (the Commodore), he was the second generation of excursion-steamer men. Now the third generation has taken over for the most part."[240]

Capt. Roy's father ran away from home and stowed away on a boat going down the river. Some years later, he acquired his own—a little packet, the *Freddie*. From that modest start, the Streckfus line grew to operate in 1967 the *Admiral* and the *Huck Finn* in St. Louis, the *President* and the *Mark Twain* in New Orleans, and the *Tom Sawyer* in Minneapolis.

In an interview with daughter Lily several years prior, Capt. Roy attributed the family's success in excursion steamers to the fact that "there was a family atmosphere on our boats.

---

240 Obituary for Captain Roy M. Streckfus, Oct 11, 1967, *St. Louis Post Dispatch*

'My father developed a clean atmosphere on the Streckfus boats [lacking in some earlier packets when gambling was rampant]. Our success stemmed from strict attention to safety, to detail and to providing a wholesome place for families.

We did so by always having a member of our Streckfus family aboard.'"

LILY'S PACKARD TRAVELOGUE, IN THE WORDS OF LILY ANN STRECKFUS SMITH

After Lent was celebrated in the spring of each year, my dad, Capt. Roy Streckfus, would depart New Orleans to escort the *Capitol* on its annual trek to St. Paul. Over the 1920s and 1930s, the sternwheeler moved northward at a measured pace and would arrive in St. Paul in early July.

Our family would follow in Dad's footsteps, on land that is, when school went into summer recess. Mother would orchestrate the migration in an oversized sedan, a Packard, and my eldest brother, Curran, would be behind the wheel. When Curran was unavailable, a chauffeur would pilot the giant auto.

Mother was Irish and we were devout Irish Catholics. Before departing New Orleans, we would all go to mass at the Holy Name Jesuit Church on St. Charles Avenue. Our adventure began at 5:00 a.m. and, as we left the city, we recited the rosary. Oh yes, a giant picnic basket accompanied Mother, Curran, Mary, R.M., Robert, me, and little brother Bill. And not to be forgotten was our nursemaid, Mrs. Gillan. It was an uncomfortably challenging entourage of eight; my brother Bob and I would sit on those little seats that pulled up from the floor.

We would pack a traditional repast of crackers and tongue. While the beef tongue was from a can, we devoured it with gusto. The first leg was not too onerous—200 miles—and brought us as far as Jackson, Mississippi. Here, as was her convention, Mother would pull up to a hotel and bargain for the best room rate possible. If the hotelier was too firm on his asking price, Mother would return to the Packard and the search would continue. After any full day of travel when room and board were elusive, the entire family would sink into the seats, exhausted and spirits deflated.

When we did locate suitable accommodation—usually a family suite with lots of beds, including Murphy beds—we would camp out while take-out food was brought in.

Each day on the highway was grueling as we would cover almost 250 miles to attain first Jackson, Mississippi, then Memphis, then St. Louis. At least 10 hours of travel if our readings of signs and markings all proved accurate. That was a rare happenstance. Instead, I can remember the sinking feeling when Mother burst the silence with "I haven't seen a sign in a while." We would just about faint as we realized we must retrace the journey until we found the correct path.

There were no interstate highways then—mostly dirt and gravel roads. Standard-issue tires were chancy, and blowouts were common. I recall one memorable blowout when the Packard went over the embankment and rolled over.

That's right—it made a 360-degree spin and landed upright. Those Packards were like military tanks. When the accident occurred, Mrs. Gillan was asleep and, as was her custom, she had removed her teeth and set them in her lap. Bob and I had a running joke of stealing Mrs. Gillan's dentures. Mother said, "Oh, is everyone all right?" Absent seat belts, all of us had miraculously avoided serious injury. But Mrs. Gillan was distraught: "I can't find my teeth."

Anther indelible memory is that of Mother going into a service station while Curran filled the gas tank. She would always purchase a Coca-Cola, one of those green, six-and-a-half-ounce glass bottles. At every filling station, Mother would purchase a new bottle and, with no hesitation, drain the whole contents without stopping.

After our second night on the road was spent in Memphis, we would make the more tolerable stretch to St. Louis. Our favorite, the Lennox

Lily's Packard Travelogue, in the Words of Lily Ann Streckfus Smith

Hotel, awaited us. The Lennox, an upscale fancy hotel on Washington Avenue, was only 10 blocks from the river. In St. Louis, we spent several days, always ate Chinese food, and toured the Streckfus steamers then operating there.

My brother Bob and I were inseparable during our childhood; one year, without permission, we bought a small pony, which we stabled behind Versailles Boulevard. Bob and I would often sneak off in the hotel to avoid the cacophony of our mother and siblings. One day we were playing in a large closet when we realized there were no sounds coming from our room in the Lennox. It was so quiet. We searched the room and went to the lobby where the manager assured us that we would be reunited.

Meanwhile, Mother, with the Packard well on its way out of St. Louis, took a roll call. The car returned and we joined the brigade on our way to Mother's hometown, Burlington, Iowa.

We always were thrilled to pull into Burlington where we would stay for a number of days visiting Mother's family. My grandmother Mary was there, as were my aunts Kathryn, Mary, and Gertrude. Aunt Kate was especially fun to visit as she and Uncle Louie had a great home on Central Avenue. Kate was a siren on the telephone and could wear out anyone, including her sister, my mother Isabel.

My dad helped support Kate and Louie after the weight of the Great Depression in the 1930s caused Uncle Louie's successful grocery store to fail. Louie eventually found work, albeit at much lower wages, as a butcher.

Liquor laws must have been lax as Uncle Louie would often bring home beer and share a glass with Bob and me. That was exceptional.

Uncle Louie was perhaps the best storyteller in all of Burlington. Family picnics—and there were a lot of them—inevitably were turned over to Louie to officiate as the master of ceremonies.

Our next stop was St. Paul. Here, we would be reunited with Dad for the balance of the summer excursion season.

When leaves began to turn in the fall, we would retrace our steps back to New Orleans, hopefully with fewer wrong paths and flat tires.

THE STRECKFUS RIVERBOAT DYNASTY

JOHN CURRAN STRECKFUS (1916-1959)

Roy and Isabel were at home on Versailles Street in New Orleans. Would the University of Notre Dame flag be flying next to the Stars & Stripes and Louisiana's pelican flag?

Excitement abounded! They and John Curran's five brothers and sisters were focused on "Curran," as he was nicknamed, and who had received a long-awaited letter from the University of Notre Dame.

Upon opening it, the first-born son of Capt. Roy and Isabel let out a whoop and a yell! The revered campus and hallowed towers in South Bend, Indiana, beckoned him!

Following in the German and Irish family tradition of favoring the eldest male heir, it was known that only Curran was to be allowed to attend a full-time university, as tuition funds were rationed and not generally available.

Younger brothers R.M., Bob, and Bill would be passed over and would, like Capt. Roy, who wasn't the eldest male among his male siblings, seek junior college training. As it was with Curran's Uncle Joe, it was preordained that Curran would go to Notre Dame. Curran's younger brothers would go to junior college.

A tall (6'2") and handsome young man when he matriculated to Notre Dame in the fall of 1935, Curran was given plenty of "scope"—parlance for thoroughly proportioned anchor line—by Capt. Roy and Mrs. Streckfus.

But though she was 962 miles away, his mother was prepared to intervene and tighten that rope at a moment's notice. And did she! Isabel flexed her muscles on that quiet autumn night in New Orleans.

Capt. Roy was home from a season of tramping the Mississippi with the *President*; Verne would now pilot her twice a day on harbor tours and weekend-evening moonlight cruises. Isabel and Roy were at the Orpheum Hall, popcorn and drink in hand and ready to take in a movie.

Preceding films at that time, rather than scores of trailers for other movies, were newsreels—short films showing recent events of national interest. That evening's newsreel included a bit about Notre Dame football including the team dashing on the field.

Isabel grabbed Capt. Roy's arm and shrieked: "There is our son, Curran!"

Not seeking permission, which he knew would be denied, Curran had tried out for Coach Elmer Layden and was picked for the varsity.

Despite Capt. Roy's energetic protests, Curran's football life came to an abrupt end the very next day. Isabel insisted that her husband contact the monsignor at Notre Dame, whom the family knew well: John Curran Streckfus was no longer Notre Dame's starting right tackle.

IN THE WORDS OF CAPT. JOHN NICHOLAS STRECKFUS (1891–1948)

I am John Nicholas Streckfus, the third son and one of nine children born to John and Theresa Streckfus at Rock Island, Illinois. I came into this world in the last decade of the 19th century, on December 6, 1891.

I have three older sisters, two older brothers and one younger brother. I lost two younger sisters—one while I was three years old; another when I was 16. The census of 1910 includes the answer to a question posed to my mother; she had replied that she had given birth to nine children, seven of whom were living.

My birth records are clear; I am named after my dad. However, although many reports list me as John N. Streckfus Jr., I am not a "Jr." My father rarely used his middle name—or his middle initial. Yet the preponderance of records where one is noted indicate John "B." It would be reasonable to ascertain that this stood for his father's name, Balthazar.

I grew up in a steamboat family and, from my earliest memories, everyone pulled his or her work weight. In my birth year, the Commodore was concentrating his energies and the riverboat assets of his Acme Packet Co. on the upper regions of the Mississippi.

In 1901, I was 10 years old when the family celebrated the launch of the *J.S.*, the first of the Streckfus Line to be wholly purposed as an excursion vessel. The immediate success of the *J.S.* was translated into great commercial results.

For our family, the next 10 years were wonderful—until the fiery tragedy at Bad Axe Island reduced the proud steamer to mostly ashes in 1910. At the time, my eldest sister, Lily, had already been working as a bookkeeper for several years, while sisters Anna and May were continuing their schooling.

I was 18 years old at the time. I had not yet joined my brothers Joe, 23, and Roy, 21, as employees. At this time, Joe was already a licensed steamboat captain, while Roy was a clerk. By the time I reached my majority at 21, I too began training to become a certified riverboat captain. Younger brother Verne, who was nearly 15 at the time of the fire, would follow in short order.

While I was told I was often singled out by the fair sex as "the most handsome Streckfus brother," I remained single for most of my life. Although it was standard Streckfus policy to discourage romantic entanglements among employees, I, like Joe and Verne, found my spouse onboard a Streckfus steamer.

On December 12, 1934, I was married at St. Patrick's Catholic Church in New Orleans at the seasoned age of 43. I had fallen hopelessly in love with a beauty, Shirley Wellnitz of St. Paul, who was a purser (cashier) onboard the *Capitol*, where she also served as executive assistant to Capt. Roy.

After our engagement and betrothal, Shirley and I planned to relocate to St. Louis where I would join my brother Joe in management. By this time, plans for acquisition of the *Albatross* were in place.

Wasting no time, Shirley and I embarked on an extended honeymoon adventure in Europe. With water travel our preference, Shirley and I proceeded to cross the Atlantic both directions. We departed New York City on the *Paris*, celebrating Christmas at sea, and arrived in Plymouth, England, on the 27th. We toured England and parts of Europe over the next 10 days and sought our return journey originating from Le Havre on the *Île de France*, returning to New Orleans on January 15, 1935.

In the Words of Capt. John Nicholas Streckfus (1891–1948)

(Whether planned or happenstance, this was the identical journey John Nicholas Streckfus's grandparents, Balthazar and Anna Marie, had made 85 years earlier.)

When I registered for the first World War (at 26), I was living at 5861 Nina Shores in St. Louis. My draft registrar noted that I was tall and stout with blue eyes and brown hair. My occupation was "Captain–Steamboat, licensed as an officer and mariner." By 1942, I had moved to New Orleans for several years and then back again to St. Louis to 1415 Lindell Avenue.

My service on the river included as master of the *Admiral*. Had you visited Vicksburg, Mississippi, in 1935 and seen the SS *Albatross*, you would never have guessed that the decrepit railroad ferry could be transformed and emerge phoenix-like as the "S.S. *Admiral*—the world's finest inland luxury liner."

After Joe, Roy, and I negotiated the purchase of the *Albatross*, I spent several weeks in Vicksburg learning the mechanical "ropes" of the giant railroad transfer.

Seemingly overnight, the *Albatross* had gone from industrial workhorse to anachronism. No longer needed to provide daily crossings for locomotives and rolling stock, the proud vessel was quiet and silent; mothballed, so to speak. On May 1, 1930, a Vicksburg bridge had opened for rail and auto traffic. The *Albatross* had been in service only 23 years at the time.

My brothers entrusted me with bringing her upriver.

I can vividly remember that cold, foggy morning when I assumed her helm and ordered her unshackled from the eastern Mississippi shore. At one time or another, I had piloted virtually every vessel in the Streckfus fleet—to wit, the *Saint Paul, Capitol, Sidney,* and *J.S. Deluxe*. Each had idiosyncrasies that were only manifest at the wheel when wind, rain, and racing current hindered maneuverability.

A few years had passed since I had guided the sidewheel *Cincinnati* from her eponymous native city to St. Louis. After she was reincarnated the *President*, I was her ship master.

Like the *President*, the *Albatross* was a massive sidewheeler—just a bigger and clumsier version. I had no trouble at the helm that day and the *Albatross*—the property of our sister company, Steamer Service Co., which would reinvent her—left her mooring under the new Vicksburg bridge and cruised north.

Soon, she glided safely to rest on the west bank of the St. Louis harbor north of Eads Bridge, where we docked her to begin a multi-year transformation into the world's largest river excursion vessel. At the end of the vision emerged the *Admiral*.

Author's note: Although the third son in the family, John Nicholas Streckfus was the first to perish. He died of heart disease on December 12, 1948, at the premature age of 56. Although his life was cut short by heart disease, he lived a terrific life. Those who knew him described him as warm-hearted and lovable. His outgoing personality was manifest in humor and great friendships. He found time to become active in St. Louis commerce as a member of the Athletic Club, the Propeller Club, and the Golden Eagle Club. A devout Catholic, he counted membership in the ranks of the Knights of Columbus and the Holy Name Society.

In a published eulogy, *The Waterways Journal* noted his passing: "As a steamboat man, Captain John had few equals in this century. As a man, he was upright and generous. As a friend, he was loyal and sincere. In his death, the river fraternity sustains a loss far above the ordinary."[241]

---

241 Meyer, "Excursion Steamboating," *The Waterways Journal,* citation. pg. 228.

IN THE WORDS OF CAPT. VERNE WALTER STRECKFUS (1895-1984)

The baby, the last of the litter (of Streckfus boys, that is): that's me, Verne Walter Streckfus. I was granted the moniker Verne in recognition of one of my father's first, memorable and most celebrated packet boats, the *Verne Swain*.

Like Roy and John, I primarily rotated service as captain of our vessels in New Orleans and St. Louis—and many tramping stops in the cities between the two, while our oldest brother, Joe, ran the company from St. Louis. In early years, I piloted our wooden excursion craft on the Upper Mississippi, including the Minneapolis/St. Paul and the Quad Cities.

Capt. Verne Walter Streckfus on the *J.S. Deluxe* (1934)
Murphy Library Special Collections/ ARC, University of Wisconsin–La Crosse.

Like my siblings, I was born in Rock Island, Illinois. On July 27, 1895, I came into this world, the eighth of nine children of the Commodore (John) and Theresa. Of all my family, I was blessed with the most durable physical makeup. [*Author's note: Verne passed on October 14, 1984; he started out in one century and darn near saw the conclusion of a second!*]

I was devoted to the river and to Streckfus steamers and continued working until 1981, at which time I was 86 and had spent more than 60 years at the maritime trade.

You have learned of the century of excursion steamboating launched by John Streckfus in 1885, carried on by my siblings and continued through our sons and daughters (and grandchildren).

There was no question that I was destined for the river. By the time I entered the scene, our father had built a solid customer following as owner of the *Freddie* and *Verne Swain*. The *City of Winona* (a.k.a. the *W.W.*) was added in 1896, one year after I was born.

The Acme Packet Co. fleet at that time were primarily packet boats focused on the transport of farm produce, sundry goods and, lastly, people. Packet commerce was the sole business of Acme until the *J.S.* became our greenfield excursion mothership.

VERNE: ESCAPE FROM THE COMMODORE

As the youngest son on board the J.S. sternwheeler, it was my duty to assume all the dirtiest, smelliest, and most unpleasant maritime chores. I was born five years before the 1900 millennial, a key year in Streckfus Steamers history. 1900 was the critical year when the *J.S.*, my dad's brand new, custom, and specially purposed excursion vessel, was launched from Jeffersonville, Indiana.

For every day of the excursion season my entire family, including my three sisters, lived on board the *J.S.* The Commodore wasted no time after the launch of the *J.S.* to put my brothers Joe, Roy, and John into non-stop action cleaning, painting, and polishing our spectacular new vessel.

We were not threatened with being keelhauled every day. However, the Commodore was a strict taskmaster and expected your best in every action you performed. My father was already 45 at the time of the vessel's christening; he suffered no fools and was quick to punish my brothers and me with the cane.

In the Words of Capt. Verne Walter Streckfus (1895–1984)

I believe it was the year 1905; I celebrated my 10th birthday in Vicksburg, Mississippi. A pandemic of yellow fever had so crippled New Orleans that our normal season there was declared unfeasible. Death hung over the Crescent City and the warnings the *J.S.* received from the NOLA health system were dire.

I remember Vicksburg as a grand and stately community. We made the most of our relocation and our sightseeing and moonlight excursions of the Vicksburg harbor were very well received. Yes, I really remember 1905.

What happened to ten-year old Verne, you ask? The Commodore's wrath!

It is true that I had been strictly warned by my brothers of the Commodore's fiery temper. Should the Commodore observe incompetence, slovenliness, or laziness among any member of the crew of the *J.S.*, his rage would be stoked and all hell would break loose. Tales of unfortunate crew members, verbally scarred and physically maimed, added to the mystique around the Commodore's wrath.

It was another Popcorn Verne day as I dutifully guided the kernels, oil, and salt into the noisy popping boiler. Making bushels of popcorn was my job and I took it seriously. As is natural while enjoying the amusements of the *J.S.*, our patrons were extremely partial to popcorn, and that kept me on my toes. When our afternoon sightseeing harbor trip had concluded, it was time to knuckle down for a thorough cleanup of my popcorn empire. This day was unexceptional, the weather delightful and the customers pleasant. What was the matter, then? My energy level was low and, after the last clean bucket was wiped and stored, I was ready for some shuteye.

Time, you ask? Well, our daily sightseeing cruises left the dock at 2:30 p.m. and returned at roughly 5:00 p.m. That gave me and the crew about three hours before the 8:00 p.m. Moonlight Music and Dance crowd would throng the gangway to board. So, I place my showdown with the Commodore at about 6:30. It was summer, and twilight was still hours away.

Popcorn Verne decided that a nap, albeit a short one, would be a just reward for a talented and industrious young man recovering from an afternoon of hard work. At this time, our *J.S.* patrons had collected their picnic baskets and personal items and disembarked. Except for the captains housed in the Pilothouse and texas on the top deck, the central two decks of the *J.S.* were bereft of customers, musicians, and deck crew. Of course, the mechanics and firemen who tended the boilers were active in the engine room, but there was no activity anywhere to speak of.

I decided to travel to the dancefloor and see if I could locate an appropriate spot upon which to become horizontal and inconspicuous. The musicians' bandstand was elevated and carpeted. How appealing was the grand piano and the hint of shade below! In a moment, Popcorn Verne was sound, sound asleep.

"I don't tolerate slackers!" So bellowed forth my father the Commodore. "I was looking for you by the popcorn stand and saw you slip away. I followed you here. What do I find? My youngest son, Verne, practicing Laziness 101!"

Shaking his fist in anger, the Commodore commanded: "Come over here son, so I can deliver you a solid taste of the cane! One you will remember, very well and for a very long time."

This is when a good son—like my brothers Joe, Roy, and John—would have acquiesced and taken a good caning from my father. But not Verne! I leaped from my somnolent crouch under the piano in such haste that I gained a large knot on my skull. Never mind, I thought: Escape!

The Commodore gave chase as I bolted down the dance floor to the stairs that led to the deck above. Here, a ten-year-old possesses a solid advantage in speed, quickness, and motivation. My mid-forties-age father was neither nimble, nor quick, but he too possessed strong motivation. As we raced from deck to deck, I tried out a variety of hiding places—closets, under stairs and chairs—only to have the Commodore's keen senses uncover each temporary lair. I had to run!

This game of "Popcorn Verne" mouse and "Commodore John" cat was surprising in its duration. "Surely," I thought, "my father will lose interest and permit me a quiet and diplomatic surrender over the family dinner." But, no!

In the Words of Capt. Verne Walter Streckfus (1895–1984)

Every good chase deserves a critical juncture, explosion, or switchback in the road.

Our moment came when I sought refuge in the Men's Restroom on the second deck. Seeking further distance from the Commodore, I entered and locked the men's toilet stall. Certainly, I was safe—I thought.

But no, a knock came to the door of the Gentlemen's W.C; I knew it was the Commodore.

Here is when the large toilet opening below the toilet seat provided salvation.

I hoisted myself above the opening and dropped down into the warm muddy waters of the Mississippi River below. It was only a relatively short drop and I had already developed strong swimming skills. I swam to the Vicksburg shore without incident. The Commodore was kind to me and never revisited the time when sleepy Popcorn Verne became Houdini.

VERNE'S SMOKE

The Streckfus family was worried about Verne. First, it was the slightly sour odor that hovered over the boy and his clothing. As time progressed, his mother, Theresa Streckfus, noticed Verne's loss of appetite and disturbingly gaunt appearance. He was still tending the popcorn station, but how much popcorn could he possibly consume? How could one justify the growing yellow stains on his fingers, lips, and teeth?

The Commodore concluded that Verne had not contracted a grave illness: the lad was becoming heavily addicted to nicotine. Verne may have been only a 14-year-old adolescent, but the evil tobacco weed was having its way with him. Smoking cigar butts was his pastime.

The power of tobacco was known at the turn of the 19th century when Rudyard Kipling penned his seminal poem on cigars ("Betrothed"). Kipling is strife torn: "For Maggie has written a letter to give me my choice between, The wee little whimpering Love and the great god Nick o' Teen."

Verne Streckfus had been seduced like Kipling: ". . . . a woman is only a woman, but a good Cigar is a Smoke."

Quietly, Verne's passion for tobacco had been stoked by the diabolical intersection of vices: unrivaled rare opportunity and outrageous and compelling value.

Master investor Warren Buffett once offered an illustration of how "cigar butt" thinking might be relevant: "If you buy a stock at a sufficiently low price, there will usually be some hiccup in the fortunes of the business that gives you a chance to unload at a decent profit, even though the long-term performance of the business may be terrible." I call this the 'cigar butt' approach to investing. A cigar butt found on the street (like those collected by young Verne Streckfus) that has only one puff left in it may not offer much of a smoke, but the "bargain purchase" will make that puff all profit.[242]

While sightseeing and enjoying the riverbanks and the flow of the Mississippi, tourists on the *J.S.* loved their cigars. Brother Roy searched and discovered that Verne had accumulated a large tin. It was no piggy bank, but it held a curated cache of discarded cigar butts that Verne had scrounged from the decks of the steamer. Let the record show that Verne's penchant for cigar stubs had been inspired by none other than the Commodore, his father.

Examining the history of tobacco and smoking, we learn that cigar smoking was quite popular on the Streckfus fleet of riverboats in the early 1900s. At the time, cigarette smoking had only a fledgling following, and Streckfus Steamers policy banned cigarette usage. Meanwhile gentlemen on the excursion craft were encouraged to puff on their cigars at will, with one important proviso: they must be smoking "Streckfus Stogies."

The Commodore recognized the inherent incendiary danger posed by a smoldering cigar butt (in the British vernacular a "dog end.") Streckfus

---

242 Warren E. Buffett, Chairman of the Board of Berkshire Hathaway Inc. Letter to Shareholders, March 2, 1990.

In the Words of Capt. Verne Walter Streckfus (1895–1984)

Stogies were rolled on deck of the *J.S.* by craftsmen who saw that these special cigars would quickly extinguish when left unattended.

It is not hard to envision that Verne's cigar butt hobby stemmed from a perfectly rational situation onboard the *J.S.*: Verne, as the lowest ranking deck hand on the vessel, was exquisitely suited to gather these tobacco discards. He just got carried away.

Over the years, the eldest brothers, Joe and Roy, were seldom seen without a cigar in hand. John was more a "fair weather" cigar smoker.

To complete the story, readers should know that young Verne received harsh punishment from the Commodore. In a public spectacle on board the *J.S.*, Verne was required to continuously puff on an oversized but low-quality cigar for an entire afternoon and evening. Folklore has it that Verne swore off cigars that day and never returned to the Stogie habit! And let the record show that Verne outlived his three brothers and left the world in 1984 at a well-seasoned 89.

MUSIC: MORE IN THE WORDS OF CAPT. JOSEPH STRECKFUS

Capt. Joseph Streckfus wrote in 1958 in his memoirs:[243]

I recall in the fall of [1920] at St. Louis when Fate Marable, Louis Armstrong and fellow musicians in the band had completed the summer season on the SS *Saint Paul* at St. Louis and were transferred to play on the steamer *Capitol*, which was enroute to New Orleans for the winter season.

This band, while at St. Louis on the *Saint Paul*, was the talk of St. Louis: All were good musicians for dancing. Had good rhythm, tempo and played jazz that was different.

Personally, I believed if this band played more variety, they could become the best band in New Orleans. I decided to go downriver on the *Saint Paul* and expected to return from Cape Girardeau [Missouri]. It was my hope that a few pieces could be rehearsed with the band in order to give them an idea, which they could perfect and rehearse each day on their way down the river to New Orleans.

At our first day's stop, we were to play Chester, Illinois, which called for a rehearsal on the way down, and [I] explained to the

---

243 Source: Streckfus Steamers family records.

THE STRECKFUS RIVERBOAT DYNASTY

musicians my object in making the trip was to possibly give them some ideas that were somewhat different from their music as played in St. Louis. I convinced them it was worth a trial.

[My] efforts at the first rehearsal didn't fare so well; they just couldn't get the idea, although they tried hard.

Our next stop was Cape Girardeau[244] and my wife and I started up the main street in Cape Girardeau. As we passed a shop with records and Victrola in the window, the idea came to me: Why not inquire if they have the records we have at home [that] we can buy and demonstrate to our orchestra what we are driving at?

Fortunately, the shop had the records, played by Art Hickman's band at the Palace Hotel in San Francisco: the first Victor Dance Music Records.[245]

We purchased the record "Avalon," which played one chorus in one key, then a few bars of modulation and into another key, playing the second chorus in that key, then a few bars of chord modulation and into another key.[246] That was the first record of its kind. We bought a Victrola and a repeater arrangement and some more records: "Love Nest" and "Young Man's Fancy," and all were delivered to SS *Capitol*.

We set the Victrola up and started playing the records, and soon the orchestra boys, who were napping on the texas, the deck above, heard dance music that they never heard before. They all came down. It wasn't long before we were in a rehearsal of these pieces by ear.

Louis Armstrong, with his trumpet his hand, came down alongside of the Victrola and would pick up on his trumpet the

---

244 Cape Girardeau, Missouri, generally shortened to "Cape," is located on the west bank 60 miles south of St. Genevieve and roughly 30 miles north of where the Ohio joins the Mississippi. Named for the French soldier Jean Baptiste de Girardot, who settled a La Louisiane trading post circa 1733.
245 Hickman played at the St. Francis Hotel in San Francisco. Also, the recordings Streckfus subsequently mentions here were published by the Columbia Graphophone Co.
246 The flip side of "Avalon" was "The Japanese Sandman."

Music: More in the Words of Capt. Joseph Streckfus

notes in the several chords in the modulation, giving the saxophone section their chords and, likewise, the brass their changes in chords. And by repeating over and over again, all chords were down pat, then playing the choruses in the different keys was easy. The other records were rehearsed likewise.

That evening, we had approximately 1,200 dancers and, when the band played "Avalon," they stopped the show. Folks crowded around the orchestra stand and applauded and applauded. They never had heard music like that. At Cairo, Illinois, the next night, we experienced the same grand reception of our music. Patrons just would not get off the boat—wanted more.

The next day, Louis rehearsed a trumpet solo. I believe it was "LaVeda," with Fate on the piano and Louis on the trumpet—[the] balance of [the] orchestra not playing. Louis Armstrong stood up alone and played his first trumpet solo accompanied with the piano. This was the first time. The applause and requests were outstanding. They repeated the number.

After that reception the band received at Cape Girardeau and Cairo, it was not hard for it to continue rehearsing and learning the music played by Hickman's band. That, I believe, was the start of the success of Louis Armstrong and Fate Marable.

The *Capitol* opened at New Orleans two weeks later, and it was not long before she was doing capacity business, due mostly to the wonderful dance music played, in the most beautiful dance hall afloat.[247]

In "A Floating Seminar; Louis Armstrong and Art Hickman's Orchestra" in *Vintage Jazz Mart* magazine, Bruce Vermazen cites Capt. Joe Streckfus's recollections of instructing the band on the style of the Hickman records.[248]

---

247 Source: Streckfus Steamers family records.
248 "A Floating Seminar; Louis Armstrong and Art Hickman's Orchestra," Bruce Vermazen, *Vintage Jazz Mart*.

One other aspect of Armstrong's later performances might stem partly from Captain Joe's imposition of the Hickman model on the Capitol band. At Armstrong's feet in the photos of that band lies a slide trumpet with a slide whistle leaning against it, presumably his doubling instruments.... What led him to take up the rather less glamorous slide whistle again in 1920, ultimately leading to his beautiful playing...? Could it have been Captain Joe's Hickman seminar? Hickman played slide whistle on a number of his orchestra's records... Hickman, however, can't "feel the positions so beautiful," so his playing is painfully off pitch and amateurish; the pupil once again far surpasses his teacher.

Captain Joe's interventions in 1919 and 1920 were apparently not his last. Baby Dodds remembered years later that his and Armstrong's resignations from the band, probably at the end of the 1921 summer season, were precipitated by Streckfus, through Marable, ordering the band, once again, to change the way they played. Dodds was irked by an order to play in "toddle time," using four beats to a measure where Dodds thought two were appropriate, apparently to facilitate dancing of the toddle, a bouncing variant of the fox trot that was very big in 1921, as well as "delightfully easy and restful," in the words of Arthur Murray....

Armstrong was tasked with something unspecified: "Louis was also to play differently from what he had been used to ... and couldn't do what they wanted him to do either." Armstrong might well have feared that his resignation would put a major dent in his income, since ... he was making more than twice as much on the Streckfus boats as he had in Kid Ory's band. Breaking his shackles was obviously worth a lot to him. But he may have gained more than money and the beginning of fame on the boats, as he returned to New Orleans with the ability to read dance orchestrations, a new approach to second-cornet parts, a new confidence in the slide whistle, and the freedom to grow in his own direction.

Music: More in the Words of Capt. Joseph Streckfus

John Chilton wrote in *Ride, Red, Ride: The Life of Henry 'Red' Allen*:[249]

Captain Joe Streckfus took a keen, if, at times, dictatorial interest in the music that was played by Fate Marable's Band, even sending away for orchestrations of tunes he felt the public wanted to hear. He also designated the tempo, insisting that the St. Louis dancers liked their music faster than the New Orleans patrons. Looking back to the 1920s, he said in 1958, "St. Louis tempo was 20 beats per minute faster than New Orleans."

. . . Discipline for the musicians was strict, both on and off the bandstand, and though the Streckfus Brothers were generally respected, their word was law. Marable simply acquiesced to the regime. While he could rehearse a band expertly, he was not particularly interested in fostering improvisation and once an arrangement had been mastered he was happy to repeat it without variation for the rest of the season. Throughout his long career Marable only ever recorded two titles—in 1924 as Fate Marable's Society Syncopators, and the overall results illustrate that Marable led a dance band and not a jazz group.

Referencing Chilton as well as other researchers' work, Dennis Owsley wrote in *City of Gabriels: The History of Jazz in St. Louis, 1895–1973*:[250]

It is apparent from these descriptions that while many of the excursion boats had Marable and others as the leader of the bands, the real bandleader was Captain John Streckfus. Streckfus dictated the tempo and duration of tunes. His crew timed tunes and counted tempos from a place above the dance floor to make certain that

---

[249] *Ride, Red and Ride: The Life of Henry "Red" Allen* by John Chilton (London & New York: Continuum; Revised ed. 2000), quoted on pg. 20 of *City of Gabriels* by Dennis Owsley (St. Louis: Reedy Press, 2006).

[250] Dennis Owsley, *City of Gabriels: The History of Jazz in St. Louis, 1895–1973* (St. Louis: Reedy Press, 2006) pg. 20.

Streckfus's instructions were followed. Transgressions to these rules often led to the firing or the fining of musicians. This practice continued until the last Streckfus boat stopped having bands to entertain customers. It did not matter whether the band or the audience was black or white.

Fate Marable also was very strict with his musicians, often firing them for small transgressions to his rules. Nevertheless, many black musicians thought of Marable's bands as a "finishing school."

Fate Marable's Capitol Revue Band, 1919 (left to right): Henry Kimball, Fate Marable, Boyd Atkins, Johnny St. Cyr, David Jones, Norman Mason, Louis Armstrong, Norman Brashear, and Warren "Baby" Dodds.
Courtesy of the Dave Thomson Collection at Steamboats.com

The Streckfus Steamer Company played a large part in the development of jazz, operating excursion boats out of both New Orleans and St. Louis. Other companies also operated excursion

Music: More in the Words of Capt. Joseph Streckfus

boats. When Streckfus hired the Paducah, Kentucky, pianist Fate Marable in 1908, it set the stage for the arrival of jazz music in St. Louis. Marable brought a band of jazz musicians from New Orleans to St. Louis in 1919. There is no question that the musicians in Marable's band were jazz musicians, but was the music played on the boats jazz?[251]

---

251 Owsley, *City of Gabriels,* pg. 17.

PART VI

Jazz & the Streckfus Steamboats

You'll never be able to swing any better than you already know how until you learn to read [music]. Then you'll swing in ways you never thought of before.

—Louis Armstrong, recalling advice from early bandmate David Jones

AS TOLD BY VERNE STRECKFUS, 1960

On September 22, 1960, Verne Streckfus, then 65 years old, was interviewed by Richard "Dick" Allen onboard the *President* while docked at the foot of Canal Street in New Orleans at what was then Eads Plaza (it was demolished in 1964 for construction of the International Trade Mart, now known as the World Trade Center).

A jazz enthusiast who became one of the music's leading historians, Allen began recording interviews in 1958 with pioneers and individuals influential in the migration of the style, as part of his master's thesis at Tulane University. The oral histories were foundational in the development of the William Ransom Hogan Jazz Archive at Tulane. Between 1958 and 1980, Allen and jazz historian William Russell "conducted 2,000 reels of taped interviews, the largest collection of jazz oral history in existence."[252]

The following first-person narrative is based on what Streckfus told Allen in the 1960 interview:

> A meaningful element of my family's success with excursion riverboats was our love of music and improvisational bands. All of us in the Streckfus family were musical: Roy and I played violin;

---

252 https://64parishes.org/entry/dick-allen

THE STRECKFUS RIVERBOAT DYNASTY

John and Joe, the piano. My father, the Commodore, was an accomplished violinist and would often join an impromptu band session on board. As entertainers, we were always scouting for the best musicians and the most innovative bands. Great music performed on the grand ballrooms of our wooden and steel steamers was a terrific draw.

Live music is a hallmark of Streckfus boats. Our first group on the *J.S.* in 1903 was a trio led by a black man. Charlie Mills was the finest piano player in the business in the early days. As a concert-level pianist, Mills toured Europe and played a command performance for Queen Victoria's grandson, Prince Arthur of Connaught, upon his marriage.

After his passing, Mills's remains were returned to his home town of Quincy, Illinois, for burial with honors as an outstanding citizen.

Mills played on the boat four or five years; it was Mills who broke in Fate Marable, an unknown piano player from Paducah, Kentucky, on calliope. At the time, Mills, the original calliope player on the boats, ranked as the best on the Mississippi.

Marable's calliope lessons on the riverboat were staged between towns for two or three hours, so that the piercing sounds wouldn't disturb the public. Marable was a world-class piano player who worked on the Streckfus steamers up and down the river for many years. Marable was first to employ Louis Armstrong in the early 1920s before a largely white audience; the band was called the "Cotton Pickers."

The Streckfus company was in the process of converting its four freight and transportation [packet] boats to excursion-only with eight- to nine-piece bands, such as are favored by the *President* and *Admiral* today. The New Orleans to St. Louis [and sometimes to St. Paul] steamers were the *J.S.* (1903–1910), the *Sidney* (1910–1929), the *Capitol* (1920–1940) and the *President* (1933–present).

As Told by Verne Streckfus, 1960

The bands on those boats were employed for only the four or five months of the summer season. Henry "Red" Allen Jr., a cornet talent out of Algiers, Louisiana, worked with Marable on the *Capitol*. "Baby" Dodds, who also worked with Marable on the *Capitol* was an exceptional drummer. [George] "Pops" Foster too, though unable to sight-read, was a heavyweight bass player anyway. Davy Jones played mellophone with Marable at the same time Armstrong was in the band; there hasn't been a mellophone player of Jones's caliber on the boats since.

The dancers on the *Sidney* liked "straight" music—fox trots and the like—and our bands played stock arrangements, "music as it was published not distorted by improvisation." Couples who danced on the *Capitol* liked the same kind of music; the bands would play some rumbas and other special rhythms, but the floor wouldn't fill until the "pretty" music was played again. Here in 1960, our Streckfus riverboat patrons still like good, danceable music—romantic music, but with good rhythm; it must have good rhythm.

Most of the musicians on the boats played by ear. Louis Armstrong couldn't sight-read musical sheet music at all when he first joined the band; however, he would learn a piece by hearing it played through once. Armstrong was very bashful at first; he had never played for white folks before he played on the *Capitol*.

My father John and brothers Joe and Roy went to Economy Hall, where Armstrong was working with Kid Ory and King Oliver. Playing a cornet loaned to him by Ory, Armstrong was recruited to Marable's band on the *Sidney*. Folklore has it that Satchmo hadn't ever stood up and taken a solo until one night at Caruthersville, Missouri, when the lights were turned down low. Louis may have been quite nervous when he was told to step forward and solo. The audience applause was deafening, and Armstrong was so elated that he wanted to do more solo improvisation.

Marable was featured on calliope and on organophone, which was like a calliope, except that it used air instead of steam and was not so loud.

By a mile, Tony Catalano of Davenport had the best band on the upper part of the river; Stacy and Bix Beiderbecke were featured working the Davenport and Burlington routes with Catalano's band in the summer months only.

Paul Mares and Leon Roppolo, who had been working New Orleans cabarets and in The Rhythm Kings at the Friars Inn in Chicago, joined a Streckfus steamer out of Evansville, Indiana, for a summer season. Santo Pecora and Turk Murphy appeared in a special concert aboard the *President* in 1955. A great clarinetist, Alfred Williams, played on the boat with master violinist, bandleader, and composer [Armand] "A.J." Piron. Piron is credited with "I Wish I Could Shimmy Like My Sister Kate" (1922) and "Purple Rose of Cairo" (1920).

Irving Fazola and his brother Blue Prestopnik played on the boat with Earl Dantin, who had his own band for a couple of years. Admittedly, I didn't think Fazola was very good at first, but I changed my mind quickly. Multi-talented Fats Pichon developed his skills as a pianist, singer, and bandleader on our boats; Pichon credits his diverse musical talents to serving as an understudy to A.J. Piron.

It was not unusual when *(sic)* our musicians played the calliope while wearing a raincoat *(sic)* to deflect the steam spray and putting *(sic)* cotton in their ears, as protection against the extreme volume. Loudness could be controlled by adjusting a regulator valve but the high-pitched instrument shriek is unavoidable.

Good calliope players practice on the 28 keys of a piano which correspond to the 28 keys of a calliope; when they have worked out a good-sounding arrangement, they play it on the calliope. Our flagship boat in St. Louis, the *Admiral*, has a calliope; our afternoon player, a good pianist, gives calliope concerts which are well attended.

Marable had charge of getting men for the band; in the case of Louis Armstrong, however, the Streckfuses knew at once that they wanted him. He was so shy then that they had to go up on South Rampart Street, where he lived, to escort him to the boat.

A Russian maestro, who was director of music at the Saenger Theatre for years, was hired to fine-tune the band. We Streckfuses didn't want to radically alter its style, but we also encouraged the band to play waltzes and other pieces a bit more gracefully. The Russian taught them how and their performances were very well received.

Dewey Jackson played on the *Saint Paul* for several years after Marable transferred his talent and band to the *Capitol*. Jackson was a local and his band was homegrown St. Louis. He was a top-shelf cornet player, but not a very good bandleader.

The best colored band from St. Louis was led by another cornet player, Charlie Creath. Creath's band alternated between the two boats (*Saint Paul* and *J.S. Deluxe*) operating out of St. Louis in the summer. His band compared favorably with any band in St. Louis.

Jules Buffano led a white band, which played on the [*J.S.*] *Deluxe* boat in the summer; he is now with Jimmie Durante. Ralph Williams of Chicago also was bandleader on the *Deluxe* boat, while a colored band worked summers on the cheaper boat, the *Saint Paul*. The *Deluxe* boat's prices were high end: $1.25 and up.

J. Burroughs Lovingood, piano player, who now lives in Washington, D.C., spoke recently with my brother Roy about returning to play the *President*'s calliope. Lovingood was the extra piano player with Fate Marable when two dueling pianos were featured on either end of the bandstand. Lovingood's style was more flowery than Marable's, who was more rhythmic. To my knowledge, Lovingood/Marable were the first two-piano team with a dance band.

Pops Foster worked on the boat for years; we bought him his first bass "of any consequence." Johnny Dodds, brother of Baby Dodds, was a superb clarinet player; the Dodds brothers, unlike earlier jazzmen, were part of a new jazz generation that was educated to read music. Fate Marable could read; his mother was a piano teacher in Paducah, Kentucky. Before Marable enforced music education among his musicians, the band members didn't have to read, as Marable would play the tune or their parts on the piano. By rote, they would learn that way. The non-readers may have had sheet music in front of them, but "it didn't mean anything."

None of our bands recorded when they were working on a Streckfus steamer. We did discourage it for commercial reasons. For another reason, the amplification systems in those days weren't very good. The first system used on our steamers was a battery-powered outfit, made by Western Electric; the next one, same maker, was part battery and part external power. The *Capitol* was equipped with an amplification system in 1920, the first such system in the city of New Orleans.

I insist that drums should always be heard—if the dancers can't hear the drums, they can't dance. The bass should be heard, too, and a piano player with a good left hand is an asset. The Streckfuses don't much interfere with the playing of our bands now, although we used to suggest changes (personnel, arrangements) within the band; if the band doesn't play well, they are not hired again.

I am fond of the band currently performing on the *President*, Phil Zito's orchestra. The lineup of Zito's band includes Mike Lala, trumpet; Hank Kmen, clarinet and saxophone (and a history teacher at Tulane); Leland Bennett, clarinet and saxophone (music teacher); Henry Gustine, piano (music teacher); Pat Easterling, bass; Phil Zito, drums and band leader.

As Told by Verne Streckfus, 1960

I like Jan Garber and Guy Lombardo and it is my opinion that Zito's band sounds better than the music on Garber's latest recording.

The beat bands of recent years have played some rock-and-roll numbers, and rock-and-roll bands have been used infrequently, but that type music *(sic)* doesn't please the bulk of the boat's customers. The boat has built up its business with "straight" music, catering to people in their 20s and older. These days our patrons on the *President* don't want kids, i.e., teenagers, as regular customers; the loud rock-and-roll music they prefer drives away our older, more established, customers.

On the recording front, I am a fan of "Frankie and Johnny" on the record Fate Marable created on the OKeh label.[253] I understand that Dewey Jackson's "Capitol Blues" recording is a tribute to our SS *Capitol*.[254] I want to point out that Eugene Sedric (with Fats Waller for several years) was a very good saxophone and clarinet player who also worked with Fate Marable's band on our vessels.

Charlie Creath, who played on the *Saint Paul* in St. Louis, emphasized rhythm. Business on our large steamer was brisk because Creath's band played the best music in town. In later years, Creath's lip went bad, but he kept a good second cornet player. Therefore, the bandleader minimized his play to only his best numbers that the people loved.

---

253 The recording was made in 1924 in New Orleans. Members of Marable's "Society Syncopaters" band on the recording were Sidney Desvignes and Amos White, trumpet; Harvey Lankford, trombone; Norman Mason and Bert Bailey, clarinet and alto sax; Walter "Foots" Thomas, tenor sax; Fate Marable, piano; Willie Foster, banjo and guitar; Henry Kimball, bass; Zutty Singleton, drums. https://www.youtube.com/watch?v=bpZyMrSNd3c

254 The song was recorded in St. Louis in 1926. It was co-written by J.J. Johnson. In the recording, Dewey Jackson is on cornet; Albert Snaer, trumpet; William Luper, trombone; William Thornton Blue, clarinet and alto sax; Cliff Cochran, alto sax; Willie Humphrey, clarinet and tenor sax; Burroughs Lovingood, piano; Pete Robinson, banjo; Pops Foster, string bass; and Floyd Campbell, drums. https://www.20sjazz.com/videos/dewey-jackson/capitol-blues.html

Creath's musicians were good but not outstanding; he had trained them to play for him, and they wouldn't have been good for anyone else. I was surprised to learn recently that Creath had moved to Chicago and dropped out of professional performances entirely.

I recall that when Creath played blues on an evening cruise he could really rock the crowd. Neither Creath nor Dewey Jackson used mutes much; Jackson, a loud player, featured himself quite a bit. Excessive loudness was one of the drawbacks of the Jackson band.

A.J. Piron was the only violinist on the boat, except Charlie Herzog, who played on the *J.S.* in the early days. Before electrical amplification, the violin couldn't be heard above the band; if it could be heard, the band had to be so soft that people weren't able to dance to it.

Since we expanded operations in 1920, Streckfus summer excursion boats operated in the upper Mississippi River as far as St. Paul and on the upper Ohio River as far as Pittsburgh. Our steamers would move from town to town, remaining a day or two at each stop; when they reached the terminus (e.g., St. Paul), they would remain about 10 days.

Then the tramping protocol would be adopted, and our excursion vessels would move up and down the rivers all summer long, primarily focused on the same territory. The towns where we stopped were about 30 miles apart; they *(sic)* would run a day excursion and a night excursion, then move to the next town. The excursions were advertised in local newspapers, on posters and through organizations, mostly women's clubs, and mostly in schools. The day trips with such groups aboard would go from one town to another; the night trips didn't stop anywhere and were only for romance under the moonlight.

New Orleans is our winter home port; there has been at least one Streckfus boat in New Orleans during the winter for the past

As Told by Verne Streckfus, 1960

57 years. Years ago, we would leave New Orleans during the summer, as there was no business of any volume to be had. It may be surprising, but a sweltering summer before air conditioning did not work as tourists didn't come to New. Orleans. Thank God our governor, Huey Long, had good roads and bridges built in the state. With New Orleans growing as a tourist destination, our summer business on the boat is now equal to the winter business.[255]

Author's Note: Huey Pierce Long Jr. (August 30, 1893–September 10, 1935) was governor of Louisiana from 1928–1932. Long was assassinated in 1935.

---

[255] September 22, 1960, Interview with Verne Streckfus on board the *President* at the foot of Canal Street. Interview by Richard Allen. Edited by Arthur L. Smith.

THE MONUMENTAL INFLUENCE OF LOUIS ARMSTRONG

No one epitomizes "jazz" and its influence on American music more than Louis Armstrong. Armstrong's immeasurable talent and irrepressible personality dominated the first half of twentieth century jazz. From the early New Orleans years of tramping the Mississippi, Satchmo (also "Satch" and "Pops") went on light up St. Louis, Chicago, New York, and the international music world. Armstrong's final days were spent in Queens, New York.

We first think of Armstrong as a virtuoso cornet player. His complete body of work showcases a public figure of immense talent as a singer, bandleader, and icon.

A young trombonist from Texas named Jack Teagarden had a memorable first encounter with Armstrong. Standing on the New Orleans levee one moonlit evening, Teagarden heard the distant sound of a cornet from across the water. After a moment, he could identify the vague form of an excursion boat gliding toward him through the mist. The sound, growing louder as the boat neared the shore, was unlike anything he had ever heard before. It was Louis Armstrong, he remembered, ". . . descending from the sky like a god."[256]

---

[256] Ward and Burns, *Jazz: A History,* pg. 76.

Armstrong was a masterful accompanist and ensemble player and raised the bar musically for all who came after him.

According to literary critic Harold Bloom, "The two great American contributions to the world's art, in the end, are Walt Whitman and, after him, Armstrong and jazz. . . . If I had to choose between the two, ultimately, I wouldn't. I would say that the genius of this nation at its best is indeed Walt Whitman and Louis Armstrong."[257]

With his instantly recognizable rich, gravelly voice, Armstrong was also an influential singer and skillful improviser, bending the lyrics and melody of a song and peppering in a unique "scat" style. In 1964, he recorded his biggest-selling record, "Hello, Dolly!," originally sung by Carol Channing for the Broadway hit show. Armstrong's version remained on the Hot 100 for 22 weeks, longer than any other record produced that year, and went to No. 1—making him, at 62, the oldest person ever to do so. Surprisingly, Armstrong's "Hello Dolly!" dislodged the Beatles.

Armstrong tended to perspire under bright lights and he was seldom seen without a white handkerchief, mopping his brow. Pops had 19 top ten records, including "Stardust," "What a Wonderful World," "When the Saints Go Marching In," "Dream a Little Dream of Me," "Ain't Misbehavin'," "You Rascal You" and "Stompin' at the Savoy."

"We Have All the Time in the World" was featured in the 1969 James Bond film, *On Her Majesty's Secret Service*.

Armstrong's legacy is founded in jazz and the Streckfus story benefits from the association with the great man. Armstrong returned to the St. Louis riverfronts on numerous occasions over the years and often was enticed to pick up his horn on the *Admiral*. One memorable visit was on the summer solstice in 1963.

Satchmo was his jovial self and spent an afternoon reminiscing with Capt. Roy Streckfus about the Marable days when he performed aboard the *Sidney*, *Saint Paul*, and *J.S. Deluxe*. The *St. Louis Globe-Democrat* posed this

---

257 Ward and Burns, *Jazz: A History*, pg. 146.

The Monumental Influence of Louis Armstrong

St. Louis Globe-Democrat, June 22, 1963
Left to right: Captain Roy Streckfus, Captain Bill Streckfus and Louis Armstong

question to Armstrong: "How does it feel to be back?" (Armstrong and his All-Stars were heading a major musical event on the *Admiral* that benefited the St. Louis Symphony.)

In his trademark gravelly voice Armstrong replied, "Man, it feels good, real good. It brings back so many beautiful memories. The all-day excursions. The crowds comin' on with their picnic baskets."[258]

Trumpet legend Wynton Marsalis said:

Louis Armstrong's overwhelming message is one of love.

Louis Armstrong (circa 1925)
Hogan Jazz Archive, Special Collections, Howard-Tilton Memorial Library. Tulane University

---

258 *St. Louis Globe Democrat*, June 22, 1963.

THE STRECKFUS RIVERBOAT DYNASTY

When you hear his music, it's of joy.... He was just not going to be defeated by the forces of life. And those forces visit all of us ... My great-great-grandmother used to say that "life has a board for every behind" and it's a board just fit to yours, so maybe your board is not going to work on someone else's behind. And when it's your turn ... that paddle is going to be put on your booty and it's going to hurt as bad as it can hurt. And Louis Armstrong is there to tell you after you get that paddling, "It's all right, son."[259]

Louis Armstrong, in His Own Words, edited by Thomas Brothers and published in 1999, contains many of Satchmo's letters and other archives that had not been previously published. A prolific writer, the legendary musician used apostrophes and underlining (converted to italics by Brothers for the book) and other punctuation marks unconventionally, as forms of emphasis:

I can remember *twice'* that I actually went to the pawn shop, and picked up some Loot on my *horn*. The first time was, to play *Cotch*, and to be around in the company of those good ol' old time Hustlers and Gamblers. I've already explained, the way they played with 3 cards, and, which, fascinated me—no end. I was working on the excursion boat—the Steamer *Sidney*—for some real fine white people' the Streckfus family. They were *real Groove* people. And love music, the way that *I did*.

"Especially" *that great man'* Captain Joe. He was really on the Ball. He went in for the finest in 'Jazz.' He understood it. And, whenever he was on the *mound'* he'd pull up a chair at our rehearsals' and *watch' look* and listen, very carefully' to every note' which came out of our instruments. *And'* Oh *'Brother* if those notes weren't, right, or those *Chords'* etc.' that's when you'd hear from him, and

---
[259] Ward and Burns, *Jazz: A History*, pg. x.

how. As for me' 'I could not play anything decent whenever I saw Capt. Joe angry. I think I am justified in saying—not only was I sort of' on' edge, when Capt. Joe was on the war path—but, there were lots others, of the Crew and Band' who shuttered the same as I. They were *Fate Marable*, Colored boy' whom the *Streckfus* Brothers, picked up on' ever since he was the size of *Sugar Child Robertson*. They *'Reared' 'Fate*. P.S. I'd—rather' my' 'way of explaining it—They' *Raised'* Fate Marable.

They discovered Fate in Paducah, Kentucky. Fate learned to play the *"Calliope"* very good. Of course, I am not trying to make myself any *too* "younger than Fate. Although, he is older than I. But—I can easily remember "Fate playing the *Calliope* on the Steamer *Sidney* when I was a boy' Selling Newspapers. I used to go out to the foot of Canal Street—out there by the L. +'N' Station—and Just sit there listening to Fate Marable 'Swing those Calliope Keys down to a low gravy. And—not with the slightest intention or knowledge that I would be, featured trumpet in his famous orchestra. It just goes to show you—it's a *small* and beautiful world.

Getting back to Captain Joe Streckfus. Not only was the musicians, waiters and checkroom folks perked up when ever he was around, but there were his devoted Brothers—Mr. Vern—Roy—John,—they also, would really get in there and really do the thing Right.

There were also a Mr. Lax, whom the Streckfus Boys raised. He was *First Mate*. And, a *Darn Good* one. It was really a great day' in St. Louis, Mo., on the Steamer *Saint Paul* the day' Captain Joe Streckfus married Lola, the young Cashier on the boat. As surprised as everyone were there were a lot of rejoicing—and everyone had a good time. Even we musicians.

They (Capt. Joe + Lola)—sure did have a lot of children. And "Ol" capt., my boy—He wasn't anybody's "Chippy. He was a big, well built' fine man' not too fat. In fact, he wasn't fat at all. His

THE STRECKFUS RIVERBOAT DYNASTY

Physique was something to marvel at. And fine—strong frame' would' sorta' make 'one say *"Gee'* I wish that I was as healthy looking as "that man."

Later on, we'd talk about Capt. Joe again. Because, in his later years, *he* and his family made a trip, all the way from St. Louis to New York to hear me play. He loved the way that I played the trumpet. *Yessir*" 'Capt. Joe was a real Jazz fan at heart. Which, to me, was really *"Somphn."* When, Joe ["King"] Oliver came from Chicago down to St. Louis to hear me play the *trumpet*, and spend *four* days of his vacation with me as my personal Guest, he [Capt. Joe] got a big boot out of watching Joe Oliver's expressions and admiration, as he watch me *play*.

And the big baskets of *lunch'* my *landlady* would fix for me, during those' all day excursions—I would not get any of it. I would turn the whole basket over to Joe. And with two Cups of Coffee and a tin bucket full of real Cold Ice Water, he would really go to town.

Honest, I used to love to see him eat. Pappa Joe, as I used to call him, as far back at 1917. He would be actually enjoying himself *So* well, as he would Devour my lunch—which was consist of 4' porkchops, a bowl of steamed corn, a bowl of rice, a half dozen slices of bread, well buttered, 2 *Hunk'* Slices of plain pound Cake' (P.S.) I Just *love* plain pound cake. Anyway" Joe Oliver cleaned the whole basket, of food to my *dee'*light. I bought a couple of ham sandwiches for myself, and was *tickled pink.*

Ever since the first time I met Joe Oliver, he always play the part of something real precious in my life. He always seemed just a little different from anyone, I had met. And, as a *kid*, I couldn't help but notice the difference in the kindness of *Mr. Joe'* as I once called him. All the rest of the musicians around New Orleans (including "Bunk Johnson") at the time when I was a kid' were full of "you "*know what*" and they never had time. They' just couldn't be *bothered, that's* all.

My step father Mr. Gabe, in my estimation, came very close to Joe Oliver, with his kindness to an 'up and coming youngster.— *Gabe*" Oh' I just *love* that name. And—I—being a *Trumpet Player*, and heard all about *Ol* Gabriel so many times, just makes me think that I' know *Gabriel personally*." Hmm—*silly Boy Satch*."

"MOVIN' ON UP"

In Thomas Brothers's *Louis Armstrong's New Orleans* (2006), Brothers describes Armstrong's time on the boats further in the chapter "Movin' On Up."

Louis Armstrong (1931)
Hogan Jazz Archive, Special Collections, Howard-Tilton Memorial Library. Tulane University

When Armstrong accepted Fate Marable's offer to play with his riverboat orchestra, he was motivated by a push and by a pull. The push came from his unhappy marriage to a woman named Daisy (formerly Daisy Parker). They had wed in early 1918, and there were problems from the start. Daisy was a rough prostitute— "the prettiest and the baddest whore in Gretna, Louisiana," said Armstrong—and some of May Ann's friends did not approve of the match.

But May Ann stayed out of it: "I can't live his life. He's my boy and if that's what he wants to do, that's that," Armstrong remembered her saying. The newlyweds fought often, and Daisy quickly discovered a point of real vulnerability: She could get him particularly upset by hitting him in the mouth, thereby jeopardizing his musical career. The last straw was when she shredded his Stetson hat with a razor. The offer from Marable started to look pretty good. Daisy was certainly not the last woman to hear from Armstrong that his horn comes first.

Marable liked to scout out the dance halls in New Orleans and the Big 25. He heard Armstrong with [Kid] Ory's band at Cooperator's Hall and offered him the job. Armstrong was only seventeen years old and reluctant to leave home. Several offers came his way during his last few years in the city, including one from Fletcher Henderson who was in town accompanying Ethel Waters, but he was too *nervous* to accept them. He had heard stories about the treacheries of traveling jobs, stories about not getting paid and ending up stranded in some desolate place that was hostile to African Americans. The initial job with Marable was less risky because it was a tethered departure: as everyone could see, the Streckfus brothers' excursion boat regularly left its dock at the beginning of Canal Street and regularly returned later that night, right on schedule.

The pull to take this job was that it could help him move forward in the music business. "I jumped at the opportunity, because I thought it was an advancement towards my musical career," he wrote some thirty-five years later. "Because Fate's band had to read, and they *did* read music, perfectly. And Ory's band didn't. It was very fine (I thought) to be in Ory's band—but being in Fate Marable's band meant an advancement to me, a youngster who had big things in mind as far as music's concerned."

He told Daisy that if he didn't take the job he might be stuck in New Orleans forever. In other words, he recognized the career limitations of playing only by ear. He knew a few musicians who had made dramatic progress in army bands. Cornetist Punch Miller rehearsed in one four hours a day and learned the tricks of rhythmic notation, fancy fingering, and good intonation. Armstrong must have had similar expectations for the riverboat job. He returned the cornet Ory had purchased for him, since he had not finished paying for it, and Captain Johnny Streckfus purchased a new one for him.

The *Dixie Belle* was based in New Orleans, and from November through April it took two-and-a-half hour trips on Friday, Saturday, and Sunday nights. *[Author's note:* Armstrong . . . the *Sidney.]* Before departure the band played on the wharf to advertise the event, just as they would at a dance hall. Marable had previously hired the Eagle Band for this job, but it failed because the players could not read music. The new band was named the "Jazz Syncopators," later changed to "Fate Marable and his Jazz Maniacs."

In May of 1919 the program shifted northward. Armstrong was once asked when he had first left New Orleans, and he answered 1919, thinking back, no doubt, to the train ride he took from New Orleans to St. Louis, where the Streckfus operation was based. David Jones, the mellophone player, was assigned to look out for him. "One of those dicty guys, very much erect in everything he did—a little too erect, I'd say," was Armstrong's reading of Jones.

Jones had traveled with circuses and other road shows, so it fell to him to escort homeboy Louis safely to St. Louis. Jones was not pleased with this assignment. "He stood by me as if I was just another colored boy going to some other direction and he didn't know me at all," remembered Armstrong. The two eventually became friends, Louis nicknaming him "Bre'r Jones." Their train ride included a stop in Paducah, Kentucky, Marable's hometown, for the purpose of joining the musicians union, which had not been a possibility in New Orleans. When they arrived in St. Louis, they transferred their membership to the local union there.

The work routine in St. Louis was one of longer excursions, the boat leaving at 9:00 in the morning and returning at 6:00 in the evening. After a dinner break they played for the "moonlight ride" at 8:30. "In the four months of summer in 1919," said Pops Foster, "most of the time we worked from eight in the morning until eleven-thirty at night. That was long playing." They also took a few extended trips up the river, stopping by Alton, Illinois; Keokuk, Ft. Madison, Des Moines, and Dubuque, Iowa; Louisiana, Missouri, and, in August, all the way up to Red Wing and St. Paul, Minnesota. Marable's band started playing on the steamer *Sidney*, which had a capacity of eight hundred patrons, and then moved over to the *Saint Paul*, a much bigger boat that held thirty-five hundred.

The boats were, of course, segregated. A couple of years earlier, Captain Streckfus had originally hired Marable to lead a white band. (Johnny St. Cyr claimed that Marable, whose Negro mother was a maid on the boats, was actually Streckfus's illegitimate son, which might explain this experiment of an inverted racial hierarchy.) This new African-American band with Armstrong, Dodds, St. Cyr, and Foster was not "allowed to mingle with the guests . . . Just play that good music for them, the same as we did in New Orleans and all points 'south,'" wrote Armstrong dryly.

People in small towns [had] never before seen African-American musicians dressed up playing European instruments, and many of them simply stood and stared—or worse. "At first, we ran into a lot of ugly moments while we were on the band stand," Armstrong wrote, "such as 'Come on thar, black boy, etc.'" But the next time the boat came into town, the people were more relaxed and started dancing. Expectations of the musicians were high and discipline was severe. Baby Dodds returned to the boat drunk one night and the boss tied him to a post, threatening to horsewhip him.

Armstrong's 2006 New Orleans narrative gives additional color to his volatile relationship with Marable.

Armstrong had been frank with Marable about his inability to read, and it is hard to imagine that Marable didn't know that already, since he knew his way around New Orleans. St. Cyr, Dodds, and Foster all joined the band without reading skills too, so it was clear that Marable was willing to hire obvious talent and work with it. He had learned one important lesson from his failed experience with the Eagle Band: now he mixed readers and nonreaders together.

In the beginning, Joe Howard, the first chair cornetist, played the lead melody for Armstrong, who memorized it and added a harmony part. The procedure worked so well that a few of the musicians thought Armstrong was actually reading parts; it wasn't until Howard got sick and Armstrong was expected to take over the first cornet part that they realized he couldn't read. A concerted effort was brought to bear upon the seventeen-year-old's skills. Bre'r Jones worked with him on the top deck of the boat for ninety minutes every day on divisions and phrasing, and Joe Howard continued to help too.

Armstrong said that Marable had hired him because of his tone: "He like the way I played. My tone, and the way I could catch on." The big, fat, round—no peashooter!—confident sound that would come to be admired all over the world was in place, or at least nearly so.

"I was piling up all kinds of experiences, that an ambitious kid usually dreams of. So Fate made me a featured man in his Orchestra. And Oh, [what a] thrill to hear those fine applause from the customers."

He [Armstrong] was the only one who took solos. He was certainly not brought on the boat to impress midwestern white patrons with the improvisational style that would begin to be documented on recordings during the mid-1920s. "We played strictly by music," said Baby Dodds.

THE STRECKFUS RIVERBOAT DYNASTY

Yet it is clear that the band eventually did bring a distinctive New Orleanian sound to these towns along the river. Pops Foster said that "the *Saint Paul* was known as the rough boat where they played jazz. The *Capitol* was known as a clean boat where they played sweet music." According to Armstrong, even dicty [chiefly in Black usage: snobby; pretentious] David Jones could swing and improvise. The band did not have the musicians to practice collective improvisation, and it is very unlikely that the Streckfus brothers would have been interested in that anyway. But with the high-level uptown rhythm section of St. Cyr, Foster, and Dodds and with Armstrong, there was plenty of rhythmic drive and swing.

The Streckfus brothers were firmly in control of musical production. "You played music to suit them, not the public," Foster remarked, and it may have been the first time the New Orleanians had encountered such strong intervention. It was certainly the first time they encountered a heavy schedule of rehearsals, essential for learning the fourteen new numbers that the band turned over twice per month.

A cashier with a good ear was assigned to keep track of mistakes the musicians made. Marable could be cruel and haughty with them. Streckfus meticulously monitored their tempos with a stopwatch. The biggest problems came when the tempo slowed down and "guys would be out on the floor doing nothing but shaking their butts very slow and dirty," said Foster.

In addition to the exotic attraction of seeing and hearing African-American musicians playing this kind of music, the excursion boats offered a giant hook-up scene. For the fifty-cent price of admission, customers received a book of fourteen dance cards on which they could make notes about arrangements later in the evening, a meeting by the candy counter, at the bar, near the pilothouse, and so forth. "Most everybody came alone, but left with someone on their arm," said Foster.

Monday-night excursions from St. Louis were set aside for African Americans. This was a relaxing night for the musicians because they could drink, smoke cigarettes, and socialize with these patrons, who crowded around the bandstand, five or six deep. It was perhaps on these nights, especially, when Armstrong and his buddies brought the uptown routine style to the northern river corridor. Jerome Don Pasquall, a musician from St. Louis, said that hearing Armstrong was a "revelation": "Louis, with all that terrific technique of his (like a clarinet almost), would play so many notes you'd be thrilled and forget all about the melody."

He [Armstrong] gained a bigger sense of the world. In Memphis he hung out on Beale Street with Howard and Dodds. In St. Louis he was amazed by the tall buildings and asked Marable what they were—Were they colleges? he wondered. One summer [Joe "King"] Oliver visited him in St. Louis for four days, his mission to persuade his prize pupil to join him in Chicago. Armstrong declined but gave his entire lunch to Papa Joe.

He continued to compose; he said that he made up the tune *Weatherbird* while playing on the boats. He made a big splash at a party in St. Louis and his reputation as a soloist was starting to spread. In 1920 in Chicago, Paul Mares teased Oliver, telling him, "There's a kid down there in New Orleans, if he ever comes up here you're dead."

The idea that commercial pressures regularly taint the authentic purity of vernacular music is a familiar one. Something like that can happen, of course. But there may also be a more positive dimension in that kind of encounter. Armstrong's riverboat experience shows a musician who grew by meeting the challenges put before him. Playing for the Streckfus brothers and their straw boss Marable meant dealing with a different order of commercial expectation than anything he and his colleagues had previously known. He mastered musical notation and gained precision in the melodic syntax of Eurocentric music. No more faking the unfamiliar keys and scales.

The whole structure of the job, with its regular schedule of rehearsing and its downtime for practicing, fostered steady progress. Baby Dodds said that the rehearsals taught the musicians precision and quickness. The experience transformed his ear playing too. Armstrong remembered Jones telling him that "you'll never be able to swing any better than you already know how until you learn to read. Then you will swing in ways you never thought of before."

"And he was right," was how Armstrong came to think of the situation. The story of Armstrong on the riverboats stands as a good example of how many of the great popular musicians take their art to higher levels through encounters with the marketplace.

STRECKFUS STEAMER MUSICIANS

The following are among the many musicians who performed on Streckfus excursion vessels.

CHARLES WENZEL "CHARLEY" MILLS

May 5, 1884–December 7, 1946

Born in Quincy, Illinois, Mills played piano aboard the *J.S.*—and also played her calliope. He also introduced pianist Fate Marable to the Streckfus brothers.

Mills was well known in Quincy, providing musical accompaniment for a variety of entertainment venues during the first decade of the twentieth century. He moved East and, in 1909, graduated from the music department of Lebanon Valley college in Annville, Pennsylvania.

The *Quincy Daily Herald* reported on Aug. 14, 1913, "He played in saloons and at the parks here for a number of years [then] went away and was lost to sight."

Rather, Mills was honing his skills and paving the path for others to follow, by performing ragtime music, which is considered by some to be the precursor to jazz. In New York, he joined other musicians to form the "Versatile Entertainers Quintet." The group performed at James Reese

"Jim" Europe's Clef Club in May 1910. Others in the core group included Anthony Tuck, banjoist, and Charles Wesley Johnson, a Chicago drummer.

The group—also known at times as the "Versatile Three" and the "Versatile Four," depending on the number of members—was hired to accompany renowned ballroom dancers Vernon and Irene Castle during the summer of 1913 on a tour of France. In November, the group's members joined with banjoist Gus Haston.

In London, the group entertained HRH Prince Arthur of Connaught, a grandson of Queen Victoria of England. A command performance followed—at Prince Arthur of Connaught's marriage to Princess Alexandra in October 1913.[260]

---

260 https://www.maryloumontgomery.com/single-post/2019/08/10/quincy-musician-performs-before-british-royalty-in-1913

FATE MARABLE-INSPIRED JAZZ LEGENDS

JOSEPH NATHAN "KING" OLIVER—CORNET

1881–1938—Born Aben, Louisiana (near Donaldsonville)

Streckfus Steamers Connection: While it appears that King Oliver never was a Streckfus Steamers musician on the river, he had great influence on the migration of jazz and mentored Armstrong in New Orleans and later in Chicago and New York.

Joseph Nathan "King" Oliver circa 1915
Wikimedia.org

King Oliver
A gifted cornet player, Oliver became "King" when he outdueled two battle-of-bands opponents in the New Orleans red-light district. In the tumultuous speakeasies of Storyville, Oliver co-led one of the hottest bands in the Crescent City with trombonist Edward "Kid" Ory.

Oliver was a jazz pioneer and virtuoso on what became known as the Harmon trumpet ("Wa-Wa") mute. Drawn to the excitement of Chicago in 1917, he led King Oliver's Creole Jazz Band, which reached out to New

Orleans' 21-year-old Louis Armstrong to forgo further Steamer work and join the 10-piece ensemble. Immediately, record companies flocked to the Royal Gardens cabaret. The Chicago market was wild about hot New Orleans jazz and in 1923, Oliver's Creole Jazz Band recorded 37 performances.

In what is widely regarded as one of the top periods of creative jazz development (1921–1929) Oliver worked with some of the greats—Armstrong, Johnny and Baby Dodds, Honore Dutrey and Lil Hardin, to name a few.

In 1927, Oliver's career took a major nosedive when he held out for a higher offer from the New York Cotton Club, which instead went to Duke Ellington. By 1935, a gum disease (pyorrhea) restricted Oliver's ability so badly that he pawned his trumpet for cash. He died in poverty of arteriosclerosis in 1938.

Honore Dutrey, tb; Warren "Baby" Dodds, d; Joe Oliver, co; Louis Armstrong (kneeling in front), slide tpt; Lil Hardin Armstrong, p; Bill Johnson, bj; Johnny Dodds, cl.

Hogan Jazz Archive, Special Collections, Howard-Tilton Memorial Library. Tulane University

Memorable Quotation:

"It was my ambition to play as he did. I still think that if it had not been for Joe Oliver, Jazz would not be what it is today."

—LOUIS ARMSTRONG

Fate Marable-Inspired Jazz Legends

JOHN ALEXANDER "JOHNNY" ST. CYR—BANJO

1890–1966—Born New Orleans

Streckfus Steamers connection:
St. Cyr was a disciple of the King Oliver Magnolia Band, which was admired by Marable. He was recruited to work the river on the SS *Sidney*, playing banjo as part of the original Jaz-E-Saz ensemble that spent 1918–1920 tramping the river from NOLA to St. Paul to sensational receptions.

Johnny St. Cyr
St. Cyr got his early start playing a "cigar-box" guitar at the age of 15. As talented as he was, St. Cyr never forgot the old maxim, "Keep your day job"; between gigs throughout his career, he labored as a plasterer in construction.

Among the great pioneers of jazz, St. Cyr worked with A.J. Piron, Marable, Dodds, Oliver, Ory, Armstrong, Doc Cook and others from Storyville, (the red-light district of New Orleans, from 1897 to 1917) to Chicago to East St. Louis. When the SS *Capitol* entered the Streckfus fleet in 1920, St. Cyr returned to New Orleans where he and Pops Foster left Marable to join the Creath band.

John Alexander "Johnny" St. Cyr, circa 1963
Hogan Jazz Archive, Special Collections, Howard-Tilton Memorial Library. Tulane University

Oliver convinced St. Cyr to travel to Chicago in 1923 where he joined at the Lincoln Gardens, a Black and Tan club, with no segregation. Chicago was his home for the next few years when he roomed with Oliver and Armstrong and Lil Hardin.

He returned to New Orleans in 1930 and returned to plaster while gigging whenever the opportunity arose. St. Cyr's banjo can be heard in recordings of Louis Armstrong's Hot Five and Hot Seven sessions. He was active in music until the end, playing in the Young Men from New Orleans group in the 1960s. St. Cyr succumbed to leukemia in 1966.

Memorable Quotation:

> *"We were going out to Canal Street with Fate and our little Ford almost hit a woman pedestrian. Armstrong said, 'You'd better watch out, You'll get arrested for emergency.' We all said, 'Emergency what emergency?' Louis replied, 'You hit that woman and you'll soon find out what emergency is!'"*

ARTHUR JAMES "ZUTTY" SINGLETON—DRUMS

1898–1975—Born Bunkie, Louisiana

Streckfus Steamers connection:
Singleton was part of the New Orleans "Jazz mafia" and worked tirelessly among the big bands of the jazz era. On the river on the SS *Capitol*, the drummer was part of Fate Marable's celebrated ensemble of 1923, the Society Syncopators.

Zutty Singleton
The musician acquired the unique moniker, Zutty (pronounced Zoo-tay) as a child. The term is Creole patois for "Cute."

He began working at the Rosebud Theater in New Orleans in 1915 at age 17. He earned a "purple heart" for his service in the Navy in World War I. Postwar he worked in St. Louis with Charlie Creath and on the Mississippi with Marable. His brief stint with Marable came when he was asked to fill in for Baby Dodds who had been recruited by Oliver in Chicago. (It was this experience with Marable which led to Singleton's oft-mentioned, "When a musician got a job on the riverboats with Fate Marable, they say, 'Well, you're going to the conservatory.'")

His New Orleans musician's pedigree and powerfully inspired drum performances were the ticket to recording sessions with Jelly Roll Morton and Armstrong. It was said, "[playing on a band with Zutty Singleton] was like trying to stay ahead of a freight train that was bearing down on you."

Singleton's unique drum style evolved over the years and can be appreciated in numerous recorded performances which survive.

Arthur James "Zutty" Singleton
Wikimedia Commons

Memorable Quotation:

"Zutty and I played together pretty nearly all our lives."
—LOUIS ARMSTRONG

CHARLES CYRIL "CHARLIE" CREATH—TRUMPET, SAXOPHONE, ACCORDION & BANDLEADER

1890–1951—Born Ironton, Missouri

Streckfus Steamers Connection:
Creath was a multi-talented musician and bandleader who was active on the *Sidney* and *Capitol* and enjoyed tramping from St. Louis to New Orleans from 1919 on. In 1927 and later he co-led popular bands with Fate Marable.

Charlie Creath

Creath got his start playing with circuses and traveling bands in the St. Louis area. In the 1920s, he was unique as a "Player Manager" directing a host of popular bands on the Mississippi riverboats while contributing sounds from saxophone, trumpet, and accordion.

After a stint in Seattle leading his own bands, Creath returned to St. Louis where he managed his own franchise and often had several groups gigging on the riverboats and local cabarets. A brother-in-law of acclaimed drummer Zutty Singleton, Creath also employed his sister Margie Creath in the popular six-piece Jazz-O-Maniacs band.

Charles Cyril "Charlie" Creath
YouTube.com

Creath is a dynamic figure in virtually every historical accounting of the early years of "Red Hot Jazz." His works with Pops Foster and the Jazz-O-Maniacs were recorded by OKeh Records between 1924 and 1927 and are considered some of the most collectable jazz memorabilia.

Quotation:

> *Creath advertisements during his franchise heyday in the early '20s: "Give a thought to Music: For Real Time, Rhythm, Jazz Dance Music call C. Creath, 4257 Kennerly Ave" and "The Water's On! There'll be a Hot Time in the Old Town."*[261]

---

261 William Howland Kenney, *Jazz on the River*, pg. 101.

Fate Marable-Inspired Jazz Legends

JOHN "JOHNNY" DODDS—CLARINET

1892–1940—Born Waveland, Mississippi

WARREN "BABY" DODDS—DRUMS

1898–1959—Born New Orleans

Streckfus Steamers Connection:

The senior brother, Johnny, and his seven-years' younger brother, Warren "Baby" Dodds, were fixtures of Fate Marable's riverboat swing jazz bands from 1918 to 1921.

At the high point of the Jazz-O-Sans ensemble's career, the Dodds brothers "tramped" with two Streckfus steamers—the *Sidney* and *Capitol*—moving seasonally between New Orleans and St. Louis and often to points north as far a Minnesota.

During the prime summer season, the brothers Dodd worked the St. Louis excursion harbor market, alternating between the *Saint Paul* and *J.S. Deluxe*.

Johnny Dodds

The elder brother started on the clarinet at 13 and, despite spending time with Marable, he eschewed reading music and played entirely by ear. He was 20 when he joined Kid Ory's group, the Crescent City's hottest jazz group, where he freelanced. He spent most of his career in Chicago, originally lured by King Oliver to his Creole Jazz Band.

Johnny worked with Oliver, Armstrong, and Jelly Roll Morton and various bands and was recorded in many numbers featured by the Hot Five and the New Orleans Wanderers. Heart complications led to his death in 1940, at a premature 48.

John "Johnny" Dodds
Jazzmusicarchives.com

Baby Dodds

Younger brother Baby derived his nickname from his mother, who distinguished him from his father, Warren. Both he and Johnny were part of a musical family growing up in New Orleans with a dad and uncle who played violin and a sister who mastered the harmonica.

There is considerably more literature written on jazz drummer Baby Dodds than on Johnny, in part because Baby influenced the very evolution of the standard drum set of today. He experimented with tom-toms, snares, wire brushes, various cymbals (including the sock cymbal). He was quoted: ". . . I felt that drums has as much music in them as any other instrument. A drummer provides a very important foundation for the rest of the musicians. You can't get into a locked house without a key, and the drum is the key to the band."

Warren "Baby" Dodds, 1935
Hogan Jazz Archive, Special Collections, Howard-Tilton Memorial Library. Tulane University

Baby and Johnny crossed paths repeatedly over the years, originally in 1918 with Fate Marable and his legendary Jazz-O-Sans ensemble, which included Armstrong, St. Cyr, Foster, Davey Jones, and Joe Howard. Soon he joined King Oliver's seven-piece Creole Jazz Band in Chicago where there was never a loss of demand for his inspired drum talent.

Quotation:

> *"The jazz played after New Orleans funerals didn't show any lack of respect for the person being buried. It rather showed their people that they wanted them to be happy."*

Fate Marable-Inspired Jazz Legends

Doddsiana

"When I first went to New York it seemed very strange to have people sitting around and listening rather than dancing. In a way, it was similar to theater work. But it was peculiar for me because I always felt that I was doing something for the people if they danced to the music."

—BABY DODDS (WIKIPEDIA)

DEWEY JACKSON—CORNET AND TRUMPET

1900–1994—Born New Orleans

Streckfus Steamers Connection:
Jackson was only twelve when his musical training in New Orleans began with the Odd Fellows Boy's Band. He led his own ensemble, the Golden Melody Band, teaming with Charlie Creath. Working closely with the Streckfus Line, Jackson was mainly active on the *Capitol* and *Saint Paul* from New Orleans to St. Louis. In 1933, his Dewey Jackson Peacock Orchestra authored an interesting original tune, the "Depression Dance,"

in support of a fundraiser for orphan boys. When the *Saint Paul* was converted to the *Senator*, Jackson led the band on its scheduled Louisville, Kentucky, to Pittsburgh run.

Dewey Jackson

A legendary trumpet soloist, Jackson was a fixture in the St. Louis and New Orleans jazz scene from the 1920s through the 1940s. His surviving recordings are limited but include the classic, "She's Cryin' for Me," and other numbers where he shared the stage with Charlie Creath.

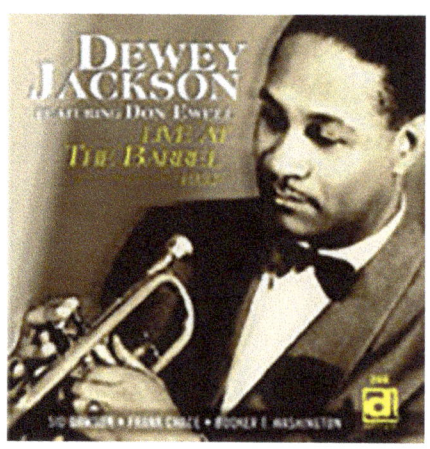

Dewey Jackson
Dewy Jackson (1952 album)

Jackson overcame the hard times of the early 1930s with nonstop musical performances leading black bands that he organized. He was a favorite of Streckfus Steamers, repeatedly joining Fate Marable and his Cotton Pickers Orchestra on the river. Marable, Jackson, and Creath were intimately connected through a variety of highly acclaimed bands.

Quotation:

> *"It seems strange that Dewey Jackson made so few recordings. He was considered one of the biggest names in St. Louis jazz and a legend of jazz in the early decades of the century. Unfortunately, Jackson was forced into part-time work in the 1940s before his revival in the 1950s."*
> —SCOTT YANOW, ALLMUSIC, INC.

Fate Marable-Inspired Jazz Legends

JESSE JOHNSON—ST. LOUIS PRODUCER/PROMOTER

?—1947? — Born Tennessee[262]

Streckfus Steamers Connection:
No discussion of the early jazz scene is complete without recognition of Jesse Johnson. Johnson, a man of wide-ranging contacts and negotiating skills, ran the entertainment show in St. Louis in the first half of the twentieth century. For many years, Johnson worked closely with the Streckfus brothers on bookings for segregated Monday night "colored" cruises. Johnson's relationship with the Streckfus Line was not exclusive; he actively promoted the expansion of segregated cruise offerings through his contacts on many excursion boats working the Upper Mississippi including the *Pilgrim, Grey Eagle, Liberty,* and *Majestic*.

In a highly charged period in 1931, the white-controlled Musicians Union Local 2 refused to allow Streckfus Steamers to implement a Depression-influenced "concession price." The union, which had unilaterally revoked the black musicians' charter earlier, then bristled when Captain Joe Streckfus threatened ". . . to use four colored bands" on the *Saint Paul* and *J.S. DeLuxe*. Reflecting the power of the white-controlled musicians union, Streckfus Steamers was forced to acquiesce and install three white and only one black band. It came as no surprise to Jesse Johnson that the Streckfus Line, limited as it was, chose Jackson, Marable, Creath, and Campbell to lead its non-white ensemble.[263]

Quotation:

> "Promoter Jesse Johnson put together a battle of the bands on board the St. Paul but neglected to limit the number of tickets sold. Five

---

262 There is not much information on Jesse Johnson. He was originally a dance instructor, teaching dance steps and leading dances in various cabarets. By 1916, he was promoting excursions on Monday afternoons and nights on the various segregated excursion boats that were on the St. Louis Levee. https://www.stlmag.com/culture/St-Louis-Jazz-Pioneer-Jesse-Johnson/.
263 Kenney, *Jazz on the River*, pgs. 101–103.

thousand people were on board and overloaded it. The captain recognized the peril of overcrowding and refused to leave shore, thereby averting a disaster."[264]

GEORGE MURPHY "POPS" FOSTER—BASS

1892–1969—McCall Plantation, Louisiana (near Donaldsonville)

Streckfus Steamers Connection:
Foster was a master of both the tuba and, more importantly, the standing string bass. Pops was an early part of the Marable Jazz-O-Sans ensemble of 1919 that included a panoply of great jazz performers then gathered on the Streckfus excursion steamer *Sidney*. He also worked with Armstrong, Oliver, and Charlie Parker over a lengthy career in St. Louis during which he was best known for his creative "slap" solid bass fiddle techniques.

Pops Foster
Foster began playing professionally in 1907 at 15; he was a unique performer who almost single-handedly raised the level of importance of the bass in Dixieland music development. He was somewhat older than the young men of the bands Ory, Oliver, and Piron led in New Orleans, hence the "Pops" nickname stuck.

Foster left the Streckfus riverboats and moved to St. Louis in 1921. He joined the Creath and

George Murphy "Pops" Foster
Wikimedia Commons

---

264 Owsley, *City of Gabriels,* pg. 32 and pg. 54.

Jackson bands when needed. In 1929, at the outset of the Great Depression, he moved to the Big Apple and spent time with Louis Armstrong's bands, among others. His talent overcame the difficult economic conditions of the times and he prospered. Foster's legacy stems from his enthusiastic playing style and strong "slap" tone that reverberated from standing bass.

Quotations:

> *"I'm just another bass player trying to make a living." (Stanford libraries)*
> *"New Orleans was one of the great melting pots of musical history." . . .*
> *"Ragtime music is different from other music because it's a happier kick, and Dixieland is an even happier kick than ragtime . . . What's called jazz today was called ragtime back then, and blues back then was called honky-tonk music." . . . "I got my nickname from Louis Armstrong."*

WALTER GABRIEL "FATS" PICHON—PIANO

1906–1967—Born New Orleans

Walter Gabriel "Fats" Pichon
Wikimedia Commons

Streckfus Steamers Connection: Pichon was raised in New Orleans and returned to New Orleans in the 1930s to lead some of the best big bands the Crescent City would ever hear. The Streckfus brothers raved over Pichon and his exceptional talent leading big bands on the company's New Orleans-based steamers.

Fats Pichon

In his early career as a pianist, Pichon performed throughout New England while he studied at the Conservatory of Music. The author is at a loss to explain why Pichon, who was of average build, was called "Fats." Lacking other explanations, one possibility is that his stage moniker reflected the rich sound of Pichon's impressive talent as jazz singer, pianist, and bandleader.

Pichon was a loved and legendary figure on the Streckfus Steamers line throughout the 1930s where he weathered the depression in hale shape. In 1940, Pichon kicked back and settled in as house pianist at Bourbon Street's Old Absinthe House, where he was a fixture for some 20 years. He was coaxing sweet melodies from the piano until he passed at 60.

Fats Pinchon and his Orchestra aboard the *Capitol*
Hogan Jazz Archive, Special Collections, Howard-Tilton Memorial Library. Tulane University

Quotations:

> *Captain Roy Streckfus had a favorite jazz musician: Fats was a virtuoso on calliope. "It takes a mastermind to play that thing, and Fats can really make it talk."*
>
> —CAPT. ROY STRECKFUS, DIXIE MAGAZINE, JULY 12, 1959

SIDNEY DESVIGNE—TRUMPET

1893–1959—Born New Orleans

Streckfus Steamers Connection: An accomplished trumpeter, Desvigne occupied the second chair next to Louis Armstrong when Fate Marable's Society Syncopators were

The *S.S. Capitol* Band led by Sidney Desvigne
Hogan Jazz Archive, Special Collections, Howard-Tilton Memorial Library. Tulane University

the headliners on the *Sidney* circa 1915. He was a soloist featured in Marable's lone recordings of "Frankie and Johnnie" and "Pianoflage." Desvigne was a performer with Ed Allen's Whispering Gold Band and later rose to bandleader of his own group of musicians on the gingerbread-filigreed sternwheeler, the *Capitol*.

ALVIN ELMORE ACORN—TRUMPET

1912–2003—Born New Orleans

Streckfus Steamers Connection: Another famous New Orleanian trumpeter, Acorn came from a musical family where, as one associate recalled he, ". . . . grew up in a time when sight-reading, good intonation and consistency were essential."

He was an early musical prodigy earning his US Musician's Union card at 15. While there are no specific records of Acorn performing on the Streckfus excursion vessels, it seems indisputable that he did so while working with the host of legendary New Orleans jazz ensembles.

Alvin Elmore Acorn
Hogan Jazz Archive, Special Collections, Howard-Tilton Memorial Library. Tulane University

Alvin Acorn

Acorn starred in many of the great bandleaders swing bands, including the bands of Kid Ory, A.J. Piron, Don Albert, and Sidney Desvigne. Acorn was a lead player in the early 1930s with Don Albert's ensemble, which was billed "America's greatest swing band." With Piron, he was a featured soloist in the Sunny South Synopators and he achieved top billing in Ory's Creole Jazz Band.

In the twilight days of his career, Acorn entertained in the New Orleans French Quarter (Pat O'Briens) and the Garden District (Commander's Palace), leading a trio of jazzmen.

CHARLES "BUDDY" BOLDEN—CORNET & TRUMPET

1877–1931—Born New Orleans

Streckfus Steamers Connection:
It is not known whether Bolden figured into the early bands which played on the Streckfus Steamers excursion *Sidney* during that vessel's days in New Orleans in the decade. Pops Foster was a contemporary and sidekick. Therefore, a Streckfus Steamers gig by Bolden was certainly a possibility. What is known is that Bolden's was a memorable, lasting original sound that is at the root of the musical genre the world calls jazz.

Buddy Bolden was born in uptown New Orleans and became an iconic figure in the earliest years of Crescent City jazz. His brand of music was distinct and his performances throughout his career were legendary. A virtuoso on the horn, Bolden is said to have led the blues/ragtime movements' metamorphosis into the earliest forms of jazz. He was one of the first jazz royalty to be anointed "King" as excited dancers shouted "Aw, play it, King Bolden!"

Regrettably, King Bolden's career was shortened by alcoholism. Later, mental health depression led to him being committed to the

Charles "Buddy" Bolden
Wikimedia Commons

Louisiana State Asylum by his family; he resided in that institution until his death in 1931.

It was said that in his prime years performing in Storyville, in Louisiana's Lincoln and Johnson parks, Bolden attracted record crowds to his gigs. One historian said, "King Bolden took the guttural moan of the blues, mixed it with the spirit of the black Baptist church, and applied a 'ragged' rhythmic feel to his songs. The result was an all-new sound that was perfect for dancing . . ."[265]

In his *City of a Million Dreams*, Jason Berry noted, "Leading small bands, Bolden fused rags, passages improvising around a melody, with a hot moaning blue in simulation of sounds from rowdy bars in the 'tango belt,' above Canal Street, just outside the Storyville bordello district, in lower Treme'."[266]

In his book *Empire of Sin*, Gary Krist explains: "But for white audiences, the music of the ODJB (Original Dixieland Jazz Band) was a sensation. Their recording of "Livery Stable Blues" became wildly popular. And soon many black bands were reaping the benefits of that success. Some black groups changed up the composition of their ensembles, eliminating the violin to emulate the ODJB lineup. They also adopted the neologism "jazz"—sometimes spelled "jass" or even "jasz" in these early years—for the music they had informally been calling "ragtime" for twenty years. Before long, black bands were recording as well, to popular acclaim. And 1917 was the turning point. As one historian put it: 'By 1917 jazz, the Southern folk music, had emerged as jazz, the profitable commodity.' Whatever its reception among the elites of its place of birth, Bolden's new sound now belonged to the world."[267]

---

[265] Source: New Orleans Jazz National Historical Park, https://www.nps.gov/jazz/learn/historyculture/bolden.htm
[266] Jason Berry, *City of a Million Dreams*. (University of North Carolina Press, paperback 2021), pg. 167.
[267] Gary Krist, *Empire of Sin: A Story of Sex, Jazz, Murder, and the Battle for Modern New Orleans* (Broadway Books, an imprint of the Crown Publishing Group, 2014; New York), pg. 249.

I take exception to the characterization of Streckfus's influence on riverboat jazz. I believe the following description by the Missouri 2021 Bicentennial page of the State Historical Society of Missouri:[268]

> Jazz is a uniquely American music genre that began in New Orleans around 1900, and is characterized by improvisation, strong rhythms including syncopation and other rhythmic invention, and enriched chords and tonal colors. Early jazz was followed by Dixieland, swing, bebop, fusion, and free jazz. Piano, brass instruments especially trumpets and trombones, and woodwinds, especially saxophones and clarinets, are often featured soloists.

JOSEPH STRECKFUS INTERVIEWS ON JAZZ AND LOUIS ARMSTRONG

Author's note: The following are reminiscences written by Joseph Streckfus.

Music: Louis Armstrong—Fate Marable 1917 (Dated 11/04/1958)
Fate Marable with his band, Louie Armstrong playing trumpet, had finished playing the summer session on the SS *Saint Paul* at St. Louis—the band was hot, the talk of St. Louis.

This band at the end of St. Louis season on the *Saint Paul* was transferred to the Steamer *Sidney*, and for three weeks played at all cities enroute to New Orleans

I was Captain, and Capt. Roy Streckfus was pilot of the *Sidney* while at New Orleans. In my opinion, I felt the tempo of the band was too fast for the New Orleans patrons. With faster tempo, the band had lost that syncopation and the beat they used to have.

One evening we had no trip scheduled, so I went up to the Orpheum Opera House on St. Charles Street and took in the show. Dedroit's band was in the orchestra pit. After the show, I went over to the Gruenewald

---

268 TheSheldon.org https://www.thesheldon.org/app/uploads/2021/05/Missouri-Bicentennial-education-jazz.pdf

Fate Marable-Inspired Jazz Legends

Hotel (now the Roosevelt) Dining Room to hear Dedroit's band play for the dancing. I could hear and feel that band had the tempo, syncopation, and rhythm, and played the right pieces for dancers. The beat was so predominant that I caught myself keeping time with my foot, so I took out my watch and counted the number of impulse beats to the minute and jotted down the name of the pieces played.

Next day, at rehearsal of Fate Marable's band, I requested they play the same pieces, just like they played them for our dancers. I marked down the tempo count, and then compared our tempo count with that of Dedroit's band, and found our band's tempo was just 20 counts faster per minute than Dedroit's band.

We did our best trying to get band to reduce their tempo to the N.O. tempo on the same pieces; wanted Leader to try the slower tempo out on our regular dance trip. Fate, Louie, and the band thought I was wrong. After two weeks, Fate waited until the last set on an afternoon trip, to play one piece at the slower tempo.

At the time I was on the bridge, Captain Roy was in Pilot House as Pilot. One headlight alongside of me started to shake, the Pilot House shook, we heard loud hollering coming from the Cabin. Both of us thought something had happened and quickly went down to Cabin Deck. The dancers were going off. I saw Louie Armstrong coming toward me with his trumpet in hand, smiling, and Louie said—"We's got it." I said what do you mean—he said—We played it slow like you wanted it, and I's put in a little swing, and they like it!

From that time on, our band put out the best dance music ever. St. Louis tempo was just 20 beats per minute faster than New Orleans, and it took Louie Armstrong's ability and his trumpet to play the syncopation, which was possible at the slower tempo, but at [the] St. Louis fast tempo was an impossibility.

Louie Armstrong was always ready and willing to try out anything for the good of the band.

When Louie was playing at the Southside in Chicago, with Joe Oliver, I went down there and arranged for Louie to come to St. Louis for our summer season. At the time the Oriental Theatre was the first theatre in Chicago putting on a specialty show in connection with films. Paul Ash was Master of Ceremonies and offered Louie Armstrong $500 to put his tights and short skirts and just play the Heebie Jeebies on his trumpet as he walked across the stage in front of curtain. It took Louie just two weeks to get up his nerve, but he did it, and made a big hit.

left Joe Strecht
J.S.
11/4/58

Music

Good dance music on our steamers was a first.

For years, we made it possible for our musicians to have good musical instruments.

I recall one spring, the musicians from New Orleans came to St. Louis on the train, to start their season on our Steamer *St. Paul*. Fate Marable was the Leader, Louie Armstrong, 1st trumpet, Bobby Dodds, drummer, Pops Foster, base violin, Nathan Story, trombone, David Jones, mellophone, Robert St. Cyr, banjoist.

Pops Foster's base violin, the boys' saxophones, Louis' trumpet were in bad shape. We arranged to buy all new instruments for them, they paying back cost price, without interest, at a rate of $5 per week.

Remember Louie Armstrong when he left Joe Oliver at New Orleans, and took his first job on his own, on our Steamer *Sidney* at New Orleans. He reported for boat rehearsal with his feet half out of his shoes, and had no trumpet; he had been using Joe Oliver's trumpet, and Oliver was mad at Louie for leaving him, for the first time. We bought new shoes for Louie and let him use a silver trumpet we had on hand. Later we bought him a good trumpet; later, his second, and last one was his best, a $225 trumpet. Louie repaid us in full. Bought Foster a bass violin at Lon Healy's Music Store in Chicago for $375, and expressed it back to St. Louis. Foster really went to town and still has that base violin in New York on Broadway.

Speaking of Broadway and New York, my wife and I, while in New York some years ago took in an after dinner theatre show at the Palais Royal on 45th & Broadway, $2.50 table cover charge I recall; Robinson, the best of dancers was leading the show, and Louie Armstrong was leading the band. When the orchestra boys learned we were there, one by one would leave the band and come to our table. There were eight of our past old steamer players in that band.

—J.S.
11/4/58

Music—Louis Armstrong—1920*

Author's note: Parts of this interview were incorporated earlier in the book

I recall in the fall of one season at St. Louis when Fate Marable, Louie Armstrong, and fellow musicians in the band had completed the summer season on the SS *Saint Paul* at St. Louis, and were transferred to play on the steamer *Capitol*, which was enroute to New Orleans for the winter season.

This band, while at St. Louis on the SS *Saint Paul*, was the talk of St. Louis—all were good musicians for dancing. Had good rhythm, tempo, and played jazz that was different.

Personally, I believed if this band played more variety, they could become the best band in New Orleans. I decided to go down river on the *St. Paul* and expected to return from Cape Girardeau. It was my hope that a few pieces could be rehearsed with the band in order to give them an idea, which they could perfect and rehearse each day on their way down the river to New Orleans.

At our first day's stop, we were to play Chester, Ill., which called for a rehearsal on the way down, and explained to the musicians my object in making the trip, was to possibly give them some ideas that were somewhat different from their music as played at St. Louis. I convinced them it was worth a trial.

My efforts at the first rehearsal didn't fare so well; they just couldn't get the idea, although they tried hard.

Our next stop was Cape Girardeau, and my wife and [my]self started up the main street in Cape Girardeau. As we passed a shop with records and Victrola in the window, the idea came to me—why not inquire if they have the records we have at home, which we can buy, and demonstrate to our orchestra what we are driving at. Fortunately, the shop had the records played by Art Hickman's band at the Palace Hotel in San Francisco—the first Victor Dance Music Records.

We purchased record "Avalon," which played one chorus in one key, then a few bars of modulation and into another key, and played second chorus in that key. Then again, a few bars of chord modulation and into another key, and one chorus in that key. That was the first record of its kind. We bought a Victrola and a repeater arrangement and some more records—"Love Nest"—"Young Man's Fancy," and all were delivered to SS *Capitol*.

We set Victrola up next to the band stand, and started playing the records, and soon the orchestra boys, who were napping in the texas, the deck above, heard dance music that they never heard before. They all came down, and wasn't long before we were in a rehearsal of these pieces by ear. Louie Armstrong, with his trumpet in his hand, came down alongside the Victrola, and would pick up, on his trumpet, the notes in the several chords in the modulation, giving the saxophone section their chords, likewise the brass their changes in chords, and by repeating over and over again, all chords were down pat; then playing the choruses in the different keys was easy.

The other records were rehearsed likewise.

That evening we had approximately 1,200 dancers, and when the band played "Avalon," they stopped the show. Folks crowded around the orchestra stand and applauded and applauded. They never had heard music like that. Just a few months ago, an elderly businessman from Southeast Missouri recalled this to us.

At Cairo next night, we experienced the same grand reception of our music. Patrons just would not get off the boat—wanted more.

Next day arranged for Louis to rehearse a trumpet solo, I believe it was Louie Armstrong stood up alone "LaVeda," with Fate on the piano and Louis on the trumpet, balance of orchestra not playing. Louis Armstrong stood up alone for the first time and played his first trumpet solo, accompanied with the piano. There were over 800 dancers on the floor. The applause and requests were so outstanding, they repeated the number. From that time on, we had no difficulty in having Louie and other members stand up and play their solo.

After that reception band received at Cape Girardeau, Cairo and Caruthersville, it was not hard for band to continue rehearsing and leaving off the records, the music played by Hickman's Band. That I believe was the real start of the success of Louie Armstrong and Fate Marable.

The Str. *Capitol* opened at New Orleans two weeks later, and it was not long before the Steamer *Capitol* was doing capacity business, due mostly to the wonderful dance music played, in the most beautiful dancehall afloat.

J.S.
11/4/58

BOARDS OF DIRECTORS AND OFFICERS OF STRECKFUS AND RELATED COMPANIES[269]

1925 Streckfus Steamboat Line, Harper House Hotel, Rock Island, Illinois
   Board of Directors: Captains John (Commodore), Joe, and John N. Streckfus, H.H. Cleveland, Joseph Schaab
   Officers: President: Captain John Streckfus (Commodore); Vice President: H.H. Cleveland; Secretary: Joe Streckfus

1926 Streckfus Steamboat Line, Office of H.H. Cleveland on 18th Street, Rock Island, Illinois
   Board of Directors: Captains Joe, Roy, and John N. Streckfus, Joseph Schaab, H.H. Cleveland
   Officers: President: Captain Joe Streckfus; Vice President: H.H. Cleveland; Secretary: Captain John N. Streckfus
   These officers were in place until the middle of 1926 when a new corporation was formed.

1926 Streckfus Steamboat Line, Office of US Corporation Company, N. 19-21 Dover Green, Dover, Delaware
   Board of Directors: Captains Joe Streckfus, E.R. Vaughn, C.J. Mangan, J.L. English, E.A. Schmid

1926 Streckfus Steamers, Incorporated, 1114 Central National Bank Building, St. Louis, Missouri
   Board of Directors: Captains Joe and John N. Streckfus, Joseph Schaab, H.H. Cleveland

---

269 Blum, *The Steamer Admiral,* Appendix, pgs. 92–94.

Officers: President: Captain Joe Streckfus; Vice President: H.H. Cleveland; Secretary: Captain John N. Streckfus

1927, 1928, 1929, 1930, 1931, 1932 Streckfus Steamers, Incorporated, office of Company at International Life Building, St. Louis, Missouri

Board of Directors: Captains Joe, John N., and Roy Streckfus, H.H. Cleveland, Joseph Schaab

Officers: President: Captain Joe Streckfus; Vice President: H.H. Cleveland; Secretary: Captain John N. Streckfus

1933, 1934, 1935 Streckfus Steamers, Incorporated, office of Company, St. Louis, Missouri

Board of Directors: Captains Joe, John N., and Roy Streckfus, H.H. Cleveland, Joseph Schaab

Officers: President: Captain Joe Streckfus; Vice President: H.H. Cleveland; Secretary: Captain John N. Streckfus

1936, 1937, 1938, 1939, 1940, 1941, 1942, 1943 Board of Directors: Captains Joe, John N., Roy, and Verne Streckfus; H.H. Cleveland

Officers: President: Captain Joe Streckfus; Vice President: H.H. Cleveland; Secretary: Captain John N. Streckfus

1944, 1945 Board of Directors: Captains Joe and John N. Streckfus, V. Dueker, H.H. Cleveland, Marie Addison

Officers: President: Captain Joe Streckfus; Vice President: Captain John N. Streckfus; Secretary: M. Bushnell

1946 Board of Directors: Captains Joe and John N. Streckfus, H.H. Cleveland, V. Dueker, Marie Addison

Officers: President: Captain Joe Streckfus; Vice President: Captain John N. Streckfus; Secretary: Marie Addison

Boards of Directors and Officers of Streckfus and Related Companies

1947, 1948 Board of Directors: Captains Joe, John N., Roy, and Verne Streckfus, Marie Addison
   Officers: President: Captain Joe Streckfus; Vice President and Treasurer: Captain John N. Streckfus; Secretary: Marie Addison

1949, 1950, 1951, 1952, 1953, 1954, 1955, 1956 Board of Directors: Captains Joe, Roy, and Verne Streckfus, Marie Addison, V. Dueker
   Officers: President: Captain Joe Streckfus; Vice President: Captain Roy Streckfus; Secretary and Treasurer: Marie Addison

1957, 1958, 1959 Board of Directors: Captains Joe, Roy, and Verne Streckfus, Shirley Streckfus, Marie Addison
   Officers: President: Captain Joe Streckfus; Vice President: Captain Roy Streckfus; Secretary/Treasurer: Marie Addison

1960 Board of Directors: Captains Roy, Verne, and Bill Streckfus, Shirley Streckfus, Lola Streckfus
   Honorary Chairman of the Board: Captain Joe Streckfus
   Officers: President: Captain Roy Streckfus; Vice President: Captain Verne Streckfus; Secretary/Treasurer: Marie Addison

1961 Board of Directors: Captains Roy, Verne, and Bill Streckfus, Shirley Streckfus, Lola Streckfus
   Officers: President: Captain Roy Streckfus; Vice President: Captain Verne Streckfus; Secretary/Treasurer: Marie Addison

1962 Board of Directors: Captains Roy, Verne, and Bill Streckfus, Shirley Streckfus, Betty Streckfus Carroll
   Officers: President: Captain Roy Streckfus; Vice President: Captain Verne Streckfus; Secretary/Treasurer: Marie Addison

1963, 1964, 1965, 1966, 1967 Board of Directors: Captains Roy, Verne, and Bill Streckfus, Shirley Streckfus, Betty Streckfus Carroll
>Officers: President: Captain Roy Streckfus; 1st Vice President: Captain Verne Streckfus; 2nd Vice President: Captain R.M. Streckfus; 3rd Vice President: Captain Bill Streckfus; 4th Vice President: Captain Bill Carroll; Secretary/Treasurer: Marie Addison

1968 Board of Directors: Captains Verne, R.M., and Bill Streckfus, Betty Streckfus Carroll, Marie Addison
>Officers: President: Captain Verne Streckfus; 1st Vice President: Captain Bill Streckfus; 2nd Vice President: Captain R.M. Streckfus; 3rd Vice President: Captain Bill Carroll; Secretary /Treasurer: Marie Addison

1969 Board of Directors: Captains Verne, R.M., and Bill Streckfus, Betty Streckfus Carroll, Marie Addison
>Officers: President: Captain Verne Streckfus; 1st Vice President: Captain Bill Streckfus; 2nd Vice President: Captain R.M. Streckfus; 3rd Vice President: Captain Bill Carroll; Secretary/Treasurer: Marie Addison

1970, 1971, 1972, 1973, 1974 Board of Directors: Captains Verne, R.M., and Bill Streckfus, Betty Streckfus Carroll, Kathryn MacKenzie
>Officers: President: Captain Verne Streckfus; 1st Vice President: Captain Bill Streckfus; 2nd Vice President: Captain R.M. Streckfus; 3rd Vice President: Captain Bill Carroll; Secretary/Treasurer: Kathryn MacKenzie

1975, 1976 Board of Directors: Captains Verne, Bill, and J. Curran Streckfus, Patricia Streckfus Clark
>Officers: President: Captain Bill Streckfus; 1st Vice President: Captain J. Curran Streckfus; 2nd Vice President: Captain Bill Carroll; Secretary/Treasurer: Shirley Lay

STRECKFUS STEAMERS, INCORPORATED STEAMERS OPERATIONS—1936 THROUGH 1943[270]

1936

STEAMER	SPRING	SUMMER	FALL
Washington	Ohio River	Ohio River	Ohio River
Saint Paul	St. Louis	St. Louis	St. Louis
J.S.	Ohio River	Upper Miss.	New Orleans
Capitol	New Orleans	Upper Miss.	New Orleans
President	St. Louis	St. Louis	St. Louis

1937

STEAMER	SPRING	SUMMER	FALL
Washington	—	Ohio, 6/30 on	Ohio, laid up 9/9
Saint Paul	Ohio River	Ohio River	Ohio, laid up 9/26
J.S.	Lower Miss.	Upper Miss.	New Orleans, laid up 9/19
Capitol	New Orleans	Upper Miss.	Laid up till 10/26; N.O. 11/11
President	St. Louis	St. Louis	St. Louis

1938

STEAMER	SPRING	SUMMER	FALL
Washington	not operating	not operating	not operating
Saint Paul	Ohio River	Ohio River	Ohio River
J.S.	Lower Miss.	Upper Miss.	laid up STL 9/15
Capitol	New Orleans	Upper Miss.	New Orleans, laid up Nov. & Dec.
President	St. Louis	St. Louis	St. Louis

---

270 Blum, *The Steamer Admiral,* Appendix, pgs. 94–95.

1939

STEAMER	SPRING	SUMMER	FALL
Washington	not operating	not operating	not operating
J.S.	not operating	not operating	not operating
Saint Paul	Ohio, open 5/4	Ohio River	Ohio River, laid up 9/6
Capitol	New Orlns 2/11 to 4/17	Upper Miss	Laid up Pad. Till 11/1, N. Orlns, 11/1
President			

1940

STEAMER	SPRING	SUMMER	FALL
Washington	not operating	not operating	not operating
J.S.	not operating	not operating	not operating
Senator	Ohio 5/2	Ohio River	Ohio River till 9/16
Capitol	New Orleans	Upper Miss.	Laid up N. Orlns. 10/3–12/25
President	New Orlns 4/15–5/18	Upper Miss. St. Paul	N. Orlns. 9/19
Admiral	St. Louis 6/4	St. Louis	St. Louis

1941

STEAMER	SPRING	SUMMER	FALL
Washington	not operating	not operating	not operating
J.S.	not operating	not operating	not operating
Senator	Ohio River 5/1	Ohio River	Ohio River till 9/6
Capitol	N. Orlns. 1/1–4/14	Upper Miss.	Laid up Pad. 9/29–10/15 N. Orlns. 11/1
President	New Orlns 4/15–5/18	Upper Miss	N. Orlns. 9/25–11/1, laid up to 12/31
Admiral	St. Louis	St. Louis	St. Louis till 9/15

Streckfus Steamers, Incorporated Steamers Operations

1942

STEAMER	SPRING	SUMMER	FALL
Washington	not operating	not operating	not operating
J.S.	not operating	not operating	not operating
Senator	not operating	not operating	not operating
Capitol	N. Orlns. 1/1	New Orleans	N. Orlns. till 9/30, laid up 10/1–11/2
President	Lower Miss. 5/11	Upper Miss.	N. Orlns. 10/1–11/2, laid up to 12/31
Admiral	St. Louis 6/3	St. Louis	St. Louis till 9/21

1943

STEAMER	SPRING	SUMMER	FALL
Washington	not operating	not operating	not operating
J.S.	not operating	not operating	not operating
Senator	not operating	not operating	not operating
Capitol	N. Orlns. 1/1–5/1	not operating	N. Orlns. 11/1–12/31
President	N. Orlns. 5/1	New Orleans	N. Orlns. laid up 11/1–12/31
Admiral	St. Louis 5/29	St. Louis	St. Louis to 9/17

Cash Dividends Paid[271]

1926 through 1930: $50,000
1931 through 1933: $0
1934 and 1935: $25,000
1936 through 1942: $50,000
1943 and 1944: $100,000
1945: $50,000
1946 and 1947: $100,000

---

271 Blum, *The Steamer Admiral,* Appendix, pg. 95.

THE STRECKFUS RIVERBOAT DYNASTY

Gross Revenues Streckfus Steamers[272]

STEAMER	1936	1937	1938	1939	AVERAGE
Washington	$106,189	$51,482	0	0	$39,418
J.S.	$112,330	$113,938	$90,040	0	$84,077
Saint Paul	$106,357	$179,589	$145,368	$150,305	$145,405
Capitol	$225,011	$241,563	$211,453	$237,428	$228,864
President	$320,417	$356,787	$317,205	$327,438	$330,462
Tug Boats	0	0	0	$3,715	$929
Booklets	$6,205	$6,768	$7,023	$6,616	$6,653
New Boat (Admiral)	0	0	0	$3,715	$929
Total Gross	$876,509	$970,127	$771,089	$725,502	$835,808
Net after tax	$100,708	$143,342	$95,145	$84,283	$105,869

STEAMER	1940	1941	1942	1943	AVERAGE
Washington	0	0	0	0	0
J.S.	0	0	0	0	0
Saint Paul—Senator	$131,135	$150,238	$11,451	$1,342	$73,541
Capitol	$30,416	$285,304	$261,222	$192,458	$242,350
President	$277,536	$322,333	$432,049	$367,550	$349,861
Tug Boats	$7,289	$15,225	$45,224	$47,895	$28,896
Booklets	$8,099	$7,705	$7,888	$6,823	$7,628
Admiral	$561,578	$601,898	$742,791	$926,583	$708,212
Total Gross	$1,216,053	$1,382,703	$1,500,625	$1,542,651	$1,410,505
Net after tax	$136,728	$100,343	$125,099	$139,550	$125,430

---

272 Blum, *The Steamer Admiral*, Appendix, pg. 96.

Streckfus Steamers, Incorporated Steamers Operations

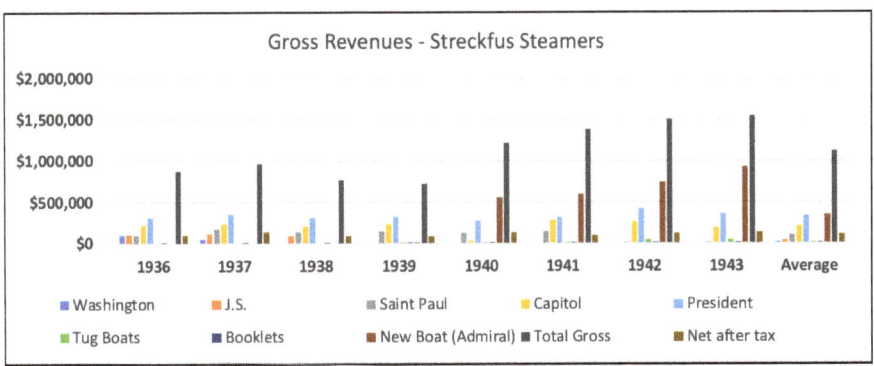

Chart created by Debra Claxton

NEWS CLIPPINGS

With more than 100 years of broad-scale excursion vessel commerce, Streckfus Steamers Inc. was often featured in the popular press. The company advertised daily and constantly promoted the riverboat bands, its star musicians, and the attraction of its Mississippi and Ohio fleet.

Over the years, Streckfus Steamers received great press centered on its popular sightseeing jaunts and romantic moonlight cruises. During the summer seasonal peaks, the mega-steamers *President* and *Admiral* might collectively entertain upwards of 40,000 excursionists per week.

However, not all the newsprint was consistently upbeat and cheerful. An anathema to the Streckfus captains: inebriated passengers, aquatic daredevils, and, in some cases, accidents from causes unknown.

Here are some newspaper clippings that also demonstrate how, in the past, race was stated regardless of whether it was relevant.

Released after Dive
July 23, 1943

John Keck, 16, of Lebanon, Illinois, was released by police yesterday to the custody of his father, Albert Keck, after the youth accepted a challenge by five companions and dived about 40 feet from the fourth deck of the *Admiral* as it passed the foot of Vietor Street Wednesday night. A strong swimmer, young Keck remained in the water five minutes before he was pulled out by crewmen of a Coast Guard patrol boat.[273]

---

273 Dunn, *The Admiral*, pg. 99.

Admiral Crew Saves Swimmer in River
June 19, 1948

A St. Louisan who said he was trying to swim the Mississippi River as he did in his youth was saved from drowning by personnel of the excursion steamer *Admiral* last night as approximately 2000 persons aboard the vessel watched.

Capt. Roy Streckfus of the *Admiral* said Ralph Sage, 56, of 3632 Adine Ave. was first observed midstream when his shouts were heard about three miles south of Rutger Street. Sage told his rescuers the swift current prevented his successful crossing.[274]

Soldier Leaps off *Admiral*, Swims Ashore to Win $5
August 2, 1948

A 23-year-old soldier won a $5 bet yesterday but he swam halfway across the Mississippi River, lost a pair of pants and stopped the excursion steamer *Admiral* for a half hour to do it. Goaded by his companions after bragging that he could swim ashore faster than the *Admiral* could get there, Cpl. Thomas Kane of Tenafly, N.J., accepted a $5 bet, shed his shoes, shirt and hat and leaped overboard from the lower deck. He hit the river about a block north of MacArthur Bridge while the *Admiral* was going upstream and barely managed to reach shore seven blocks south.

After a 330-yard swim he climbed ashore into the hands of waiting police who returned him to his outfit. The *Admiral* stopped in midstream and sent four men in a lifeboat out to the rescue. When they saw that he was doing a good job of swimming they stopped rescue efforts but stayed around until he made shore. "If it had been another 30 yards, I'm afraid I wouldn't have made it," Kane said.[275]

---

274 Dunn, *The Admiral,* pg. 99.
275 *Ibid.*, pg. 98.

News Clippings

Deckhand Missing after Fall into River
July 3, 1949

Burl B. Sidney, 25, of 6202 Wells Wellston, a deckhand for Streckfus Steamers apparently drowned last night after he fell into the Mississippi River from the wharf at the foot of Washington. Sidney, a negro, was working on some lines used in docking the steamer *Admiral* when he suddenly lost his footing and fell into the water, several other deckhands told police. They say they threw a line to Sidney but he failed to grasp it.[276]

Asks $3000 in Damages for Injuries Inflicted by Jitterbug Dancer
January 11, 1955

A Florissant woman charged she suffered a broken ankle from a form of dancing sometimes referred to as "jitterbugging" in a $3000 damage suit filed yesterday in the St. Louis District Court. Mrs. Betty Mayers of 34 St. Celeste Dr. alleged in her petition that on June 5, 1954, a jitterbug broke a number of bones in her right ankle as she was dancing aboard the SS *Admiral* owned by Streckfus Steamers Inc. against whom the suit was filed.[277]

Man Jumps from Steamer *Admiral*
September 3, 1958

George R. Nelson, 32, of New York City was in fair condition in St. Mary's Hospital, East St. Louis, yesterday after jumping from the steamer *Admiral* about 11:45 p.m. Sunday, swimming to the east shore and being pulled to safety there by two nightwatchmen. Mr. Nelson was seen to jump from the *Admiral* on the Coast Guard Auxiliary boat, *Communicator*.

---

276 Dunn, *The Admiral*, pg. 99.
277 *Ibid.*

The cruiser and a boat from the *Admiral* launched a search for him. William Dammann, a watchman at the Alton & Southern Railroad's Fox Terminal near the eastern end of MacArthur Bridge, pulled Mr. Nelson to safety with the aid of a companion after hearing his cry for help. Mr. Nelson was registered at the Sheraton-Jefferson Hotel.[278]

Body of Vet Sought After Dive Off Boat
May 29, 1960

The search was being made yesterday for the body of Frank Heiderie, 24-year-old Army veteran who dived into the Mississippi River from the excursion boat *Admiral* Friday night after telling companions he had always wanted to jump into the river from the boat for a swim. The excursion boat was headed upstream near Lesperance Street when Heiderie jumped from the top deck. A chauffeur, his address is 3231 Ohio.

A boat was lowered immediately but Heiderie could not be found. A watchman six blocks south reported that a few minutes later he heard cries for help from the middle of the river. He turned a spotlight on the river but could see no one. Miss Mary Cardillo of 3018 Marconi, who went with Heiderie and two other couples aboard the *Admiral*, told police they thought he was joking when he proposed to jump.[279]

Body Discovered in *Admiral* Paddle
August 1960

A man's body was taken from the paddle wheel of the Steamer *Admiral* at the foot of Washington Avenue at 8:55 a.m. Tuesday, August 3, 1960. Police said it had apparently floated downstream and caught on the wheel

---

278 Dunn, *The Admiral*, pg. 97.
279 *Ibid.*, pg. 99.

during the night. The body was that of a white man, six feet tall, weighing about 180 pounds and clad in blue shirt, blue jeans and black shoes. It was taken to the morgue. The Coast Guard removed the body from the paddle wheel when it was discovered by a steamer employee.[280]

Body Caught in Paddle Wheel
April 26, 1968

The body of an unidentified white woman about 50 years old was found caught in the paddle wheel of the excursion boat *Admiral* at the foot of Washington Ave. Thursday, police said. A painter working on the side of the vessel saw the body about 11:00 a.m. when he reached down to retrieve a brush handle he had dropped in the Mississippi River. Police said the body had apparently been in the water for several weeks.[281]

Female Lifeguard Jumps from *Capitol*
Date Unknown

On a dare, a young female lifeguard dove off the upper deck of the *Capitol* as it neared St. Paul. The captain dispatched a lifeboat, and the crew were incredulous as she refused help. Finally, she was exhausted when her legs became ensnarled with underwater weed growth and she was hauled to safety. Back on board the sternwheeler, the brazen lass pointedly questioned the *Capitol's* master, "Will my name and picture be in tomorrow's newspaper?" His answer, "As far as I am concerned, it should be published in the local 'Police Gazette.'"[282]

---

280 Dunn, *The Admiral*, pg. 97.
281 *Ibid.*, pg. 99.
282 Source: Lily Streckfus Smith

Missed the Boat
Date Unknown

Streckfus folklore includes the episode of the delayed passenger who "missed the boat." Hurrying in near darkness to catch the late Moonlight Cruise, the would-be excursionist raced up the gangplank and demanded that the entry gate be opened. Safely aboard the wharfboat, he plopped down in a nearby couch to regain his breath. He handed the surprised security guard his ticket. With the *Admiral's* evening voyage well under way by this time, he exclaimed "Whew, that was a close call, I almost missed the boat!"[283]

---

283 Source: Lily Streckfus Smith

THE STRECKFUS FAMILY

The Children of Commodore John Streckfus and Theresa Bartemeier Streckfus

Elizabeth Mary, called Lily, was born in 1881. In 1906, she married Fowler Manning. They lived in upstate New York and had one son, Streckfus. Lily died in 1974. Fowler Manning held high positions with Hoover Vacuum Cleaner Co., Diamond Watch Co., and Smith Corona Typewriter Co.

Anna Cecelia was born in 1883 and married Edward Manthey. She died in 1965 at the age of 81. Edward died at 60. They had three children: Edward, Gustave, and Anna May. Anna May married Dr. Charles Odom, who became Gen. George Patton's personal physician during World War II.

Mary Theresa Anna, called May, and lovingly known as Aunt May or Miss May, even to the boat crews, was born in 1884. She did not marry or have children. She died in 1973.

Joseph Leo was born in 1887. In 1919 he married Lola Laux, who was from East St. Louis, Illinois. Lola's father died when she was very young, but her mother remarried and gave birth to Lola's half-brother, Elmer Herr. Joseph and Lola's daughters were Elizabeth (Betty), Jeanne, and Maysie. Joseph died in 1960. Betty married Bill Carroll from Boston, who became a steamboat captain. He worked for Streckfus Steamers for 50 years on the Mississippi River. Jeanne and her husband Vernon (Bud) Meesey had 13 children. Maysie married Harry Schreier in 1952. Several days after giving birth to their third child, Maysie was waiting in the hospital for Harry and the children to pick her and the baby up. Harry was in an automobile accident; Harry survived, but tragically, the two children perished. Two years later they lost another child to leukemia.

Roy Michael was born in 1888 and married Isabel McPartland of Burlington, Iowa. Isabel had been raised by her uncle, John Curran, and her aunt, Mary. Her uncle was the proprietor of a cigar store and later the postmaster in Burlington. Roy and Isabel were the only couple with the Streckfus surname to have sons who would be able to carry on the family name. Of their seven children, four were boys. The children were John Curran, who was named in honor of Isabel's uncle, Roy Michael "R.M." Jr., Isabella Mary, Robert, Lily, Mary Isabelle, and William. R.M. had a son, Roy Michael III, who died in 1972 at the age of 21 in an accident on an inboard motorboat. Roy Michael Streckfus Sr. died in 1967.

John Nicholas, born in 1891, married Shirley Wellnitz in 1934, but they did not have children. He died in 1948.

Theresa Agnes was born in 1894 and died the same year.

Verne Walter, born in 1895, married Louise McCants. They had two daughters, Barbara and Patricia. Verne died in 1984.

The ninth and last child born to John and Theresa Streckfus was **Nina Agnes**. She was born in 1897 and died in 1907 at age 10.

The Streckfus Family

The Family Tree of the Commodore—Captain John Streckfus

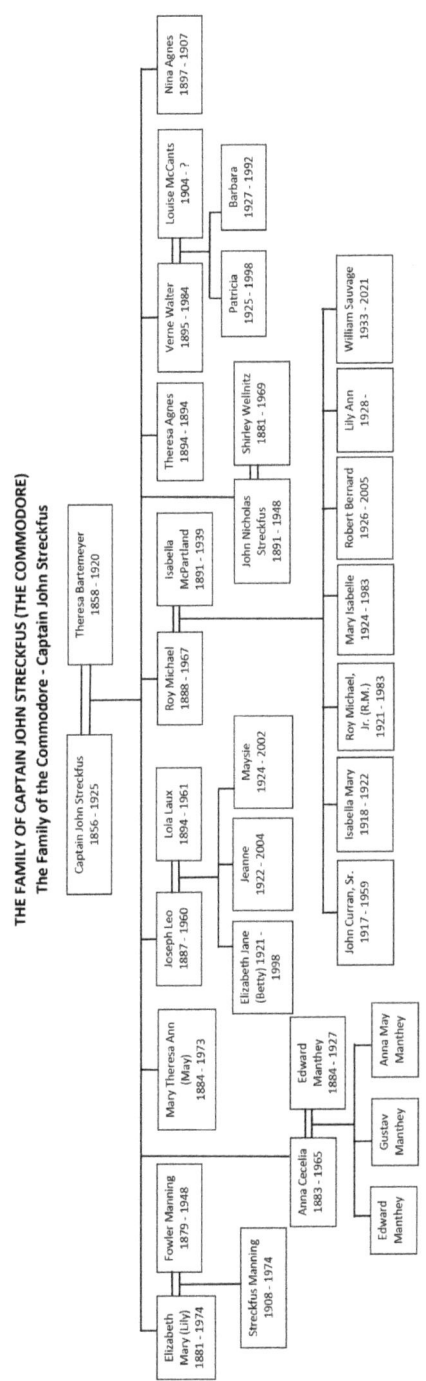

THE STRECKFUS RIVERBOAT DYNASTY

The Captains of Streckfus Steamers, Inc.

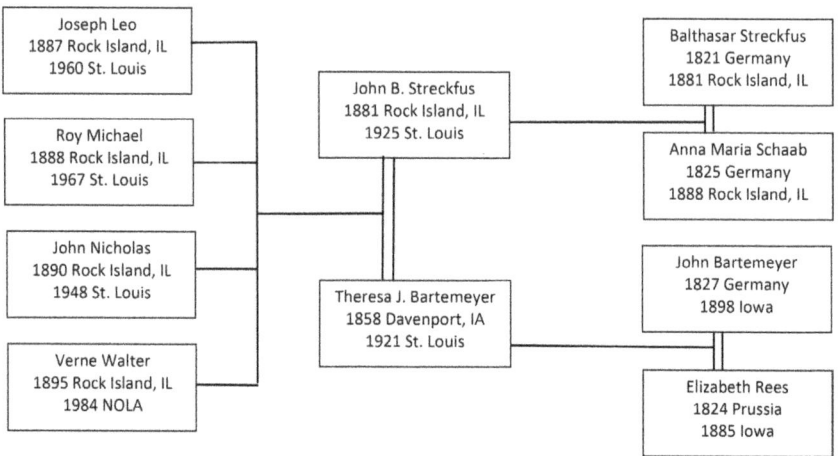

EPILOGUE

This narrative focuses on the last several decades of the nineteenth century and the first half of the twentieth. After the Commodore passed in 1925, Streckfus Steamers enjoyed some of its greatest years of profitable operations when Joe, John, and Roy Streckfus commanded the helm of the enterprise.

However, the second half of the twentieth century was not kind to excursion steamboating.

For fans of the magnificent Mississippi ocean liners created by the Streckfus brothers, the *President* and *Admiral* were the iconic centers for enchanted evenings of jazz, dance, and romance. While centered on their home ports of New Orleans and St. Louis, Streckfus excursion craft brought nightlife and entertainment up and down the Mississippi and Ohio rivers.

The popularity and profitability of the Streckfus fleet peaked in the latter years of World War II. The lion's share of Streckfus Steamer income in the 1940s came from the *President* (24%) and the *Admiral* (60%). The Diamond Jo's wooden hull, the *Capitol*, was scuttled in 1943.

We knew that the really good times for the Streckfus Line eventually had to come to an end.

THE COMPETITIVE LANDSCAPE

The 1960s and 1970s brought a slow but serious deterioration in the operations and financial health of the once-mighty steamer line. The glory days of excursion steamboating faded along all the inland rivers and gradually morphed into a struggle for survival. For Streckfus Steamers, there was new competition for tourism on the river, which the company addressed by adding additional, smaller 400-passenger propeller-driven vessels, including the *Mark Twain*, *Huck Finn*, *Tom Sawyer*, and *Becky Thatcher*. Notwithstanding their faux sternwheels, the smaller MV riverboats were well-received. With this growth in four separate cities: St. Paul, St. Louis, Baton Rouge, and New Orleans, the Streckfus Line was building an active sightseeing and chartering line of business that was healthy and profitable. It was clear that the problem with Streckfus Steamers was the failure to address its aging behemoths.

Outdated and shop-worn, the *Admiral* and *President* were both too large, capacity-wise, and too expensive to operate profitably. Large crew requirements and never-ending repairs to maintain the vessels were financial millstones.

But there were a host of other factors at work.

- Times were changing, and the interest of the public in moonlight cruises with great bands and rollicking music was slowly waning.

- While economic times were great and disposable income was climbing, entertainment tastes were rapidly changing. The post-war Great Generation was building a new, "modern world."

- The two flagship Streckfus Steamers vessels moved at a leisurely pace of 10 miles per hour on the river. Complaints were becoming common that sightseeing was "boring" and the two-plus hour excursions "way too long." It seems that with the changing times would-be SS patrons now set their sights on driving vacations to Disneyland, NASCAR events, and novel forms of fast-paced entertainment.

In his address to Streckfus Steamer shareholders in 1957, Captain Joe bemoaned the evolving consumer who favored television, radio, drive-in theaters, and the like. Meanwhile, seemingly frozen in time, the giant steamers found their operating margins crushed—passenger traffic dwindled but fixed costs and payroll did not.

Epilogue

Arguably, Streckfus family executive management, which had been so prescient in creating the mega vessels the *President* and *Admiral*, was woefully slow to adapt to the enormous structural changes taking place in the domestic economy during the second half of the twentieth century.

OPERATIONAL CHALLENGES

True to their German roots, the Streckfus brothers were close-knit, strong-willed, powerful . . . and incredibly stubborn. This intractable nature led Streckfus Steamers to continuously square off with authority.

Fighting the IRS over the "Excess Profit Tax" (1942–1947) took its toll for more than a decade (although the company eventually prevailed in Tax Court in 1953).

There were also numerous commercial challenges:

- Stamps and licensing for amusement games.

- Liquor licenses for the *Admiral* from both the State of Missouri and the City of St. Louis.

- Extensive negotiations with St. Louis and the National Parks over the construction of the Gateway Arch and the impact on access and egress.

- Access to suitable wharf space in New Orleans on the Canal and Toulouse Street landings.

- Taxation of crew wages on the river.

- Removal of segregation-related restrictions on the operations of all Streckfus Steamer boats were slow to be implemented.

> Ongoing issues to assure that new bridges being built would comply with an 80-foot vertical and 500-foot horizontal separation.

Joe passed in 1960 at 73, and Roy passed in 1967 at 79. Verne was on the docks in New Orleans in 1984, working until his last days, dying at 89. John died in 1948 at just 57 years.

PASSING THE TORCH, RELUCTANTLY

John Curran Streckfus

Modernization and diversification initiatives put forth by Roy's eldest son, John Curran ("Curran"), had fallen on Chairman Uncle Joe's deaf ears. Curran, a true Streckfus river rat, had become a master pilot at 22 and had taken over the bridge of the *Admiral* when Uncle John died unexpectedly. Before that, while operating the *Capitol* between New Orleans and St. Paul, Curran repeatedly clashed with Captain Joe's authoritarian brand of leadership. Curran argued for diversification on the river, identifying great post-war expansion opportunity in tugs and barges. Eventually, Roy's eldest son became so disgruntled that he turned to alcohol and quit the Streckfus Line. Returning dejectedly to New Orleans, Curran's business pursuits languished, and he died prematurely at 41. Notably, the riverboat baton was passed to his son John Curran Jr. who also became a master pilot with Streckfus Steamers. Later, Curran Jr. owned and operated his own excursion vessel operating out of Baton Rouge, Louisiana.

Roy Michael Streckfus Jr.

Roy's second son, Roy Michael Jr. ("R.M."), was active in the business for most of his professional riverboat life. Resembling Clark Gable, R.M. was stationed in New Orleans and oversaw operations as an executive and captain of the *President*. Like Curran, R.M. too became discouraged—reportedly from showdowns with Uncle Verne—and he became so uncomfortable that he resigned in 1974. Like his mother, R.M. Jr. was felled by a rare genetic heart condition several years later, at 54. Tragedy had earlier stuck R.M.'s family when son Mike (R.M. III) was killed in a freak motorboat fire in 1972 at age 21.

Robert Bernard Streckfus Sr.

Robert, Roy's third son, did work for some years for the Streckfus fleet out of New Orleans. However, Bob found his own way on the river, shunning Streckfus Steamers to become a talented and highly compensated river pilot working between the 100-mile stretch of the Mississippi from the Gulf of Mexico to Baton Rouge. Bob passed in 1990 but his sons, Robert Jr., and Steven, followed in their father's footsteps. Now retired, the two brothers enjoyed rewarding careers on the Mississippi as river pilots. (NB: Verne, R.M. Jr.'s youngest son, has also spent his life as a successful river pilot; Verne now works the commercial stretch from Baton Rouge to New Orleans.)

William Sauvage Streckfus

Of Captain Roy Michael Sr.'s four sons, the youngest, William ("Bill") spent virtually his entire life devoted to Streckfus Steamers. Bill, who hailed from New Orleans and married there, was transferred to St. Louis. He assumed command of the entire fleet of Streckfus vessels after Captain Verne ceded operating control and the title of chairman.

Stationed in St. Louis, Bill found the mega-vessels *President* and *Admiral* caught in a vise of declining health, failing ridership, and inadequate reinvestment. Efforts to pivot to a younger clientele with shorter excursions had been encouraging at first but the new smaller vessels cannibalized traditional big-boat business, invited keen competition, and lacked the scale economies that had propelled Streckfus Steamers into excursion riverboat dominance.

Pressed against the wall, the firm had been forced to divest both the flagship *Admiral* and its sister craft, the *President*. The problems were obvious: age and an avalanche of investment demand—not the least of which was the conversion from steam-driven sidewheel to propeller-driven motor vessel (MV). On June 3rd, 1982, the aptly named Boatman's Bank of St. Louis seized the last two vessels of the Streckfus fleet, the *Huck Finn* and *Tom Sawyer*. That date marked 98 years since Captain John "the Commodore" Streckfus had begun operations between Andalusia, Illinois, and Rock Island, Illinois.

A faithfully true account was that the vessels (carrying the weight of earlier modernization investments for the *President* and *Admiral*) had been slowly drowning from $2.3 million of debt. A $468,673 principal payment was overdue. Boatman's Bank stated: "We regret that it has become necessary to institute legal action in the federal courts in order to collect the delinquent debt which Streckfus Steamers owes to Boatmen's National Bank."—*St. Louis Post-Dispatch*.

By this time, Captain William F. Carroll had been appointed President of Streckfus Steamers. To be fair, Captain Carroll assumed the leadership of Streckfus Steamers after virtually all avenues of economic recovery had been fruitlessly pursued. After leaving Streckfus Steamers in 1979, Captain Bill Streckfus pursued a variety of endeavors—including captaining one of the casino ships docked in St. Louis—before he passed in 2021.

NB: Bill's daughter, Lisa, graduated from the Coast Guard Academy and became a proficient master pilot whose career took her on inland riverways throughout the U.S.

NB: Like Captain Lisa Streckfus, Captain Verne's niece Joy Manthey also took to the river and became an experienced master pilot. Captains Lisa Streckfus and Joy Manthey are some of the most celebrated female master pilots to flourish in what had been a purely masculine-only occupation.

TAPS FOR THE *ADMIRAL*

The painful saga had been initiated in St. Louis on May 16, 1979, when grim news was reported that a Coast Guard inspector's hammer had pierced the *Admiral's* 74-year-old hull during a regular seaworthiness

Epilogue

inspection. Regular cruises for the season were cancelled, deposits were returned to groups which had organized events for the summer, and the *Admiral* ceased sightseeing and moonlight dance excursion operations. Ostensibly, there would be a pause in operations to allow for hull repairs to be completed in New Orleans where the only drydock existed which could accommodate the monstrous craft.

Looking back, the *Admiral's* years of sailing on excursion cruises came to an end on that date in 1979 when she became shore-bound permanently. While she was never to sail again, the next thirty years of the *Admiral's* existence were hardly uneventful, as is chronicled in the timeline on page 370. The saga includes the Six Flags organizations' $26.6 million conversion to an amusement center and then entrepreneur John Connolly's investments in various incarnations of the *Admiral* as a riverboat casino and gambling hall. The mighty hull was ultimately sold for scrap and melted down in 2011.

TIMELINE

1856	Commodore John B. Streckfus born.
1884–1900	Acme Packet Company is formed and runs three vessels: *Verne Swain*, *Freddie*, and *City of Winona*.
1901	Commodore designs and builds the first purposed excursion steamer, the *J.S.*, launched from Howard Shipyards in Jeffersonville, Indiana.
1910	Tragic *J.S.* fire: the vessel burns to the waterline with only two casualties. On Aug. 18, 1910, within eight weeks of the *J.S.*'s demise, the Streckfus Steamboat Line Company is organized.
1911	Streckfus Steamboat Company acquires Diamond Jo Line to operate four packet steamers. Sternwheeler *Sidney* is converted to excursion and heads to New Orleans; Streckfus Company relocates to St. Louis from Rock Island.
1917	*W.W.* excursion sold. *St. Paul* sidewheeler conversion, retains name at first, becomes *Senator* in 1939.
1919	*Quincy* sidewheeler is converted to *J.S. Deluxe*.
1920	Sternwheeler *Dubuque* is converted to *Capitol*.
1921	*Sidney* sternwheeler is converted to *Washington*; relocates to Cincinnati, Ohio.
1925	Death of John B. Streckfus (69), the Commodore
1926	New corporation name: Streckfus Steamers, Inc.
1931–1933	Steel-hull sidewheeler *Cincinnati* acquired; transformed into excursion flagship *President*.
1936–1940	Railroad transfer sidewheeler *Albatross* acquired and transformed into art deco excursion mega-ship *Admiral*.
1948	Death of Capt. John Nicholas Streckfus (57).
1939–1950	All four original Diamond Jo packets—*Senator*, *J.S. Deluxe*, *Washington*, and *Capitol* retired and dismantled.

THE STRECKFUS RIVERBOAT DYNASTY

1960	Death of Capt. Joseph Leo Streckfus (74); Roy now president.
1963	New M/V *Mark Twain* launched.
1965–1966	New M/V *Huck Finn* and M/V *Tom Sawyer* launched.
1967	Death of Capt. Roy Michael Streckfus (80); Verne president.
1973	Capt. R.M resigns as an executive and captain of the *President*; Capt. Bill Streckfus becomes president.
1973	A miscalculation of the tidal river crest causes the *Admiral* to attempt to pass under the Poplar Street bridge. The accident shears off the top-deck pilot house and texas on *Admiral's* opening day. (Six feet of smokestack, pg. 65 Blum book).
1973	Conversion of steam to diesel power commences on *Admiral*.
1974	M/V conversion of *Admiral* completed; it winters in New Orleans.
1974–1975	Generators and A/C installed on *President*.
1977–1978	M/V and dieselization conversion of *President*; *Admiral* sails out of New Orleans.
1978	*Admiral* enjoys a full St. Louis summer season.
1979	*Admiral's* 74-year-old hull fails audio gauging hull tests; new concerns emerge over deteriorated rivets.
1979	Shore-based parties only for *Admiral*; riverboat excursions cease after nearly forty years since introduction in June 1940.
1980	Coast Guard performs drydock inspection of *Admiral* and declares the vessel "unfit for passenger service." Entire hull needs replacement.
1980	With Streckfus Steamers already carrying $2MM of debt from diesel conversions of *President* and *Admiral*, Boatmen's of St. Louis refuses to extend additional loans.
1980–1981	Popular "Save The *Admiral*" campaigns in St. Louis are waged, including *City* purchase with Port Authority bond issue. Public "Save The *Admiral*" donations fall well short and $60K proceeds are given to United Way.
1981	*Admiral* sits vacant at Avondale shipyard in New Orleans and is plundered. No progress is made for new capital to complete repairs.

Timeline

1981	Streckfus Steamers sells three New Orleans vessels, including *President*, to competitor New Orleans Steamboat Company; Boatman's Bank receives entire $2.2MM.
1981	Southern Scrap Company offers $500K to dismantle *Admiral*.
1981	Entrepreneur John Connolly acquires *Admiral* for $600K. After relocation to St. Louis, Connolly plans permanent move of *Admiral* to Pittsburgh to operate as a dockside entertainment center.
1982	St. Louisans are outraged and label Connolly the "Pittsburgh Stealer." Mayor Schoemehl orchestrates repurchase of *Admiral* for $1.6MM financed by local businesses.
1982	Wharf docks sold; *Admiral* temporarily relocated to Paducah, Kentucky.
1982	Connelly buys out Boatmen's loan of $500K to control *Huck Finn* and *Tom Sawyer*; both managed by Capt. Carroll.
1982	City of St. Louis chooses Six Flags to convert *Admiral* to floating amusement park.
1983	Six Flags announces major $26.6 million renovation to transform vessel to riverside amusement attraction.
1984	Death of Capt. Verne Walter Streckfus (89)
1984	*Admiral* returns from Kentucky to St. Louis to begin renovations that ultimately are much delayed and soar to $36.9MM.
1987	Five years after purchase by the St. Louis consortium, the Six Flags *Admiral* entertainment complex opens. After great hoopla, the public reception is decidedly unenthusiastic; reviews are critical of its appearance and cost of admission. Mazie Krebs tours and gives a thumbs down. Attendance is one third of projections.
1987	Less than six months from its official Grand Opening in May, the Six Flags *Admiral* Entertainment complex is shuttered in November after hemorrhaging cash throughout the summer.
1987	Connolly invited back to St. Louis where he agrees to pay off *Admiral* debts and invest $1MM in a major renovation and refurbishment.

1988	To great fanfare, the "New *Admiral*" reopens in May. Connolly's improvements fail to generate sufficient interest; the complex closes in November. Connolly loses $5MM on this venture with *Admiral* but vows to return.
1989	Legislation passed in Iowa to permit riverboat gaming.
1990	Connolly receives license from Davenport City to operate *President* as casino.
1990	Looking forward, Connolly re-acquires *Admiral* from St. Louis partnership for $4MM.
1991	*President* is transformed to the first and largest legalized gambling venue with major investment by International Gaming Technologies (IGT). *President* Casino opens doors for legalized gambling at home port of Davenport, Iowa.
1994	*Admiral* is the first riverboat casino to operate in Missouri.
1998	Barges towed by the *Anne Holly* break loose and ram *Admiral*; gambling patrons are evacuated.
2000	*Admiral* Casino moved to Laclede's Landing.
2000	Riverboat casinos proliferate; 60 operate on inland waterways and Gulf Coast.
2002	President Casinos, owners of both *President* and *Admiral* casino vessels, files bankruptcy.
2006	*Admiral* Casino purchased for $31.5 MM by Pinnacle Entertainment. Pinnacle plans major St. Louis casino additions near *Admiral's* berth.
2007–2008	*Admiral* Casino gaming income slumps under strong regional competition; Pinnacle petitions Missouri Gaming Commission.
2009	*Admiral* hull recertification denied. Missouri Gaming Commission rejects Pinnacle proposals. *Admiral* license is later awarded to city of Cape Girardeau.
2010	*Admiral* Casino listed for sale on eBay for $1.5MM; remaining items are auctioned as souvenirs.
2011	In July, after her 104-year life, the *Admiral/Albatross* was towed to Columbia, Illinois by the Luhr Bros. Company and stripped of her superstructure. Afterwards, the hull was towed to mile 14 of the Tennessee River and scrapped.

AFTERWORD

From 1950 on, the Streckfus Line chronology of minor progress and larger setbacks is both depressing and intriguing. It is an episode that itself offers a grand canvas for a sequel to *The Streckfus Riverboat Dynasty*. With some inspiration from the muses, I will return to the second half of the Streckfus story in a separate work.

ACKNOWLEDGMENTS

I promise not to bore you with an Oscar winner's litany of "thanksters." That said, a heartfelt THANKS and to all you "Big Smoke Canoe" fans:

A call to action:
Take the longest and most scenic Mississippi river cruise possible:
You will not regret it!

The Inspiration: My mom, **Lily Streckfus Smith**, planted the seed and, rightfully, doubted that any book would ever emerge. Well, here it is. From the blacksmith Balthazar in the 1850s to the *Admiral*'s return to scrap iron in 2011—it was a lot of ground to cover.

The First Team in the Clubhouse: **Debra Claxton** and **Nissa Darbonne** were instrumental in all phases of the book's creation. Admittedly, our research efforts sometimes crawled along at a glacial pace. Debra, an English major, should really share authorship with me, so important were her innumerable contributions.

The Bench: All of my Streckfus cousins — **Robert, Steve, Lily, Donna, and Verne** — offered recollections from their first-hand river experience working on the Streckfus excursion boats. We enjoyed some especially riotous dinner and cocktail sessions that were chock full of great Streckfus folklore. Cousin Verne introduced me to Clarke "Doc" Hawley and Verne was a great source of Streckfus photos and memories.

In the Stands: Alaina W. Hebert at the Hogan Archive of New Orleans Music and New Orleans Jazz, a unit of Tulane University Special Collections and the Howard-Tilton Memorial Library. The University of Wisconsin-La Crosse, Murphy Library Special Collections. Nori Munster at Steamboats.com (Dave Thomson Collection). Dolores Jane Meyer—*Excursion Steamboating on the Mississippi with Streckfus Steamers*; Annie Amantea Blum—*The Steamer Admiral and Streckfus Steamers*; Ronda Rawlins and the folks at 1106 Design.

Smith Family: Finally, I thank my wife Holly and my wonderful Smith family who have been there to provide inspiration and support along the way. I love you all. Beware: I may have another book or a screenplay still in me!

Arthur L. Smith
September 2023

INDEX

A

Acme Packet, Anchor Line Co. and, 83–88
Acorn, Alvin Elmore, 331–332
the *Admiral,* 72, 199–200
  Albatross and, 211
  arcade, 205–206
  Armstrong, Louis, summer solstice 1963 show, 302–303
  Glamour powder room, 203–204
  Ladies Lounges, 201–204
  Main Deck Amusement Midway, 204
  operations end, 366–367
  riverboat miniatures, racing, 205
  souvenirs, 207
air travel, 174
the *Albatross,* 244, 246–247
alcohol
  family friendly practices, 108
  J.S. fire, John Plein, 117–119
  W.W., Water Wagon nickname, 125–127
Algonquian people, 9
An American Primer (Whitman), 4
Anchor Line Co.
  Acme Packet, 83–88
  sidewheelers, 86
  steamer accidents, 87–88
Armstrong, Louis "Satchmo," 282–285, 293
  the *Admiral,* summer solstice 1963 show, 302–303
  the *Dixie Belle,* 309
  early career, Marable, Fate, invite to play, 307–308
  Jones, David, 309
  Louis Armstrong, in His Own Words (Brothers, ed.), 304–307
  on Marable, 310–311
  Parker, Daisy, 307–308
  reputation spreads, 313
  segregated boats, 310
  St. Louis
    Monday-night excursions, 313
    work routine, 309–310
  Streckfus, Joseph, on, 334–336, 337–339
  Teagarden, Jack, and, 301
Art Hickman's Orchestra, 282–284
Audubon, John James, 51

B

Bad Axe Island, *J.S.* fire, 120–121
Bartemeyer, Elizabeth Rees, 360
Bartemeyer, John, 360
Bartemeyer, Theresa J., 360
Bates, Alan, *The Excursion Boat Story,* 209–210
Beiderbecke, Stacy and Bix, 294
the *Belvedere,* 49

Boards of Directors and Officers, 341–344
Bolden, Charles "Buddy," 332–334
Buffano, Jules, 295
Business Men's League, 232

C
Cairo, Illinois, 31–33
calliope, 131–133
　Marable, Fate, 135–139
canal proposal, 61–62
canoes, 37
the Capitol, 154
　brothers' argument, 211–212
　drydocking, 249
　retirement, 189
　upgrades, 169–171
Carlisle & Finch, 94
Catalano, Tony, 294
Chain of Rocks, 259
Chapman Electric Co., 94
Charles Hegewald Co., 94
the Cincinnati, 191–193, 240–241
the City of Providence, 110
the City of Winona, 76–77, 89–92, 125–127
　W.W., 220–222
Civil War, 30
Clemens, Samuel. *See* Twain, Mark
the Clermont, 43
conversions, 156–159
Corps of Engineers. *See* U.S. Army Corps of Engineers
the Corwin H. Spencer, 87
Crawley & Johnston, 94
Creath, Charles Cyril "Charlie," 321–322

Creath, Charlie, 295, 297–298
crimes on steamboats, 83–88

D
Dantin, 294
de Frontenac, Louis de Buade, 15–17
de Pineda, Àlvarez, 12
de Soto, Hernando, 11–13
de Tonti, Chevalier Henri, 20
de Vaca, Cabeza, 12
Desvigne, Sidney, 330–331
Diamond Jo Line
　demise, 149–150
　the Dubuque, 152
　fleet retirement, 189–190
　purchase, 150–155, 230–231
　the Quincy, 152
　the Saint Paul, 152
　the Sidney, 152
Dickens, Charles, 50–51
the Dixie Belle, 309
Dodds, "Baby," 296
Dodds, John "Johnny," 323
Dodds, Johnny, 296
Dodds, Warren "Baby," 323–325
the Douglass Boardman, 76–77
the Dubuque, 152, 157
　the Capitol, 154, 167–172
dugout canoes, 37
Durbin, Deanna, 201–202

E
Eads, James Buchanan, 59–60
　Humphreys and, 60–62
Eads Jetties, 62
Eagle Packet Co., 233

Index

the *Eastland* accident, 161–162
   the *Wilmette,* recommission, 163
the *Effie Afton,* Rock Island Bridge, 54
E.J. Howard & Co. shipyard, 93
the *Enterprise,* 46–47
entertainment
   bands, addition to vessels, 77
   showboats, 41–42
the *Essayons* barge, 61
E.W. Vanduzen Co., 94
The Excursion Boat Story (Bates and Hawley), 209–210
explorers, early, 7–9
   de Frontenac, Louis de Buade, 15–17
   de Tonti, Chevalier Henri, 20
   French, 11–13
   Jolliet, Louis, 15–17
   LaSalle, 19–23
   Marquette, Pere, 15–17
   Nicolet, Jean, 13

F

Fashionable Tour, 49
Fazola, Irving, 294
Fink, Mike (The Snapping Turtle), 37–39
Fitzgerald, F. Scott, xix
flatboats, 35–36
the *Floating Circus Palace,* 41–42
The Floating Palace, 41
Foster, George Murphy "Pops," 328–329
Foster, Pops, 296
the *Freddie,* 71–72
Fulton, Robert, 43–44
   the *Clermont,* 43

G

Garbo, Greta, 202–203
Garden Steamer, *J.S. Deluxe,* 177–178
the *Gem City,* 67–68
Great Depression, 191–193, 238–239
the *Greater New Orleans,* 237–238
the *Greater Pittsburgh,* 240–241

H

the *Harriet,* 122
Hawley, Clarke "Doc," *The Excursion Boat Story,* 209–210
Henie, Sonja, 203
Hertzog, Carl, 130
Hertzog orchestra, 130
Houdini, Harry, 111–112
Hubbard, John, 192–193
Humphreys, Andrew Atkinson, 57–59
   Eads and, 60–62

I

the *Island Queen,* 110, 223–224

J

Jackson, Dewey, 295, 325–326
jazz, 129–133, xix
   Streckfus Steamer Co., 286–287
Jazz Years, xix
Jefferson Expansion Memorial (Gateway to the West), 216–217
the *Jo Long,* 75–81
Johnson, Jesse, 327–328
Jolliet, Louis, 15–17
the *J.S.,* 93–97
   burning bridge in Dubuque, Iowa, 116

fire, 116
   Bad Axe Island, 120–121
   the *Harriet,* 122
   Marable, Fate, 119
   the *North Star,* 122
   Plein, John, 117–119, 121
   maiden voyage, 99–102
   New Orleans excursion, 106–110
   sand bar, 103
   storm damage, 103
the *J.S. Deluxe,* 153, 234–235
   Garden Steamer, 177–178

K

Kahlke, John, 105
Kahlke, Peter, 105
Kahlke Brothers yard, 105
keelboats, 35
   Fink, Mike, 37–39
Killeen, John, 155
   the *Dubuque/Capital* and, 168–169
   the *Quincy* repair, 174
Kohnke, Quitman, 115–116
Krebs, Mazie G., 195–199, 244–246

L

Ladies Lounges, 201
   Hollywood names, 201–203
LaSalle (René-Robert Cavelier, Sieur de La Salle), 19
   Louisiane, 21–22
   Texas expedition, 22–23
Life on the Mississippi (Twain), 4, 49, 51
Lincoln, Abraham
   flatboats and, 35
   Rock Island Bridge lawsuit, 53–56

Livingston, Robert R., 44
locks and dams, 27–28, 259
Long, Joseph Newt, 75–81
Louisiana Purchase, 37
Louisiane, LaSalle (René-Robert Cavelier, Sieur de La Salle), 21–22
Lovinggood, J. Burroughs, 295
Lower Mississippi, geography, 31–33

M

Manning, Lilly Streckfus, 151
Manthey, Anna Streckfus, 151
Marable, Fate, 119, 135–139, 281–282, 285–287, 292
   Fate Marable and his Jazz Maniacs, 309
   Jazz Syncopators, 309
   Streckfus, Joseph, on, 334–336
Mares, Paul, 294
Marquette, Pere, 15–17
McPartland, Isabel Lourdes, 254–257
McPartland family, 254–255
the Merriams, 130
Mills, Charles Wenzel "Charlie," 315–316
Mills, Charlie, 130–131, 292
Minuit, Peter, 44
Mississippi river
   comparison to other major rivers, 32
   history, 3–5
   states along, 33
Mississippi River Improvement and Levee Association, 106
Mississippi Valley
   de Narvaez, Panfilo, 12

Index

de Pineda, Àlvarez, 12
de Soto, Hernando, 11–13
de Vaca, Cabeza, 12
exploration, early, 7–9
French explorers, 11–13
Native Americans, 4
monopolies, protection, 146
Montgomery, Zebulon, 38
music and musicians
    Acorn, Alvin Elmore, 331–332
    African Americans, Monday-night excursions, 313
    Allen, Henry "Red," Jr., 293
    Armstrong, Louis, 282–285, 293
    Art Hickman's Orchestra, 282–284
    Beiderbecke, Stacy and Bix, 294
    Bolden, Charles "Buddy," 332–334
    Buffano, Jules, 295
    Capitol as rough boat, 312
    Catalano, Tony, 294
    Creath, Charles Cyril "Charlie," 295, 297–298, 321–322
    dance cards, 312
    Dantin, 294
    Desvigne, Sidney, 330–331
    Dodds, John "Johnny," 296, 323
    Dodds, Warren "Baby," 293, 296, 323–325
    Fazola, Irving, 294
    Foster, George Murphy "Pops," 296, 328–329
    interview of Verne by Richard Allen, 291–299
    Jackson, Dewey, 295, 325–326
    Johnson, Jesse, 327–328
    Lovinggood, J. Burroughs, 295
    Marable, Fate, 119, 135–139, 281–282, 285–287, 292
    Mares, Paul, 294
    Mills, Charles Wenzel "Charlie," 130–131, 292, 315–316
    Oliver, Joseph Nathan "King," 317–318
    Phil Zito's orchestra, 296–297
    Pichon, Walter Gabriel "Fats," 329–330
    Piron, A.J., 294
    Prestopnik, Blue, 294
    The Rhythm Kings, 294
    Roppolo, Leon, 294
    Saint Paul as rough boat, 312
    Singleton, Arthur James "Zutty," 320–321
    St. Cyr, John Alexander "Johnny," 319–320
    Streckfus, Joseph L., 281–287, 334–339
    Williams, Alfred, 294

N

Native Americans, Mississippi Valley, 4
New Orleans
    J.S. excursion, 106–110
    traffic in 1940, 210
    yellow fever, 115–116
the *New Orleans,* 38, 45
news stories, 351–356
Nichols, George, 117
Nicolet, Jean, 13
the *North Star,* 122

O

Oliver, Joseph Nathan "King," 317–318

P

Page, John, 121
the *Petoskey*, 162
Phil Zito's orchestra, 296–297
Pichon, Walter Gabriel "Fats," 329–330
Piron, A.J., 294
Plein, John, 117–119, 121
the *President*, 71
    Krebs, Mazie G., 195–197
    Ladies Lounges, 201–203
    move to New Orleans, 213–214
Prestopnik, Blue, 294

Q

the *Quincy*, 152, 157–158
    the *J.S. Deluxe*, 153
    port of Quincy, 173
    sinking in 1906, 173
    speed, 174–175

R

races
    Le Claire, Iowa, 76–77
    Streckfus wins, 77–78
the *Racine*, 162
railroads, monopolies, 146
The Rhythm Kings, 294
the *Rochester*, 162
Rock Island, 53–54
Rock Island Bridge
    the *Effie Afton*, 54
    lawsuit, 53–56
Roosevelt, Nicholas, 38
Roppolo, Leon, 294

S

the *Saint Paul*, 152, 157–158
    drydocking, 249
    the *Senator*, 154–155, 179–183
sawyers, 30
Schaab, Anna Marie, 65, 360
Schoon, Mazie G. *See* Krebs, Mazie G.
scrip, 109–110
secrecy in Streckfus family, 218–220
segregation, Armstrong, Louis, 310
the *Senator*, 179–183, 185–187
Showboat musical, 42
showboat years, 41–42
    the *Floating Circus Palace*, 41–42
Shreve, Henry, 30–31, 46
sidewheelers, 47
    Anchor Line, 86
    the *Freddie*, 71–72
    the *J.S. Deluxe*, 153
    the *Quincy*, 153, 173–175
    the *Saint Paul*, 154, 179–183
the *Sidney*, 152, 156–157
Singleton, Arthur James "Zutty," 320–321
Smith, Lily Ann Streckfus, Packard travelogue, 263–265
snags, 30
St. Cyr, John Alexander "Johnny," 319–320
St. Louis
    African Americans, Monday-night excursions, 313
    freeze in harbor, 165–166

Index

Jefferson Expansion Memorial (Gateway to the West), 216–217
river levels at historic low, 149–150
Twain, Mark on, 147
states long Mississippi, 33
steamboat expansion, 45–52
steamers
  Admiral, 72, 199–207, 211, 366–367
  Albatross, 211, 244, 246–247
  Anchor Line Co., accidents, 87–88
  Capitol, 154, 189
    brothers' argument, 211–212
    upgrades, 169–171
  captains, chart, 360
  Cincinnati, 191–193, 240–241
  City of Providence, 110
  City of Winona, 76–77, 89–92, 125–127, 220–222
  Clermont, 43
  Corwin H. Spencer, 87
  Dixie Belle, 309
  Douglass Boardman, 76–77
  Dubuque, 152, 154, 157
    Capitol, 154, 167–172
  Enterprise, 46–47
  Freddie, 71–72
  Gem City, 67–68
  Greater New Orleans, 237–238
  Greater Pittsburgh, 240–241
  Harriet, 122
  Island Queen, 110, 223–224
  Jo Long, 75–81
  J.S., 93–97
  J.S. Deluxe, 153
  Keystone State, 221
  Majestic, 221
  Majestic II, 221–222
  New Orleans, 45
  North Star, 122
  President, 71–72, 193, 195–200
    move to New Orleans, 213–214
  Prince, 221
  Quincy, 152, 157–158, 173–175
    J.S. Deluxe, 153
  Saint Paul, 152, 157–158
  Senator, 154–155, 179–183, 185–187
  Sidney, 152, 156–157
  Washington, 154
  steamers in operation 1936-1943, 345–349
  Van Metre, 221
  Verne Swain, 71–72, 73–74
  Washington, 47
  W.W., 125–127, 153, 220–222
sternwheelers
  Dubuque, 154
  J.S., 93–97
  Sidney, 154
  Verne Swain, 72
Streckfus, Anna Cecelia, 357
Streckfus, Balthazar, 227–228, 360
  birth, 65
  death, 69
  marriage, 65
  move to New York, 66
  son stows away on *Gem City,* 67–68
Streckfus, Elizabeth Mary, 357
Streckfus, John Curran, 266–267, 364
Streckfus, John N., 151, 228, 358, 360
  personal story, 269–272
Streckfus, John "The Commodore," 68, 143, 151, 228

children
- Anna Cecelia, 357
- Elizabeth Mary, 357
- John Nicholas, 358
- Joseph Leo, 357–358
- Mary Theresa Anna, 357
- Nina Agnes, 358
- Roy Michael, 358
- Theresa Agnes, 358
- Verne Walter, 358

family friendly practices, 108
family tree, 359
the *Freddie*, 71–72
stowaway on *Gem City*, 67–68
vision for the new venture, 146

Streckfus, Joseph Leo, 144, 151, 228, 357–358, 360
- Business Men's League, 232
- career beginnings, 230
- on music, 281–287, 336–337
  - on Fate Marable, 334–336
  - on Louis Armstrong, 334–336, 337–339
- personal story, 227–250
- St. Louis, 234–235

Streckfus, Mary Theresa Anna, 357
Streckfus, May, 151
Streckfus, Nina Agnes, 358
Streckfus, Robert Bernard, 365
Streckfus, Roy Michael "Dean of the Mississippi," 144, 151, 228, 254, 358, 360
- obituary, 261–262
- personal story, 251–259

Streckfus, Roy Michael Jr., 364–365
Streckfus, Theresa Agnes, 358

Streckfus, Theresa Bartemeier, 151
Streckfus, Verne W., 151, 228, 358, 360
- interview by Richard Allen, 291–299
- personal story, 273–279

Streckfus, William Sauvage, 365–366
Streckfus family
- Catholicism, 83
- portrait, 151
- positions in company, 152
- secrecy in, 218–220

The Streckfus House, 69
Streckfus Steamboat Line Co., 230
- The Commodore's vision, 146
- founding, 143–144
- line closure, 249–250

Streckfus Steamers Inc., 192, 236–237
- challenges, operational, 363–364
- Directors Meeting, 244–246
- jazz, development of, 286–287
- steamers in operation 1936-1943, 345–349
- tourism competition in 60s and 70s, 361–362

the *Suzie Hazard*, 186

T

Theodore Roosevelt, 162
Titanic, 161–164
tourism competition in 60s and 70s, 361–362
Trollope, Frances, 49
Twain, Mark, 48
- death, 146–147
- *Life on the Mississippi*, 4, 49, 51
- nutritiousness of river water, 51
- on St. Louis, 147

Index

U
Upper Mississippi
 geography, 31–33
 locks and dams, 27–28
 wing dams/dikes, 32–33
U.S. Army Corps of Engineers, 27–28
 Stairway of Water, 29

V
the *Verne Swain,* 71–72, 73–74
The Versatile Three, 131

W–Z
Washington, George, 8
the *Washington,* 47
Wellnitz, Shirley, 270–271
Whitman, Walt, 4
 An American Primer, 4
Williams, Alfred, 294
the *Wilmette,* 163
Wilson, Woodrow, 232–233
wing dams/dikes, 32–33
Wisherd, Walter, 125–127, 220–222, 247–248
 the *Island Queen,* 223–224
World War I, 165–166
World War II
 Excess Profits Tax, 214–215
 the *Senator* and, 185–186
the *W.W.,* 125–127, 153, 220–222
 sinking, 159
WW I, 165–166
yellow fever, 115–116

ABOUT THE ARTHUR

A native of New Orleans, **Arthur L. Smith** received his A.B. from Duke University and his MBA from New York University. His undergraduate focus in English and Zoology and his graduate concentration in Economics and Finance gave him a perfect tabula rasa from which to become a Wall Street energy investment analyst. After ten years Art left Wall Street to acquire the highly-respected oil industry valuation expert, **John S. Herold, Inc.** For more than 20 years **Herold** prospered with Smith as CEO as the firm strengthened its locations in Norwalk, CT and Houston, TX while stretching its reach among the global oil and natural gas industry. Smith divested Herold to NYSE-listed **IHS**, (now S&P Global) and formed the investment and consulting firm, *Triple Double Advisors*. Previously Smith authored *Something From Nothing*, a biography of oil legend Joe B. Foster.

Over his career, Art has been blessed to serve on the boards of directors of many leading energy companies including **Plains All American** and **Pioneer Natural Resources**. Today Smith serves on the boards of **Evergreen Natural Resources** and **Mammoth Energy Services** and non-profits **Dress for Success Houston** and **Memorial Assistance Ministries**.

Art loves Galveston where he maintains a bay house with an excessive collection of boats, jet skis, golf carts, and miscellaneous games and beach toys. A self-professed professional angler and would-be charter boat captain, Art fishes anywhere and anytime but prefers Alaska and the Gulf of Mexico. Enjoying his semi-retirement with Holly, Art is very proud of his outstanding children and stepsons and six remarkable grandchildren.

www.ingramcontent.com/pod-product-compliance
Lightning Source LLC
Chambersburg PA
CBHW042030050526
44107CB00124B/1446/J